About the author
Julian Sher was born in 1953 in Montreal, where he
still lives. After graduating from McGill University he
worked as a freelance journalist; his articles have
appeared in *Canadian Dimension, Goodwin's* and the
Centre for Investigative Journalism's *Bulletin*. He is
currently a producer for CBC Radio's Current Affairs
program in Montreal.

WHITE HOODS

WHITE HOODS

CANADA'S KU KLUX KLAN

JULIAN SHER

New Star Books • Vancouver

Copyright 1983 by Julian Sher

Canadian Cataloguing in Publication Data

Sher, Julian, 1953-
    White hoods

Bibliography: p.
ISBN 0-919573-12-6 (bound). -- ISBN
    0-919573-13-4 (pbk.)

1. Ku Klux Klan (1915-) - Canada - History.
I. Title.
HS2330.K63S53 1983   322.4'2'0971   C83-091358-0

1 2 3 4 5 87 86 85 84 83

This book was published with the assistance of a grant from the
Multiculturalism Program, Government of Canada. The Minister of State for
Multiculturalism and the Multiculturalism Directorate disclaim any
responsibility in whole or in part for the views and opinions expressed and for
the completeness or accuracy of information included in this publication.
    The publisher is grateful for assistance provided by the
Canada Council.

PRINTED IN CANADA

To my mother and father,
who taught me
never to hate anything—
except injustice

Acknowledgments

THIS BOOK IS ONE JOURNALIST'S ACCOUNT of the events and people surrounding the Ku Klux Klan in Canada, and the movement which sprang up to fight the Klan. This is not a sociological study of racism; I leave that task to others more qualified. But I hope it will be useful to people concerned about racism in our country.

This book could not have been written without the help of many people. Given the nature of the topic some of them must remain anonymous. I do wish to thank Dr. William Calderwood of the First United Church of Lethbridge, Alberta; Raymond Huel, associate professor at the University of Lethbridge; and Allan Seager of Simon Fraser University for their kind permission to quote passages from their unpublished theses. The assistance of journalists Terry Glavin, Neil Louttit, Joe Kotler, Elizabeth Escobar, Larry Colle, Zuhair Kashmeri, and Steve Overbury has been invaluable, as was the aid of lawyers Stuart Rush and Paul Copeland. I would like to thank John Thompson, co-ordinator of Canadian Studies at McGill University, for his helpful comments. The efforts of the staff of New Star Books, particularly Ralph Maurer and Lanny Beckman, made this book possible. Finally, I extend my heartiest appreciation to my colleagues and friends who gave me support and encouragement, and especially to my wife for all her patience.

Julian Sher
Montreal
July, 1983

Contents

"Not in Canada, we say. Canada is different. But is it?...The Klan has been bringing its message of hate to Canadians...they can't be ignored."

—James Fleming, federal
minister of state
for multiculturalism,
April 22, 1982

Introduction: "They are here"

HE WALKS QUIETLY into the restaurant where he had suggested we meet on this day, early in 1982. It's a small, modern bar in midtown Toronto, crowded with fashionably-dressed people from the offices and university nearby. Rock music pounds over the sound system. Not the kind of place you expect the leader of the Canadian Ku Klux Klan to frequent.

But then, James Alexander McQuirter is not the kind of person you would expect to lead the Klan. He is 24, tall and slender, with neatly-combed black hair and a clean-shaven, almost boyish face. He does not bother with a hat or gloves despite the blizzard outside. He could be the boy next door. (In March, 1980, only a few months before he became known as the Canadian chief of the Klan, McQuirter's smile earned him a pin-up spot as the Toronto *Sun*'s Sunshine Boy. "He'd like to find himself a seat on Parliament Hill," read the caption under his photograph.) He could be the boy next door, but he is not. The moment Alexander opens his mouth, he becomes the Grand Wizard McQuirter, national

13

director of the Canadian Ku Klux Klan.

"We are racists and we're proud of it," he boasts. "We're a racist organization. We want to see Canada as an all-white country. We dismiss the notion that all humanity, that all the races are equal."

"Is it true you're a fan of Adolf Hitler?" I ask.

McQuirter smiles and leans back in his chair. "Well, if I say that, you're going to write: 'He's inspired by Mr. X who killed six million people.' As far as I'm concerned, I'd like to see a neutral history written on the second world war, of what really happened. The Holocaust was the biggest hoax of the twentieth century." But McQuirter concedes his admiration for Hitler. He says he has read and enjoyed *Mein Kampf*: "There are a great many things in that book that I like and things that I have applied."

And so our conversation continued. I listened, sometimes increduously, as the Klan leader described calmly and confidently how he had built up the most visible and frightening extreme right-wing organization Canada had seen in years. I knew that McQuirter's boasts were not empty: between 1980 and 1982 there had been a flurry of Klan activity across the country. In Halifax, Moncton, Montreal, Toronto, Hamilton, Vancouver, Victoria and in many smaller cities and towns, the Klan's message had been heard. It was broadcast in interviews on dozens of radio and television shows, featured in newspaper stories, scrawled on billboards, and printed on thousands of pamphlets and newsletters which found their way into schools, factories and shopping centres. The KKK also developed less subtle ways of spreading its creed. Cross burnings lit up the night skies in southern Ontario and British Columbia. Racial violence took its toll: beatings in subways and bars, firebombings of houses, harassment and intimidation of Klan opponents. Before this wave of Klan fever was over, six Klan members would be charged with public mischief and one Klan organizer and his wife would die in a suspicious fire. Two Klan members would find themselves in American jails and another in a Caribbean prison for an attempt to topple a Caribbean state. McQuirter himself would be convicted of conspiracy to overthrow a foreign government. He, along with two other Klan members, would also be convicted of conspiracy to commit fraud and murder.

As I sat there listening to McQuirter, some questions kept racing through my mind. What were the origins and history of this mysterious American-born organization? How much influence did it exert over its Canadian branch? What about the Klan's history in Canada itself, the tens of thousands of members it was reputed to have here in the 1920s? What led to its rebirth in the 1980s? And, most disturbingly, why were the authorities and governments doing so little to stop such activity?

The story I uncovered is told in the following pages. The answers to my questions were not always reassuring. The modern Canadian Klan has never attained the strength, either in numbers or influence, of its American counterpart; it remains basically a marginal group in our country. In 1982 James Fleming, the federal minister of state for multiculturalism, said in a speech:

> In the past five years, the Ku Klux Klan has doubled its U.S. membership and Klansmen in the U.S. have been convicted of such crimes as shooting into the homes of blacks, bombing black churches and Jewish synagogues, beatings and lynchings...
> Not in Canada, we say. Canada is different. But is it?
> ...The Klan has been bringing its message of hate to Canadians. However trivial their numbers in the context of all these things that have been happening in Britain and the United States, they can't be ignored. They are here, they are bringing their message of hate. The KKK claims cells in every province except P.E.I. and it's been recruiting at schools in B.C., Alberta and Southern Ontario.

Precisely because it is an extreme and to some degree exceptional political phenomenon, the Klan is a litmus test for society. For while the Canadian Klan never achieved the prominence of its U.S. parent, its emergence on the Canadian scene does force everyone — governments, the police, the media, schools, communities, labor unions and ordinary citizens — to take a position. Not everyone passes the test.

A study of the Klan can tell us some things about the social system within which the KKK can flourish, things which some people would prefer to deny, ignore or hide.

Part I The Birth
of an Empire

"Fanatic Klansmen, roaming like Alexander for new worlds to conquer, cast their eyes upon Canada."

—Montreal *Standard*, July 19, 1930

1. The Klan heads north

1868: A FREED BLACK SLAVE is murdered in Georgia by the mysterious Klu Klux Klan, the new group of hooded riders emerging in post-Civil War America. He dies from 900 lashes with stirrups.

1978: Lee Andre Carruthers, a 19-year-old black, is shot to death in his jail cell by a deputy sheriff, an avowed Klansman.

Two of the victims in more than a century of organized violence in the United States by the Ku Klux Klan — the KKK. Official records indicate that between 1892 and 1950, some 3,500 blacks were lynched in the American South by Klan members and sympathizers. No one knows the total body count of blacks (and some whites) who were whipped, shot, lynched and burned to death by the Klan.

The American Klan rose to prominence during three distinct periods in U.S. history. In the Reconstruction years (1865-1877) the original Klan fought against the new freedom of southern blacks; in the 1920s and 1930s a revived Klan widened its targets to include Jews, Catholics, labor and communists; and from the mid-fifties until today the black civil rights movement, coupled with an increasingly serious economic crisis, gave the modern Klan new fuel for its cross burnings and its hate campaigns. Two constants have characterized the Klan in each of its three stages: a systematic reliance on violence and terror, and its aid to and support from sections of the American economic and political elite.

It was in the dark days of the American South that the Ku Klux Klan was born; a South where tens of thousands of black men, women and children were literally kept in chains; a South where huge cotton plantations were kept prosperous by the sweat and blood of human chattel.

The Ku Klux Klan was created in December, 1865, in Pulaski, Tennessee, by six young men, one of them the editor of the local newspaper, and several of them Confederate army officers.* They took their name from the Greek *kuklos*, meaning circle or band. Other Klan groups sprung up and attracted some respectable members, including Gen. John C. Brown, who in 1870 became governor of Tennessee and later was to become president of the Tennessee Coal and Iron Company. In April, 1867, various local Klan groups met in Nashville, Tenn., to band together. As their first Grand Wizard, or leader, they elected Gen. Nathan Bedford Forrest of the Confederate army. Forrest had become wealthy as a slave trader in Memphis; after the Civil War, he went on to expand his fortune as a railroad and insurance magnate.

The defeat of the Confederate South in the Civil War had brought about many unpleasant changes in the lives of Gen. Forrest and his friends. The barbaric system of slavery, which had lasted for well over a century, was shaken to its roots. Freed slaves and poor white farmers were demanding a program of democratic reform known as Reconstruction. About 700,000 blacks and almost as many whites registered as new voters between 1865 and 1877. Dozens of ex-slaves and their new-found allies among the poor whites were elected to state assemblies, which began pushing for major political and economic transformations. The Klan, which had begun as little more than a social club for disaffected, wealthy young whites was turning into

*A plaque commemorating the Klan's founding still stands in Pulaski, and 2,500 people gathered there during the American bicentennial in 1976 to celebrate the KKK's first century.

something much more ominous. Donning white robes and rampaging on horseback in the dark of the night, Klansmen became the shock troops of a displaced Southern aristocracy determined to undermine a new popular order and restore the old way of life. A campaign of bloodshed was unleashed, the likes of which the U.S. has not seen before or since. Blacks who dared stand up for their freedom and whites who stood in unity with them were terrorized into submission. In state elections in 1868, Klan assassinations and harassment helped break the power of the Reconstruction forces. In Georgia, there were 142 killings, 43 shootings, five stabbings, 55 beatings and eight whippings. In Louisiana, an estimated 2,000 people were killed before the elections. The Klan razed newly-built schoolhouses and killed teachers of former slaves and poor whites. Klan terror was so pervasive in the winter of 1870-71 that in some regions in South Carolina many blacks took to sleeping in the woods for safety.

Eventually the Klan's violence and lawlessness became too excessive even for the sympathetic authorities. Congressional investigations, martial law and the arrests of a few hundred Klansmen led to the disbanding of the organization, but not before the Klan had helped to crush the democratic movement in the South, and the former plantation owners and southern aristocrats were back in power. By 1900, blacks had lost the right to vote in every state in the South and not a single elected black official remained in office.

The first revival of the Ku Klux Klan began in 1915, when a group called the Invisible Empire of the KKK was founded in Atlanta at a showing of America's first feature-length film, D.W. Griffith's *Birth of a Nation*, a lavish tribute to the old Klan and the Southern social order it fought for. The first world war and the period immediately following was a time of turmoil for the United States. Blacks still hungered for their rights; many of the 14 million immigrants who had flocked to America's shores since the start of the century saw their dreams of freedom crushed by the realities of ghetto misery and economic hardship. A militant labor movement began to grow. The Klan adopted a new American jingoism with a fervor, branding anti-war protests and strikes as "anti-American". Jews, Catholics, Asians and other immigrants joined blacks on the Klan's list of "racial inferiors". By 1921, the Klan claimed to have 500,000 adherents in 45 states. Cross burnings, whippings, lynchings and tar-and-feathering became favorite Klan sports. An exposure of KKK violence and internal corruption by the New York *World* newspaper in 1921 and subsequent U.S. House of Representatives hearings failed to stem the organization's growth.

After all, the Klan enjoyed the patronage of prominent members of the American establishment. In 1922, Klansman Earl B. Mayfield was elected to the U.S. Senate from Texas, a state where the Klan's members "literally constituted a Who's Who of business."[1] By the mid-1920s, the Klan also dominated state governments in Oregon, California, Indiana, Oklahoma and Arkansas. In Colorado the Klan, with business support, elected two U.S. senators. The state governor, as well as the mayor and police chief of Denver, were Klansmen. In Ohio, Klan-backed mayors won elections in a dozen cities and towns, and a Klansman became mayor of Youngstown. A senator from Alabama, Hugo L. Black, who later was named to the supreme court by Roosevelt, had joined the Klan in 1923 and publicly credited it with helping him get elected. The Klan itself was rapidly becoming a big business. It ran its own publishing company, a real estate firm and a manufacturing company producing Klan regalia. Advertisers in the Klan's national publication *Searchlight* included such corporations as Coca Cola and Studebaker. In August, 1925, 40,000 KKK members from across the country gathered in Washington for a massive parade to show off their force. Some of the white-robed marchers raised outstretched right hands in the fascist salute. A cross was burned as the national anthem was sung. It is estimated that by 1925, there may have been as many as 4 to 5 million members of the KKK. But after that a series of scandals and squabbles wracked the Klan's leadership, causing a brief decline in membership and KKK activities.

The onset of the new depression breathed new life into the KKK, giving it a new source of unrest to tap, and new targets: trade unions and communists. The Committee for Industrial Organization (CIO — later to become the Congress of Industrial

Organizations) was making inroads in the South. The press reported Southern businessmen as saying that if the Klan was against the CIO, then they were for the Klan. And the Klan made no secret of where it stood on the union question. "Parts of the open-shop South, particularly in textile, were penetrated and organized by CIO men and women who were flogged, tarred and feathered — some killed by the Ku Klux Klan — but who stayed in the South, organizing."[2] Not only were unions in general — and the CIO in particular — "subversive, radical, Red" organizations in the eyes of the Klan, but, worst of all, they sought to unite black and white working people. "The CIO wants whites and blacks on same level," screamed one angry headline in the Klan paper *The Fiery Cross*. When the National Textile Workers Union helped to set up a biracial unemployed workers' council in Greenville, South Carolina, 100 masked Klansmen raided one of the committee's meetings and beat up the blacks present, along with any whites who tried to protect them. The local press reported that the police stood by without interfering because they felt the Klan was putting a stop to "Communist" organizations in town. In Tampa, Florida, police raided a meeting of a municipal reform group that was helping in labor organizing drives, and turned several militants over to Klansmen. One victim was "flogged, castrated, caked with tar and had his leg plunged into the boiling tar-bucket;" he died nine days later.[3] Among those indicted in the affair was Tampa's chief of police, but after two trials and a Florida supreme court reversal of a guilty verdict, the accused were set free.

It was during its revival in the 1920s that the American Klan sent its first emissaries north to spread its creed of white supremacy. "Fanatic Klansmen, roaming like Alexander for new worlds to conquer, cast their eyes upon Canada," read one rather poetic contemporary newspaper account.[4] The first attempt to establish a base in Canada was in Montreal. Later Klan activity spread to the Maritimes, Manitoba and Ontario. Only in the latter province did the KKK succeed in becoming anything of a serious force in eastern Canada, and even there its influence was minimal compared to the strength it mustered in the west.

"Ku Klux Klan being organized in city; trouble expected," read the headline in the Montreal *Daily Star*, October 1, 1921. The article reported that a branch of "the famous Ku Klux Klan...is already in existence but has not, as yet, become a chartered branch" of the U.S. organization. The Montreal Klansmen had forwarded a letter to KKK headquarters in Atlanta requesting official affiliation and help from an organizer. "Like other branches of the Klan," the newspaper wrote, "the infant Montreal portion is anti-negro and anti-Jewish in the extreme." Some members of the group warned of "trouble in the future...on account of the large proportion of Hebrews in Montreal."

"While we are anti-Jewish and anti-negro, we shall not confine our actions to these sects or colours," an unnamed leader assured the press. "We feel that we are keeping well within the law in joining what we believe has been an unduly criticized organization in our continent." Three days later, the *Star* reported that the Montreal branch of the Klan held a meeting in an abandoned quarry:

> A band of masked, hooded and silent men gathered recently in the northwest part of the city, behind the Mountain, to discuss business.
> Of all sorts and sizes and gowned and hooded in various colours and fashions, they presented a motley appearance.[5]

Apparently, the Montreal Klansmen were waiting for the U.S. head office to send regulation hoods and robes, along with the paid organizer they had requested. But help was not forthcoming; in a letter sent to the Montreal branch by an Atlanta KKK official and published in the October 20 *Star*, the U.S. Klan disavowed any intentions of "applying for a charter in any other country."

In their request for affiliation with the American Klan, the Montrealers had noted that their membership was "entirely Protestant". Perhaps realizing the difficulties of making headway in a province where Catholics, a favorite Klan target, composed 80 per cent of the population, the Montreal Klan had asked for the "right to use discretion in their attitude toward the huge majority which differs with us in religious belief." That "discretion" did not endure. In 1922, a rash of fires destroyed or damaged several

Catholic institutions, including a rest home in Oka, and there was some suggestion in the media that the Klan was behind the blazes. The expansion of the organization into Quebec caused consternation in the French press. "Ku Klux Klan plans big projects," warned *La Presse*, reporting statements by Rev. Oscar Haywood, a New York Klan spokesman, that a Canadian recruitment drive, in response to a supposed flurry of membership requests, was imminent. An editorial cartoon showed a hooded Klansman pointing to a Canadian map and saying, "That's where I'll establish my field of action."[6]

But little more was heard of the Klan in Quebec, although its presence in Montreal was reported as late as 1931. The Klan doubtless found it harder to spread hatred against a strong Catholic majority than an unprotected Catholic minority.

By 1923, several Klan organizers were touring Canada, vowing that the hooded empire "will soon be operating over all the Dominion."[7] A Boston organizer was "offered" the territory of New Brunswick in early 1925; by August of that year, a half dozen or more Klan lodges were reported in towns such as Woodstock and McAdam. Local newspapers reported cross burnings in three other cities, including Saint John. "Speakers from the United States have taken part in public gatherings" of the Klan, one newspaper said.[8] The Klan also tried to get a charter in Nova Scotia and there were rumors of Klan activity in Prince Edward Island.

There was also a flurry of scattered activity in Manitoba. James R. Bellamy, a Klansman from Oklahoma, spent several days in Winnipeg during the summer of 1924 trying to stir up Klan support. He told Winnipeg citizens that Canada "is being overrun with undesirable sects and beliefs" and that "we to the south have decided that you will welcome our aid in freeing you from these sinister influences."[9] (Just what "aid" against what "sinister" influences Bellamy had in mind can be gleaned from an incident that occurred two years before his arrival. St. Boniface College, near Winnipeg, was destroyed by a fire that killed ten Catholics. As in the Quebec fires, the Klan had sent a warning message beforehand; after the fire, Klan officials in the United States denied their organization had anything to do with the affair.[10])

Bellamy vowed that "in two months' time, the sheeted figures of loyal subjects of the Invisible Empire will ride at night." But it took four years until the Klan took root in Manitoba, and then only in a limited fashion. A Klan organizing meeting was held in Winnipeg in June, 1928, with lectures and rallies following in Virden and St. Boniface.[11] The Winnipeg Klan appeared still to be in existence in 1930, when it passed a resolution condemning bilingualism. But by and large, the KKK night riders never swept through the towns and cities of Manitoba as Bellamy had predicted.

It was in Ontario that the Klan established its strongest base in eastern Canada. W.L. Higgett, an American Klan organizer touring Toronto in 1923, expressed confidence in the manifest destiny of the Klan's continental expansion:

> Our idea is a confederacy, . . . a more definite alliance between the two great English-speaking countries in this continent. We have a definite programme in view that will be of the greatest benefit to all. Confederacy would prohibit the dumping of European emigrants on this continent, would absolutely forbid a further influx of Orientals, and would establish a mandate over Mexico.[12]

In case some Canadians did not take kindly to the Klan's proposals for a union between Canada and the U.S., other KKK promoters offered a more low-key approach. Another American Klan official, R. Eugene Farnsworth, visited Toronto in September, 1923. Perhaps with an eye to the bad publicity the Klan's violent activities were receiving south of the border, Farnsworth assured Torontonians that

> We propose not to punish with tar and feathers, but to avenge wrongs. We propose not to indulge in law breaking, but in distributing retribution. We call upon all good, native-born Protestants to join us in our work.[13]

This would not be the last time the Klan would paint itself as a nonviolent avenger of an abused majority. But in the 1920s, as in the 1980s, it would not take long for the Klan's taste for terror to reveal itself.

In late November, 1923, the Klan appeared in Hamilton. "Ku Klux Klan rears head with 32 initiations," exclaimed one newspaper headline; Almond Charles Monteith of Niagara Falls was reported to have signed up the members in two weeks.[14] He was arrested at an Orange Lodge Hall by police while he was administering a membership oath to two women, and when he was searched, police found not only a revolver and the 32 names on a membership list, but also a detailed expense account for $200 for a cross burning. Monteith was tightlipped when authorities asked him if he had had anything to do with the fiery crosses that had been seen on the mountain overlooking the city.

The Klan's growth in Ontario began to pick up significantly in 1925. By May, it boasted 1,102 members and by June, one newspaper estimated (probably generously) that 8,000 people had joined the Toronto Klan.[15] Typically, splits developed and rival Klan groups were set up. One faction calling itself the Ku Klux Klan of the British Empire criticized the American connection of its competitors and rallied around the Union Jack. Two Klan factions even staged a debate in London, Ont. at a rally in August, 1925. But this infighting did not prevent the Klan from extending its influence, and locals were established in St. Thomas, Exeter, Sault Ste. Marie, Belleville, Kingston, Ottawa and Richmond.[16]

Anti-Catholicism continued to be the mainstay of Klan activity in Ontario. In Ottawa, the mayor received a nasty letter from "the Ku Klux Klan of Canada, Dominion No. 31," warning that if he did not pay more attention to Protestant taxpayers when assigning aldermanic positions to city wards, "concerted action" would be taken in the next election. In other cities, the Klan's anti-Catholic crusade went beyond letter writing. In Sarnia, two Klansmen robbed a Catholic church, destroying religious symbols in the process.[17] In Barrie, a Klansman was convicted of blowing up a Catholic church.

Prejudice against blacks was also exploited by the Klan. One particular incident is worth recounting in detail. On the last Friday night in February, 1930, 75 Klansmen suddenly appeared in Oakville, a small city halfway between Toronto and Hamilton, marching "through the principal streets clad in their white gowns and black hoods."[18] As hundreds of citizens came out to watch, the strange army set fire to a huge cross in the middle of Third Street. The Klansmen stood in silence until "the last bit of timber was consumed by flames." Then, "the invaders headed for a house which was occupied, it is alleged, by a coloured man and a white girl." The two, in fact, were visitors at the house, in the home of the man's aunt. The Klansmen, determined, they said, "to stop a menace to the purity of the Anglo-Saxon race," took the woman, Isabelle Jones, to her mother's house. The man's family was warned that "if their son was ever again seen walking in the street with a white girl the Klan would attend to him." The reaction of the police during this incident was remarkable. As one contemporary account put it:

> On their way out of town, these "Knights of the Invisible Empire" were met by the chief of police; they informed him of the action they had taken and (incredible though it may seem) were allowed to proceed to Hamilton whence they had come.[19]

Said police chief David Kerr: "There was no semblance of disorder and the visitors' behaviour was all that could be desired."

The wide publicity which the Oakville "invasion" received, however, obliged the provincial attorney general to ask Oakville's police chief to prepare a report on the affair. On March 7, summonses for four Klansmen involved in the raid were served, but only three eventually stood trial, under a clause in the Criminal Code which made it illegal to wear masks or disguises at night without a lawful excuse. Oakville's small magistrate's court was crowded when the trial opened on March 10. When one of the lawyers for the Klan members said "there are hundreds of mothers who would be eternally thankful that such a step had been taken," he was cheered by the spectators who packed the room.[20] Two of the Klansmen were acquitted because they apparently wore only gowns, not masks. The third, a chiropractor named William E. Phillips, was found guilty and fined $50.*

The black community in the Hamilton-Oakville-Toronto area,

---

*Phillips appealed, but the Ontario supreme court "pronounced the Oakville magistrate's leniency a travesty of justice and imposed a sentence of three months imprisonment."[21]

which had followed the case closely, was understandably upset by the entire affair. Many others were also outraged by the court decision. *Canadian Forum* complained bitterly about the double standards of the law:

> A meeting of Communists, held in daylight before the city hall of Toronto, was broken up by police, some of those who tried to speak on political questions being freely knocked about while others were run into police cells. If Ontario were true to its much vaunted British traditions, Communists would be allowed to speak and meetings of masked Klansmen would be dispersed with night-sticks.[22]

The labor movement also voiced its disgust and fears. A Toronto local of the Labour Party, one of the many socialist groups active in trade unions at the time, passed a resolution condemning the incident: "We view with alarm the lawlessness as was manifested by the Ku Klux Klan by their action in interference with the rights of citizens of Oakville, and their threats to continue this method of procedure, and even to extend it through intimidating certain sections of the labour movement."[23] The outcry over the Klan's activities by minorities, progressives and the trade unions and the lenience of the police and the courts toward the Klan was a pattern that would be repeated 50 years later when the KKK re-emerged.

Undoubtedly, one of the reasons the Ku Klux Klan had gained more influence in Ontario than anywhere else in eastern Canada was the willingness of at least some prominent members of the community to endorse its activities. The press reported, for example, that the Klan's Oakville raiding party included "some prominent businessmen" from Hamilton and a pastor from a Hamilton church. And among the Toronto members of the KKK were "a number of outstanding figures in the life of the Dominion," as the Montreal *Star* put it (or as one radical paper said at the time, "some of Toronto's 'best peepul' — lawyers, real estate sharks and other white guards").[24] Still, the eastern Klan never was the political force it would become in western Canada. It never held the many massive public rallies, never lobbied successfully for changes in government policy, never allied itself closely with a mainstream political party to achieve considerable clout, as it would in the prairie provinces and British Columbia.

Why was this so? As an organization devoted to fostering white supremacy and protecting white Protestant interests, the Klan, if it was to flourish, needed something to develop that supremacy over and protect those interests against: it needed a minority group as a target, a minority sizeable enough to generate anxieties among the majority, prejudices that could be exploited by the Klan. The minority group which best fit this bill for the Klan was the hundreds of thousands of immigrants who flocked to Canada in the 1920s. But a relatively small proportion of the immigrants stayed in Ontario and the other eastern provinces; the Klan would find the going much easier in the west. In the east there seemed to be less need for an organization like the Klan, as a 1923 editorial in the Toronto *Globe* explained bluntly.[25] The "racial and religious" problem of French Catholic Quebec, the *Globe* reasoned, had been kept under control by "statesmen and political leaders." As for Canada's blacks, the *Globe* argued that the "colour question is of little importance to Canada" because, though at one time there was "a considerable African population, still it gave Canada no trouble" and "in recent years has declined relatively, if not absolutely." The only remaining problem, in the *Globe*'s eyes, was the flood of "Oriental" immigration — but that was only "a question of interest in British Columbia" and hopefully could be solved by restricting immigration.

What is fascinating about this assessment of the Klan's usefulness in Canada is the *Globe*'s frankness. No abhorence at the racist nature of the Klan, nor shock or anger at its activities in Canada, are expressed here. The *Globe* merely calculated that there was no need for such an organization, given the other methods in use to keep race problems in check. As the *Globe* put it, "so crude a device as the Ku Klux Klan would seem like sticking a lever into a delicate piece of machinery." Presumably, if the conditions and the times warranted, that "delicate piece of machinery" could be adapted to make use of the Klan. That is precisely what happened, first in regard to the bothersome "Orientals" in British Columbia.

*"[A] fraudulent, alien, terrorist organization
known as the Ku Klux Klan is attempting to
organize in British Columbia. . .the record of
this society is one of murder, indecent assault
and unspeakable crime."*

— Resolution presented to
B.C. legislature, 1926

2. Keeping B.C. white

THE KU KLUX KLAN'S BEGINNINGS in Canada's westernmost
province began with a small advertisement placed in the
November 17, 1922 edition of the Cranbrook *Courier*:

KU KLUX KLAN!
Applications for Membership in the Cranbrook Klan No. 229
will be received by the undersigned during his two-day stay
in Cranbrook, B.C., December 8th and 9th, when Klan No.
229 will be organized.
ALL APPLICATIONS MUST BE IN WRITING
All applicants must be British subjects, between the ages of 21
and 40 and must be qualified horsemen possessing the
necessary skill and daring to uphold the law and order at all
costs. — H. Moncroft,
Chief Klansman, Can. Division[1]

A few days later, the Vancouver and Victoria dailies ran stories
suggesting that the Cranbrook ad was "the first indication of an
attempt to establish the Ku Klux Klan in British Columbia." The
advertisement suggests that Moncroft was an American organizer

trying to make some money by setting up a "Canadian division" of his organization. It is not known how many Cranbrook residents applied for membership. But it does appear that few, if any, got a chance to exercise their night riding skills, for little else was heard about the Klan's efforts in Cranbrook and the KKK soon turned its attention to the larger urban centres. The Klan undertook a membership drive in Vancouver in 1924, but its efforts may have been hampered by its image as an American organization: the application forms it handed out even pledged allegiance to the constitution of the United States, and stated that the KKK was devoted to "Closer relationship between capital and American labour; Preventing unwarranted strikes by foreign labour agitators" and the "limitation of foreign immigration."[2]

B.C. Klan activities gained momentum, though, when the organization latched on to the anti-immigrant hysteria then growing in the province. Local chapters of the KKK cropped up in Vancouver, Victoria, Nanaimo, Ladysmith and Buxton, thanks at least in part to the help from three Oregon Klan organizers who arrived in 1925.[3] More than 500 people attended the Klan's first major public rally in Vancouver. By 1927, the Klan claimed a B.C. membership of 13,000, including 8,000 in Vancouver and 3,000 in Victoria. Klan headquarters in Vancouver were located at the Glen Brae mansion in Shaughnessy — now a private hospital — and Klansmen would parade from that house on Matthews Street down Granville to the city's centre. In June, 1927, a reported 10,000 people lined the streets of Vancouver to watch a Klan parade. Only 200 of the announced 5,000 Klansmen turned out to the march, however, an indication that Klan membership figures were likely exaggerated. But the small turnout did not seem to dampen the Klansmen's enthusiasm. The parade ended with a Klan bonfire on Kitsilano Beach.

Fueling the Klan fires burning in B.C. was the anti-immigrant phobia then reigning in the province; racism was not introduced to the province by the Klan. By choosing as their target "the Orientals", as both Asian immigrants and the emerging Chinese and Japanese Canadian indigenous minorities were labelled, Klansmen were simply selecting a group that had already been victimized for decades. As far back as 1860, the then-colony's governor, James Douglas, expressed the establishment's two-sided view of Asian immigrants: "They are certainly not a desirable class of people, but are for present useful as labourers."[4] Douglas was in good company. Sir John A. Macdonald, Canada's first prime minister, said that "a Mongolian or Chinese population in our country...would not be a wholesome element for this country...At present it is simply a question of alternatives — either you have this labour or you cannot have the railway."[5]

About 15,000 Chinese were admitted into Canada as cheap labor for the transcontinental railway then being built. It is said that for every mile of track laid, a Chinese worker died. But when the railway was completed, the Chinese were suddenly no longer welcome (though they continued to be exploited in other business sectors; for example, B.C. mining magnate Robert Dunsmuir used Chinese workers as strikebreakers in 1883, 1903, and 1912-14). The Chinese Immigration Act, passed in 1885, barred virtually all Chinese through its various discriminatory rules, not the least of which was a $50 head tax which was raised to $500 in 1903. "For my part, I have very little hope of any good coming to this country from Asiatic immigration of any kind," said Prime Minister Wilfrid Laurier.[6] Local authorities in B.C. must have shared Laurier's doubts. In 1901, the Victoria School Board segregated whites and Asian students. Anti-Asian racism was whipped up to such a state that in 1907 a major riot broke out in Vancouver against the Chinese and Japanese. "The local newspapers, respectable individuals and organizations played a very prominent role in at least preparing the groundwork and instigating the violence...The timing of the riots seems to have been related to white workers' alleged fears of economic competition, especially at a time of recession," noted one study.[7] "Stand for a White Canada" read the banners as 8,000 people marched through the Chinese quarter of the city, destroying property and terrorizing the population.

The Chinese were not the only "Orientals" to feel the sting of officially-sanctioned racism. In 1907, Ottawa obliged Japan to sign a "voluntary" agreement limiting emigration to Canada. The following year, the federal government enacted a regulation making it nearly impossible for East Indians to enter the country.

By 1910, racism was formally written into Canada's Immigration Act. The act gave the government the power to

> prohibit for a stated period, or permanently, the landing in Canada...of immigrants belonging to any race unsuited to the climate or requirements of Canada.

This law remained on the books until 1978. In 1914, the infamous *Komagata Maru* incident took place in Vancouver. Three hundred and seventy-six East Indians were confined to the *Komagata Maru* while the ship waited at anchor for two months in Vancouver's harbor, because immigration officials would not allow them to enter Canada. At one point the passengers seized control of the ship and successfully fought off a midnight raid of 150 immigration officers and policemen. But in the end the ship was forced to set sail with only 22 passengers let ashore (all of whom had been previous residents in Canada).

This kind of racist hysteria reached frightening proportions after the first world war. In 1920, the Vancouver Board of Trade and the Victoria Chamber of Commerce called for segregated schools and curbs on Asian property ownership. "We strongly feel that we should do everything in our power to retain British Columbia for our own people," said the Vancouver Board of Trade in 1921.[8] All Chinese, Japanese and East Indians, including those who were Canadian citizens, were prohibited from voting in B.C. The Liberal government of premier John Oliver enforced a clause in government contracts which prevented contractors from employing Asians. A.M. Manson, the province's attorney general and labor minister, was one of the leading anti-Asian orators on the lecture circuit. It was also the B.C. government which in 1923 pushed hardest for passage of a new federal Chinese Immigration Act, superseding the 1885 statute. "Chinese Exclusion Act" would probably have been a better name for the new legislation. It barred entry into Canada to virtually any Chinese; the Chinese in Canada — even those who were born here — were not permitted to sponsor family or relatives. Between 1924 and 1930, only *three* Chinese immigrants entered the country![9] A statement by premier Oliver to his fellow Liberal, prime minister Willian Lyon Mackenzie King, sounds disturbingly similar to the Klan's ideology:

> The stopping of Oriental immigration entirely is urgently necessary, but that in itself will not suffice, since it leaves us with our present large Oriental population and their prolific birth rate. Our Government feels that the Dominion government should go further, and by deportation or other legitimate means, seek to bring about the reduction and final elimination of this menace to the well-being of the White population of this Province.[10]

But the anti-immigrant crusade waged in B.C. by politicians and businessmen was based on flimsy evidence. How much of a "menace" to British Columbia's whites could the Asian immigrants pose when, in 1921, they represented only 39,000 of the province's 524,000 people — about 7.5 per cent? Perhaps the campaigns against immigrants served a more fundamental purpose for the powers that be: they helped divert attention away from the more serious problems in the country, unemployment and an economy in crisis. In any case, the widespread approval of anti-immigrant racism from respectable quarters certainly gave the emerging Ku Klux Klan a needed boost. Klan organizers skilfully played on the "Oriental" question to expand fairly rapidly in the province.

Typical of the Klan's anti-Asiatic propaganda was a resolution passed by the Vancouver Klan No. 1 in February, 1927. "EXCLUSION OF ALL ASIATICS IS SOUGHT — Removal of Orientals from Canada," read the headline over the Vancouver *Province*'s report on the Klan meeting. The resolution called for the "complete prohibition of Asiatic immigration into Canada, repatriation of Asiatic immigration into Canada, repatriation of all Asiatics at present domiciled in this country and expropriation of their property here." Speakers at the Klan rally stressed the "desirability of maintaining Anglo-Saxon standards in the Dominion...by the preservation of the right of selection of immigrants."[11] As part of its anti-Asian campaign, the Klan forwarded the meeting's repatriation resolution to the federal and provincial governments and to local business and labor groups. In 1928, the Klan even circulated a petition in Vancouver demanding that "Orientals" not be hired on government steamships; it is not known how many signatures it collected.

The B.C. Klan relied on the authorities' acquiescence to carry out and expand its activities. In November, 1925, a resolution which condemned the Klan was voted down in the provincial parliament. Though attorney general Manson and premier Oliver both feigned support for the motion, which had been introduced by a Labour parliamentarian, the ruling Liberals did little to ensure the resolution's survival. Conservative house leader R.H. Pooley led the attack against the anti-Klan resolution: "There was no right to presume that these people (the Klan) would break the law and if they did there was machinery to deal with them," he said.[12] Thus was initiated the standard excuse for non-action against the Klan which would be repeated by politicians to this day: "Wait until they break the law and then maybe we'll do something about it." Another Conservative politician, C.F. Davie, went so far as to turn the tables on Klan opponents and suggested that the resolution — but not the Klan — was "calculated to stir up racial and religious dissension." Davie moved an amendment declaring that "it was not in the public interest to take up the time of the House" in discussing the Klan; the amendment was carried by a vote of 24 to 20. (In 1980, the government in British Columbia would go one better than its 1927 counterpart and prevent a motion condemning the Klan from even getting on the legislature floor for debate.)

Other levels of government also seemed willing to help the Klan; the Vancouver city council did by granting the necessary permit allowing the KKK to hold its 1927 parade in city streets. The media and some church figures also contributed to the Klan's growth. Newspapers throughout B.C. and including the major dailies like the *Sun*, the *Province* and the *Morning Star*, popularized anti-immigrant myths and "yellow peril" scare stories, as well as giving KKK activities front page coverage.

The much-publicized Klan resolution calling for the exclusion of all Asiatics from Canada was endorsed at a Klan meeting at the Wesley Church in Vancouver. A Rev. C.E. Ratzold addressed the gathering.[13] Another church leader, Rev. Duncan MacDougall, published a newspaper in Vancouver called *The Beacon* which was clearly allied to the Klan.[14]

The anti-immigrant sentiments expressed by government leaders, business groups and the media were echoed and amplified by much of the labor movement. Still relatively weak and fighting for recognition, trade unions tended to regard immigrants as competitors for jobs who helped lower wages. The Trades and Labour Congress held an anti-Asiatic position throughout the 1920s and both the Vancouver and Victoria labor councils pushed for restrictions on the flow of immigrants.

It fell to the more militant and radical elements within B.C.'s labor movement to lead the opposition to the KKK. Just seven days after the Klan announced its presence in the province with its advertisement in the Cranbrook paper, the *Federationist*, the B.C. Federation of Labour organ, attacked the KKK in an article entitled "B.C. workers and a Canadian Ku Klux Klan."[15] The article, based on a familiar theme in the radical labor press at the time, drew the link between the Klan and similar organizations:

> In Italy it is the Fascisti. In Ireland it was the Black and Tans. . . and in the United States the American Legion and the Ku Klux Klan have functioned very effectively. In fact, terrorism has become the weapon of the ruling class the world over.

Anticipating the kid glove treatment which governments would accord the Klan, the article pointed out the futility of relying on the authorities to stop the KKK:

> Every country has seen intensified organization on the part of the ruling class. The means may not have been legal, but those who make the laws can place what interpretation on them they wish.

The *Federationist* went on to inform its readers that "the Ku Klux Klan was exposed in the New York *World*,* all its rottenness and its infamies were laid naked before the public." The *Federationist* warned its audience that given the Klan's avowed anti-unionism and pro-U.S. stance, its first objective was the open shop and the "American Plan". The article concluded with this call to battle:

*See page 22.

It therefore behooves the trades unionists to tighten up their ranks; ere the "white terror" strikes them and destroys their organizations.

In the following years, sectors of the B.C. labor movement continued to counter Klan organizing drives with lengthy denunciations and exposures in its press. When the Klan arrived on the scene in Vancouver in the autumn of 1924, the labor newspapers warned that the Klan "relies upon organized force and will only respect a more highly organized and more powerful force than itself." Labour Party members of the provincial parliament carried the anti-Klan battle into the legislature. Frank Browne, the Labour member for Burnaby, tried (unsuccessfully) to pass a motion "expressing disapproval of the action of the Klan in organizing in this Province" when the Oregon Klan organizers first appeared. The resolution read in part:

> "We regret, however, that a fraudulent, alien, terrorist organization known as the Ku Klux Klan is attempting to organize in British Columbia. And that the purpose of this body is to perpetuate hatred amongst our citizens and to substitute lynch law for duly constituted authority. And that the record of this society is one of murder, indecent assault and unspeakable crime."[16]

The Klan was sufficiently upset at these and similar actions that one Labour parliamentarian, Tom Uphill, received an ominous note from the KKK. The note simply said: "You are known."[17]

Klan attempts to use racism to split the labor movement were also rebuffed, though not without difficulty. Anti-immigrant sentiments were defended most vociferously by the narrow-minded craft unions. When the KKK forwarded its 1927 resolution against Asiatics to the Vancouver and New Westminster Trades and Labour Council, the executive of that body recommended the motion be rejected. But a delegate from the Plumbers' Union "stated that his union had endorsed the principle of the resolution at its last meeting." His position, however, was not shared by his trade union brothers. According to a newspaper report at the time, "other delegates arose and protested against any consideration being extended to the proposals of 'men who hid behind masks.'"[18] The "great majority" of the union delegates then voted to throw the KKK proposal "into the wastepaper basket."

It was this kind of opposition which helped prevent the Klan from making anything but temporary headway in B.C. The local KKK did continue to press governments for immigration restrictions and other measures until at least 1932, but its energies had been largely dissipated by the end of the 1920s and the organization fell apart. The hooded empire would have to look elsewhere in western Canada for recruits to its campaign of hate.

"Pure patriotism, restrictive and selective immigration... one flag and one language — English."

— The by-laws of the
Alberta Klan, 1932

3. Scapegoats in Alberta

KLAN ORGANIZERS FIRST MOVED into Alberta from British Columbia in 1925 and 1926. As in B.C., the Alberta Klan found a public receptive to its message. Here, though, it was not Asians but Central and Eastern Europeans who were the abused immigrants. And a new element was added to the racist broth: anti-Catholicism, directed against some of the immigrants and the French Canadian minority in the province.

Immigration to Western Canada in the first few decades of the century had a checkered history. Policy was determined by two not always complementary considerations: the desire to recruit "English stock" to preserve Canada's Anglo-Saxon nature, and the manpower needs of labor intensive industries. Between 1900 and 1914, more than a million immigrants came to work on Canada's farms and in the booming rail and resource industries. The war put a halt to the flow, and the postwar depression — unemployment reached 16 per cent among organized workers in 1921 — gave businesses much of the excess cheap labor they needed. In 1923, Ottawa placed Poland, Yugoslavia, Hungary and Romania on its "non-preferred" list for immigration. But certain business interests pushed for more open immigration, especially after the economy picked up. The rail companies, along with the coal and lumber interests, sought workers to do the work for which "other Canadians" had shown "an aversion", as the Railway Association of Canada put it.[1] Responding to these corporate pressures, the federal government and the railways signed an agreement in 1925 to facilitate the immigration of thousands of Central and Eastern Europeans, and 185,000 immigrants were brought to western Canada. This traffic not only meant settlers for the rail companies' land and revenues for their steamship lines and passenger trains, but also cheap labor for industries like the southern Alberta sugar beet fields. Immigration allowed businessmen to depress wages; in some cases immigrants were used as strikebreakers.

Abused by the companies which had fought for an "open door" immigration policy, these Europeans also found themselves the target of those who wanted to close the door. In the 1920s about half of the people living in the largest western Canadian cities were immigrants, and a third spoke primarily a foreign language. In Alberta in 1921, 40 per cent of the population was of neither British nor French origin. Anti-immigrant sentiments among the local population were inflamed; church leaders, the press and the Orange Lodges in the prairies warned of the threats to Canada's supposed British heritage. Conservative members of the federal parliament from Alberta decried the flood of "illiterate peasants" from Europe. After 1929 the depression slashed wages and big business no longer needed immigrants to provide cheap labor. The railway agreement was scrapped and immigrants came under renewed attack from government and business. Lazy and troublesome foreigners were blamed for the failure of over-burdened government relief programs. Immigrants were also indiscriminately labelled as "Reds"; between 1903 and 1928 deportations from Canada averaged 500 a year, but in 1931 the number of deportations jumped to 5,000.

Immigrants were not the only group to feel the heat of prejudices. The 200,000 Catholics, including a small French Canadian minority, in Alberta during the 1920s were under intense pressure to assimilate and abandon their culture. Government leaders had no sympathy for the French Canadians' efforts to preserve their language and their education rights. The rabidly anti-French Orange Order was well established throughout Alberta and helped to entrench anti-Catholic feelings in the province.

It was in this atmosphere that the Ku Klux Klan began selling memberships in Calgary, Edmonton and several other cities and towns in southern Alberta in 1925 and 1926. By 1927, it claimed a membership of 1,000.[2] The organizing drive stalled when the Klan's leaders disappeared with the funds, but the show was put back on the road with the help of Saskatchewan organizers, including the professional anti-Catholic campaigner and Klan leader J.J. Maloney. By the end of 1930, eleven Klan locals had been set up and within a year another 40 towns and villages boasted "Klaverns", as local Klan clubs were known. Edmonton had seven branches, while other towns with active Klaverns included Camrose, Forestburg, Irma, Jarrow, Wetaskiwin, Red Deer, Stettler, Milo, Rosebud, Ponoka and Vulcan.[3] Edmonton was chosen as the headquarters for the Alberta Klan, whose newspaper, *The Liberator*, claimed a circulation of 250,000. Maloney claimed that by 1933 he had addressed 100,000 people on his many road trips to sell the Klan. But actual Klan membership in the province probably peaked at between 5,000 and 7,000.[4]

To ensure its growth, the Klan played on the widespread anti-immigrant and anti-French prejudices. The Klan's official charter limited membership to "white Protestants" devoted to the principles of "Protestantism, pure patriotism, restrictive and selective immigration, one national public school, one flag and one language — English."[5] Playing on the insecurities many Albertans felt in troubled times, the Klan — like its modern-day descendants — sought to blame the immigrant population for every imaginable problem. Foreigners made up "the largest contribution to our crime list and by far the largest proportion of inmates in our insane asylums," Klan literature asserted.[6] With the help of the leader of the Orange Order in Alberta, J.J. Maloney also circulated a petition in Edmonton against the "promiscuous use of French on the radio." The Klan organized boycotts of Catholic businesses. Cross burnings dotted the prairie landscape for several years. The first took place at Drumheller on the night of November 1, 1929. The following year, on July 29, a 50-foot cross blazed for two hours on a hill overlooking Edmonton's Riverdale Flats. On the night of August 8, 1932, firemen were called to extinguish one large burning cross and four smaller ones at the Edmonton racetrack. Occasionally the Alberta Klan resorted to the terror tactics more traditionally associated with the organization in order to enforce its beliefs or silence its critics:

> In May, 1930, the first act of violence in Alberta ascribed to the Klan occured when Lacombe blacksmith Fred Doberstein was abducted by six masked men, stripped naked, and taken by car to a location in the bush west of Blackfalds, where he was tarred and feathered.
>
> The men told Mr. Doberstein they were Klan members. They accused him of being intimate with women at Lacombe and Innisfail and made him promise that he would "take the first train south and never return."[7]

Though top Klan leaders denied their organization had anything to do with the affair, the Klan did gain much notoriety during the trial of the two men charged with the assault in Red Deer, a strong Klan base.

As elsewhere, the Klan in Alberta could rely on direct and indirect support from influential segments of society. The Klansmen joined with the Conservative party in criticizing the Railway Agreement favoring immigration, and supported the Conservatives' call for more stringent immigration controls. The KKK "has been primarily a Conservative political organization," wrote a Klan official to Premier J.E. Brownlee in the late 1920s.[8] The Klan also took credit for the election of Don Knott as mayor of Edmonton in 1930 as a result of their campaign against the "Catholic sympathies" of the incumbent, a Liberal. In June of the same year, the Klan backed the Conservatives in the federal election; in the East Edmonton riding, a cross was burned to celebrate the victory of Tory Ambrose Bury, whose candidacy had been actively supported by the Klan.[9] Premier Brownlee denied the claim made by Klan leader Maloney that several cabinet ministers and Brownlee himself were Klan members — a boast that was probably exaggerated.* But Brownlee's United Farmers Party government did issue an official charter to Maloney and the Alberta KKK through the provincial Registrar of Joint Stock Companies, the only province to do so. Brownlee, like politicians before and after, took refuge behind the law to justify his hands-off approach to the Klan:

> If the KKK, or any other organization, observes the laws of the country...it will not be molested. (The) government has not given any instructions to the police, or any other agency or body, to make any investigation of the matter, for no need of such action has arisen.[11]

Brownlee's minister of agriculture, George Hoadley, went so far as to condone the Klan's politics. Any "political action the Ku Klux Klan may take in Alberta is likely to be along Dominion lines," he asserted. Noting that his government had already made clear its opposition to French language school rights, Hoadley asked: "What else could the Klan have against our government?"[12]

Such co-operation from the highest levels of government was not the only helpful support the Alberta Klan enjoyed. At one point, 40 leading businessmen and mine owners in the coal mining town of Drumheller signed up with the KKK.[13] The Orange Lodges, whose membership included many prominent citizens and business leaders, were always willing to help the Klan build its anti-French crusade. The Orangist newspaper *The Sentinel* reported favorably on Klan actions. Orange Lodges also gave Klan organizers membership lists to use during their tours throughout Alberta.

Other sectors of the populace were less enthusiastic about the doctrine of the Klan. French Catholics and European immigrants obviously had little love for an organization which thrived on victimizing them. These groups did a fairly good job of keeping the KKK out of areas of the province where they represented a

---

*Several years later, however, David B. Mullin, a one-time Klan member from Edmonton, did become the provincial minister of agriculture in the Social Credit Party.[10]

significant proportion of the population. Klan locals were concentrated in towns and villages with a 14 per cent Catholic population, whereas the provincial average was 23 per cent.[14] The Klan was also successfully kept out of centres heavily populated by Eastern Europeans, such as the southern beet fields.

In some towns, Maloney was prevented from speaking. Individual citizens also displayed remarkable courage at times in standing up to Klan terror. One such man was C.B. Halpin, the editor of the Lacombe *Western Globe*. Halpin saw it as his duty to campaign against the hate crusade of the Ku Klux Klan. For his efforts, he received a letter from the Klan in June, 1930, threatening that "your place of residence will be burned to the ground" unless he let up on his attacks on the Klan. But Halpin did not flinch; he carried out his campaign, and the Klan never made good its threat.[15]

The labor movement provided some of the most vocal opposition to the Klan in Alberta. When the Klan announced its presence in Alberta in 1925 through an advertisement in an Edmonton newspaper, trade unions began their counteroffensive. "This pernicious organization has raised its dirty head in the capital city of Alberta," warned the *Alberta Labour News* in December, 1925. Anti-Klan education was not new to the *Labour News*. Four years before the Klan ever set foot in Alberta, the newspaper had informed its readers that the United Mine Workers had amended its constitution so that "no person who is a member of the Ku Klux Klan may become or remain a member" of the union.[16]

The Crowsnest Pass strike of 1932 created a showdown between the Klan and most of its principal targets — European immigrants (many of whom were Catholic), labor unions and communists.[17] Less than half the work force in the coal mines of the area — owned by the Canadian Pacific Railway and French and American multinationals — were English Canadian. Most were immigrant Slovaks, Italians, French or Belgians. The mines had been a centre of labor militancy for several decades; when the depression set in, the workers were represented by the Mine Workers Union, affiliated to the Communist Party-led Workers' Unity League. Company threats to cut wages in 1932 and an attempt to break the union led to a wildcat strike in one mine in February, and the conflict quickly spread to the other mines. The employers first tried to use force to end the strike, but the strikers and their wives resisted RCMP efforts to break up their picket lines. The mine owners then resorted to more subtle means, employing racism and anti-communism to divide the work force. Attempts were made to split the "True Blue British" element (as the English Canadian workers were called) from the immigrants and labor militants. A manager at one of the work sites, the Blairmore mine, had warned before the strike that he intended to turn the town into a "White Man's Camp". As the strike progressed, company propaganda stressed that the British way of life had to be protected from the foreigners and the Bolsheviks.

On February 13, 1933, the Klansmen arrived to reinforce the employers' arsenal. The KKK gathered on a hillside near Blairmore to burn a cross. One sign paraded during the ceremony read: "Beware Reds!" The Klan's terrorism began to have its desired effect. In one union meeting in nearby Coleman, Anglo-Saxon miners who supported the strike were hooted down by right-wingers in the union who invoked the Klan's racist ideas to justify their refusal to continue the walkout. Two union leaders were driving to a meeting when they were fired on — by a Klansman, they charged. At yet another contentious meeting, in Coleman, a KKK member helped provoke a riot. The meeting ended in complete disarray and marked the end of the Mine Workers Union in that town. A scab contract was signed and 100 workers were blacklisted from the mine.

But in Blairmore, it was a different story. The divide-and-rule ploy used by the employers and the Klan ran into stiffer resistance here. Demonstrations and other activities united workers of different ethnic origins. The Communist Party, through its influential newspaper *The Worker*, appeared to have a good measure of success in counteracting the racist ideas being spread by the Klan. A Mrs. A. Lucas, one of five women arrested during a violent confrontation on the picket lines, wrote a letter to the *Worker* which stated, "In spite of the KKK, police terror and boss agents, we are standing as solid as before...On with the struggle!" With that kind of determination, the Klan and the mine owners were forced to retreat. In September, the company signed a contract recognizing the Mine Workers as the miners' bargaining agent. In municipal elections the following February, a slate of miners' candidates defeated a group that was identified with the mine owners.

The Crowsnest Pass strike did not cause the collapse of the KKK in Alberta. But it did show that when people held their ranks, the Klan's racism made little headway. As the depression set in, at least some people realized that the hard times demanded solidarity among the down-and-out more than ever. Internal malaise also hastened the Klan's demise in Alberta. In 1933, the Klan's leader, J.J. Maloney, found himself in the midst of scandal. Various charges of theft, fraud, vandalism and slander led to jail terms. The shell of the once-vibrant Klan organization lingered on in Alberta for several years. In 1937, for example, a Klan picnic attracted 250 people. But by and large the Klan in Alberta was a spent force.

"Every organizer in it [the Klan] is a Tory. It costs over a thousand dollars a week to pay them. I know it for I pay them."
— Regina Conservative
W.D. Cowan, 1928

4. Political clout in Saskatchewan

IT WAS IN SASKATCHEWAN that the Ku Klux Klan reached the height of its influence during the 1920s. Before it disappeared in the early 1930s, the Saskatchewan KKK would boast tens of thousands of members, 125 local chapters, and the successful toppling of a government. The two things which the KKK always required for its success were abundantly present in Saskatchewan at the time: a large and vulnerable minority group to attack, and an influential section of the establishment willing to use the Klan's extremism to further its own goals. The old American South had its ex-slaves and a bitter land-owning aristocracy; Saskatchewan had its Catholics and French Candians and a Conservative Party hungry for power.

The Klan moved into Saskatchewan in late 1926. Three American KKK organizers — Hugh F. Emmons, L.A. Scott and his son Harold — distributed a pamphlet in Regina entitled *Why I Intend to Become a Klan Member*, and took out newspaper ads announcing public lectures on "The Ku Klux Klan — What is it? What is it doing here?" The Saskatchewan Klan grew rapidly in the year that followed. It claimed 1,000 members in Regina, a local branch in Moose Jaw, and nine chapters in various smaller towns. The tiny community of Woodrow reportedly had 153 of its 218 residents sign up as Klan members![1] The Moose Jaw local quickly became the largest Klan chapter. It was there, on June 7, 1927, that between 7,000 and 8,000 people attended the Klan's first major public rally in Saskatchewan. More than 400 people came to the rally from Regina in a special train provided by the CNR.[2] The Klan's endemic internal squabbling, and the subsequent rapid succession of various leaders, only seemed to spur rather than stunt its growth in the province. In late 1927, Emmons and Scott tried to make off with an estimated $100,000 in KKK funds.* But the publicity the Klan got during the Emmons trials in 1928, widely covered in the press, seemed to help rather than hurt the organization. J.H. Hawkins, an American and a former Ontario Klan organizer, stepped in to replace Emmons as the chief Klan organizer in Saskatchewan. He managed to push the number of Klan locals over the 100 mark and spread the organization's tentacles into the northern reaches of the province before he was deported in the summer of 1928. J.J. Maloney, a longtime anti-Catholic spokesman and writer who later led the Alberta Klan, soon replaced Hawkins. Gala cross burnings seemed to be a favorite pastime of the Saskatchewan Klan, and attracted large crowds. About 2,000 people crowded into the Regina city hall auditorium one winter night in 1928 for a Klan rally at which, according to the Regina *Leader*, "a fiery cross of electric red lights was burned."[3] On May 23, 1928, another 1,500 attended a spectacular burning of an 80-foot cross in the city. The next day, in the town of Melfort, and estimated 5,000 to 10,000 people witnessed the burning of two 20-foot crosses at a giant rally. Speeches by Klan leaders and Protestant clergymen were followed by the singing of the "Maple Leaf Forever" and "Onward Christian Soldiers".

Total membership in the Saskatchewan Klan of the 1920s is difficult to pinpoint; estimates range from 10,000 to five times

---

*Emmons and Scott had a history of shady dealings. They were both Klan organizers in Indiana, where the KKK leader, David C. Stephenson, had been convicted of murder in 1925. Emmons turned informer at U.S. Senate hearings into Klan violence and electoral fraud.

that number. Liberal premier James Gardiner put it at 13,000; newspapers reported it was much larger ("an organization of 40,000 to 50,000* men and women," said one account).[4] The true figure was probably somewhere in between, but in any case the Klan was undeniably a formidable force.

The Klan's remarkable success in Saskatchewan was mainly the result of its ability to fan and feed off of the xenophobic atmosphere which existed at the time toward the French minority and immigrants. As organizer Emmons put it, the Klan "fed people 'antis'. Whatever we found that they could be taught to hate and fear, we fed them."[5] The Klan would campaign against everything from government corruption in Moose Jaw to juvenile delinquency in Regina in order to widen its appeal. But time and time again, it came back to blaming French Catholics and immigrants for all of Saskatchewan's problems.

The French Canadians in Saskatchewan made up about 5 per cent of the population. Roman Catholics as a whole accounted for 233,000 of the province's 1927 population of 850,000 — about 27 per cent. Descendants of some of the prairie's first settlers, the French found themselves battling for their survival as a distinct nationality. Separate Catholic schools offered some protection for their language and culture; official government policy stipulated that English had to be used in all schools but French was allowed as a primary course. In the Catholic schools, that usually meant that French was taught for the first four or five years at least. But a tougher regulation introduced in 1918 specified that French could not be used as a language of instruction beyond the first grade. On the political scene the Conservative party, the province's official opposition, made no secret of its anti-French bias.† Even more ominous for the French Catholics was the virulent anti-French prejudice being whipped up by the powerful Orange Order. Fanatically Protestant and pro-British, the Orangemen, whose newspaper *The Sentinel* had a circulation of

---

*Klan membership of 40,000 would mean that five per cent of Saskatchewan's population at the time was in the hooded empire.

†In 1916, the Conservative Party was insisting that "the English language should be the sole language of instruction in the public school."

40,000, raged against separate French schools, the French language, and Catholicism. With words that bear a striking resemblance to those of the anti-bilingual crusaders of today, *The Sentinel* chastised what it saw as Ottawa's attempts to spread French and "the whinings of Quebec" across Canada. It denounced the bilingual stamps and the new bilingual post office in Regina as "repugnant to the whole English-speaking population."[6]

While reserving most of its hatred for the French, the Orangemen also took shots at Saskatchewan's immigrant population. In 1926, for example, *The Sentinel* condemned the immigration of 12,000 "foreigners" into the province. The same kind of anti-French and anti-immigrant diatribes were also delivered from many Protestant pulpits in the province. "Saskatchewan went through what you could call a period of violent intolerance," recalls Emmett Hall, a former supreme court judge who at that time was a young lawyer in Saskatoon. "The Klan found fertile ground in Saskatchewan."

The Ku Klux Klan plowed that fertile ground for all its worth by attempting to champion various racist causes. At its first rally in the province in 1927, the Klan made its anti-French Catholic bias clear. Klan chief Emmons told a Regina audience that every man who did not support the Union Jack should be deported (an ironic comment, considering Emmons was American). "One language — English" was the policy Emmons favored. "The Klan stands for Unity among Canada's population and we do not want this part of Canada divided by language," the organization told premier Gardiner.[7] In 1927, the Klan helped mobilize opposition to a request by a French-language association for government aid for training bilingual teachers. In 1929, the Saskatchewan Klan's second annual "Klonvokation" called on the government to require school trustees to be fluent "in the English language." And a resolution passed at the following year's convention in Regina protested against federal departments for "giving the French language equal status with the English language." In campaigning against the alleged spread of French-language education and facilities in the province, the Klan was raising a false bogey. Of the 4,776 school districts in Saskatchewan in 1927, only 31 had

separate or minority schools — and eight of these were Protestant
schools set up in districts where the majority was Catholic.[8] But
the truth never seemed to deter the Klan. With French Catholics in
the 1920s, as it would with immigrants in the 1980s, the Klan simply seized on popular myths and fears to fan the flames of hatred.

One incident clearly revealed the thrust of the Klan's
anti-French crusade and the extent of the KKK's influence. In the
Gouverneur school district, some Protestants opposed to the
teaching of French in the schools decided to keep their children
home. Five were eventually charged with breaking the law by
keeping their children out of school. They were defended in court
by J.F. Bryant, a well-known Tory lawyer and an open Klan
sympathizer. The two presiding justices of the peace, both of them
members of the Klan, dismissed the case.[9]

The Saskatchewan Klan seasoned its anti-Catholicism with a
dose of the KKK's more traditional racism toward blacks and
immigrants in general. "God never intended to dilute the white
race with inferior colored blood," Klan organizer J.H. Hawkins
told a Moose Jaw rally. "The races were meant to be separated."
Hawkins decried the "scum that refuse to assimilate" and warned
of "a Canada composed of men who jabber all the tongues." By
painting central and southern European immigrants as Catholics,
the Klan neatly rolled up its anti-French, anti-Catholic and
anti-immigrant hate campaign into one ball. Said Hawkins at a
Regina rally:

> The Klan takes this unalterable stand — that the permitting
> of any race of people to enter Canada that cannot be
> assimilated and become heart and soul Canadians, the permit-
> ting of the entry of those people is a detriment to that coun-
> try...Prior to 1920 Canada was in every sense of the word a
> British Dominion...Less than 47 (per cent) of the people
> living in Canada today are of British descent...Then do you
> wonder why the Klan has been called into being?[10]

Klan leaders told a Montreal *Gazette* correspondent that the "Klan
believes in Protestantism, racial purity (and) restrictive and
selective immigration."[11] In 1930, the Klan tried to blame "an
unemployment situation which has no parallel in the history of
Canada" on the "dumping into Canada for the last three years (of)

thousands of Central Europeans."

The Klan's successful exploitation of existing racist sentiments in Saskatchewan was not the only reason for its unparalleled growth in the province, since it used that trick everywhere else as well. What set Saskatchewan apart from all the other regions in the country was the alliance of interests which emerged between the Klan and other political forces in the province, especially the Conservatives.

The newspapers in the province, especially those in smaller towns and rural areas, generally gave the Klan lengthy and sympathetic coverage. The Kerrobert *Citizen* gave its editorial approval to the Klan, while the Esterhazy *Observer*, the North Battleford *Optimist* and other papers supported it indirectly. In Regina, the daily *Standard* once complained that a Klan rally was not adequately covered by the local radio station.[12] The Conservative Regina *Star* also echoed the Klan's anti-immigrant and anti-French message.

Sections of the religious establishment also lent the Klan credibility. At least 26 Protestant ministers, including many prominent and powerful ones, dressed the Klan's racism in a religious garb and used their pulpits to situate God on the side of the KKK. Two well-known religious leaders were frequently featured as keynote speakers at Klan rallies: Rev. S.F. Rondeau, former moderator of the Presbyterian Synod of Saskatchewan, and Rev. T.J. Hind, pastor of the largest church in Moose Jaw. Rev. Rondeau boasted that "about 30,000 ministers belonged to the Klan" in the United States and he praised "the Klan in Canada which has not committed one immoral deed...I am a Klansman." Rev. Hind, for his part, was one of the original members of the Saskatchewan Klan.[13]

Far more important than the co-operation of the media and the church, though, was that of the Conservative Party. At the time, the Tory party provincially was not very powerful; nor were there any federal Conservative MPs from Saskatchewan for most of the 1920s. The connection was not so much a conspiracy as a confluence of interests. If the Conservatives had any hope of capturing power provincially, they had to win over the votes of the small farmers and working people in the towns, the same people the Klan was attracting. Both organizations realized that playing on people's prejudices and fears was the ticket to power.

Many top men in the Klan were Conservatives ("The Klan leaders openly proclaim their adherence to the Conservative Party," said one contemporary newspaper report[14]) and a good number of leading Conservatives were Klansmen. J.W. Rosborough, who was temporarily chosen as a Klan leader after Emmons's embarrassing departure in 1927, was a member of the Orange Lodge and a well-known Conservative. Klan orator J.J. Maloney was cheered by 2,000 people at a February, 1928 Regina rally when he boasted that he was and would always remain a Conservative. Lawyer J.F. Bryant, who defended Klansmen in three separate trials, was a prominent Tory who eventually became minister of public works in the provincial Conservative government of the 1930s. The Saskatchewan Klan's secretary, G.H. Ellis, was a Tory. Dr. Walter D. Cowan, the Klan's treasurer, was the federal Tory MP for Regina from 1917 to 1921, and for Long Lake from 1930 to 1935. He reportedly refused the leadership of the Klan at its 1927 convention only because he felt his close connection with the Tories might prove embarrassing. Nevertheless, during Emmons's trial for misappropriation of Klan funds, the Klan chief insisted that he had lost effective control over the organization to Cowan, Conservative Party leader Dr. J.T.M. Anderson and other Tory bigwigs. (The Conservative politicians denied the charge and vowed to produce affidavits to prove their claim, but their evidence never did appear.[15]) As the Klan grew stronger and the Tories grew hungrier for power, the co-operation between them became increasingly extensive and open. At the Tories' annual convention in March, 1928, a large number of the delegates were Klansmen, including the "King Kleagle" (leader) and his secretary from Regina, and provincial organizer J.H. Hawkins. Klansmen leafletting the convention were asked to stop, but only after virtually every delegate had received the Klan's literature. Tory lawyer Bryant observed that KKK members were very active in the policy seminars. There were also rumors that organizers had manoeuvred to have as many Klan members registered as possible.

The Saskatchewan Conservatives' close ties with the Klan were observed with interest by R.B. Bennett, the federal Conservative leader who became prime minister in 1930. As early as 1927, he was sufficiently aware of his party's close links with the KKK to instruct local Conservatives to be careful about making the relationship too public during the scandal trial of Klan organizer Emmons. In 1928, Bennett was informed by Walter Cowan, the Klan treasurer and leading Regina Tory, that the KKK

> is the most complete political organization known in the west. Every organizer in it is a Tory. It costs over a thousand a week to pay them. I know it for I pay them...Smile when you hear anything about this organization.[16]

Bennett was also kept posted by J.F. Bryant about the Klan's role during the 1928 provincial party convention. In the months after the convention, Bennett began to take a more direct interest in making sure his party would topple the ruling provincial Liberals in the next elections. In April, Bennett, a millionaire, helped found the new Tory organ, the Regina *Daily Star*. With a by-election coming at the end of the year and general elections expected shortly, the Conservatives needed a newspaper to spread the party's message. Bennett sat on the board of the *Star*, which became a mouthpiece for anti-French Toryism* and one of the most openly favorable press allies of the Klan.

The by-election in Arm River in October, 1928, gave the Klan and the Tories a test run for the general election which followed the next year. The Tory candidate was an Orange Order member who had denounced premier Gardiner for his criticisms of the Klan and who was virulently anti-French. The Klan had nineteen organizers and six lecturers ready to swing into action the day the by-election was announced. It also had chapters active in fifteen of the towns in the riding. The KKK organized many meetings in several towns and villages to garner votes for its Tory friends. At one election rally in the town of Davidson, Klan lawyer J.F.

---

*One *Star* editorial insisted that Quebec was "outraging history and the constitution by asserting the baseless claim that French is an official language in Canada outside the border of Quebec." It was the same kind of language found in Klan propaganda: "All our troubles, all the sedition, plotting and plans against the national school system are hatched in Quebec."[17]

Bryant was joined on the stage by a young Conservative from Prince Albert named John G. Diefenbaker. Diefenbaker complained about French being made compulsory as a language of instruction in public schools in his area.[18] The Klan-backed Tory candidate failed to win the election, but came within 59 votes of the victorious Liberal candidate. It was an omen of what was to come.

The general elections in the province the following June saw an impressive joint attack by the Tories and the Ku Klux Klan. The school question, the French language and the immigrant issue — all favorite whipping boys of the Klan and the Tories — dominated the campaign. "The Klan is opposed to the teaching of the French language," Klan leader and Conservative J.W. Rosborough said. Klan speeches during the election campaign also focused on the evils of European immigration. The Klan put its full forces behind the Tory electoral machine, and when the ballots were counted the alliance had paid off. The Conservatives found themselves with 24 seats, just two short of the Liberals' total;* but after a brief period of confusion, Conservative leader Anderson was able to form a minority government with a smaller third party and independent members of the legislature. It was the first time in the province's 24-year history that the Liberal party was not in power.

The new Anderson administration wasted little time in carrying through some of the anti-French policies which the Klan championed. In May, 1930, after premier Anderson appointed an inquiry into the conditions in French school districts, he admitted to an angry Association Culturelle Franco-Canadienne de la Saskatchewan that the inquiry had been set up to satisfy the Klan.[19] The committee conducted only an incomplete and prejudiced investigation before concluding that the primary course in French be abolished because it prevented students from learning English. In February, 1931, Anderson brought down legislation to abolish French as a language of instruction in the first grade. Candidates for school trustee posts were also obliged

---

*The Liberals dropped from 52 to 26 seats; the Conservatives increased their number of seats from 4 to 24; Progressives had 5 seats and there were six independents.

to be able to conduct meetings in English, a demand raised by the Klan two years earlier.

In the federal parliament the Liberals alleged, not without basis, that the Tories and Klan were working hand-in-hand to stir up anti-French feelings in Saskatchewan. During a particularly stormy debate in the House of Commons in 1931, one angry Liberal asked Cowan why he didn't wear his "nightshirt" in parliament. Read the front-page headline of one newspaper report of the debate: "Ku Klux Klan cry is raised in Parliament — Liberal charges secret society aided Conservatives — M.P. Alleged Member." Quebec Liberal MP Jean F. Pouliot produced official 1929 Klan documents showing that Cowan, as treasurer, had overseen the collection of more than $40,000 in dues and donations in the province. The KKK financial statements also indicated that Cowan was paid a salary of $2,170 and Maloney $1,284 for expenses. Pouliot also charged that Ambrose Bury, the Conservative MP from Edmonton, was a Klan member and noted "that body celebrated his victory by burning flaming crosses on the side of a hill near Edmonton." In 1934, Pouliot reiterated his accusation that Cowan, Bury and new Regina MP F.W. Turnbill "and other members of the Ku Klux Klan" were sitting in the Tory side of parliament. Other Conservative MPs, if they were not Klan members, were certainly willing to defend the racist organization. Said John Evans, the MP from Rosetown: "As regards the Ku Klux Klan, these people are not in any way what we might call hot-headed and they are absolutely against any violent or unconstitutional way of doing things."[20] But the Liberal charges stung enough to oblige Tory newspapers across the country to run articles countering the allegations. One article from a special correspondent of the Montreal *Standard* tried to show that prime minister Bennett "made it quite clear that the Federal Conservative Party will have no truck nor trade with Klansmen."[21]

If the Conservatives gave the Klan valuable help in becoming a political force in Saskatchewan, several other forces in society were equally adamant in opposing the Klan and eventually helped drive the organization out of the province. There were individual churchmen and newspaper editors who spoke up against the Klan's hate propaganda. Rev. Charles Endicott introduced a motion before the Presbytery of Saskatchewan in October, 1927, calling on the United Church not to support the KKK in any way. (The resolution, however, was not adopted by the church's provincial conference in June of the following year.)[22] A few newspapers editorialized against the Klan, although in many cases — such as the Regina *Leader* — they tended to be Liberal papers and thus had vested political interests in attacking the Tories' cross-burning allies.

One editor who took on the Klan and paid for it was Gerald Dealtry. In his Saskatoon *Reporter* in 1928, Dealtry described Klan leader J.J. Maloney as "a well-known hatred breeder." Maloney brought Dealtry to court over criminal libel charges. Emmett Hall, then a 30-year-old lawyer called to defend Dealtry, recalls the case: "The other newspapers were treating Maloney fairly tenderly. Dealtry was the only one with enough guts to take the Klan on. He let it roll. He published an article giving a pretty accurate background of Maloney. He called him what he was — a damn scoundrel and a professional anti-Catholic organizer. We were not inhibited about what we could say about Maloney in the addresses to the jury and some of them didn't like it. I know at the time the Klan held one of their cross burnings and I was one of those burned in effigy. It was a surprise to me, though — with a number of Saskatoon businessmen on the jury — that Dealtry was convicted. But he was found guilty."[23] The judge, however, was more sympathetic, according to Hall, and Dealtry was only fined $200.

Not surprisingly, the most vocal opposition to the Klan in Saskatchewan came from those minorities who felt the brunt of its hatred. The French-speaking Catholic population used all its resources to counter the Klan. Newspapers like *Le Patriote de l'Ouest* decried the obvious connection between the Klan's racism and the officially-sanctioned discrimination:

> We regard the tolerance towards the Ku Klux Klan at the present time only as an incident of a systematic campaign against us in which the Government is liable to sacrifice its friends instead of muzzling a band of fanatics.[24]

Le Patriote also made an appeal for unity in the face of Klan hatred: "English, Polish, German, Ruthenians, Franco-Canadians, etc., we must all get together (against) the common enemy." The St. Jean-Baptiste Society and the Franco-Canadian Association joined in the battle against the Klan. The small Jewish community in Saskatchewan (numbering only about 5,000 at the time) also stood up against the KKK. The *Western Jewish News* condemned the Klan's "racial prejudices" and the *Canadian Jewish Review* did likewise.[25] The general population, as well, at times expressed opposition to the Klan. At a September, 1928 meeting in Meota, Klan leader Maloney was pelted with rotten eggs, and a small riot broke out. In Hudson Bay Junction the next year, more fighting erupted when the townspeople objected to a Klan cross burning. One man was almost blinded and another had his ribs broken during the melee.[26]

These and other signs of resistance to the Klan no doubt contributed to its demise in the province. By 1929, attendance and interest in Klan meetings began to taper off. The Saskatchewan Klan's annual meeting in January, 1930, boasted of "increased membership", but it was the last convention the organization held in the province. Some leaders went looking for greener pastures in Alberta, others to the Maritimes, and the once-powerful KKK in Saskatchewan collapsed.

"I was once a Nazi."
— KKK organizer Wolfgang Droege

5. White robes and brown shirts

WHY DID THE KLAN in Canada fade in the late 1920s and virtually disappear for almost half a century? Several factors are responsible. Internally, the Klan was weakened by constant bickering among its leaders and scandals which saw some of them (like Emmons and Maloney) brought to trial for fraud, theft and other charges. The Klan in Canada also never really succeeded in becoming a co-ordinated national organization. Though attempts were made to amalgamate the various Klan groups across Canada in the fall of 1927, nothing came of the efforts and each provincial organization was left to its own. Externally, opposition to the KKK often took time to get organized, but once it took shape — whether it was labor, French Catholics or individual newspaper editors — the Klan's expansion was made more difficult.

But there was another reason for the Canadian Klan's early failure, a reason that stemmed from the fundamental difference between the Klan in Canada and the Klan in America. In the U.S., the Klan modified its causes and campaigns with the changing times, but it owed its birth and continuing activities to the existence of the black population. Making up an eighth of the American population and an even larger percentage in several southern states, blacks were a permanent and prominent feature of American political life, and provided the American Klan with a constant target. The Klan in Canada, on the other hand, espoused all the basic racist tenets of the U.S. organization, but tended to become much more of a single-issue group adapted to the specific politics of each province. It attacked Asians in B.C., Eastern Europeans in Alberta, French Catholics in Saskatchewan. As long as these issues remained burning ones — and that meant as long as at least some segments of the establishment had an interest in keeping these issues alive — the Klan would have fertile ground to grow in. But if these conditions changed, the Klan's base disappeared. French-Canadian minorities, for example, became a less visible issue because government policies had by 1930 succeeded in eating away at many of their education and language rights. In Saskatchewan, once the ruling Tory government began applying many of the anti-French measures which the Klan had been demanding, and anti-French fanatics among the general population no longer felt threatened, the need for and interest in the KKK diminished. Immigration also began to fall off dramatically as the 1920s ended, both as a result of government policy and the onset of the depression. Immigration from Asia had been reduced to a trickle in British Columbia, for instance, and until the late 1930s, anti-Asian prejudice remained at a low ebb.[1] Government officials, the media, business groups and church leaders gave less prominence to anti-immigrant sentiments which the Klan could play upon. The KKK lost another of its favorite issues. Born around specific causes, the Canadian Klan failed to adapt to changing times.

The Great Depression, which began in late 1929 and hit full force in the early thirties, changed much in Canada. Economic stagnation swept across the country, leaving hardship in its wake. It was a period of social upheaval, marked by soup lines and foreclosures, poverty and marches of the unemployed. The chasm between rich and poor widened and the conflict between them seemed to overshadow every other issue. The faith many had in the system was understandably shaken, and socialist ideas enjoyed an unprecedented influence in Canada. The Co-operative Commonwealth Federation, forerunner to the New Democratic Party, was formed in 1933, while the Communist Party gathered recruits in strikes and demonstrations.

For those forces in Canada sympathetic to extreme right-wing ideas, fascism became the savior, and the enemies were not so much blacks, immigrants and French Catholics now, but communists and Jews. In the U.S., the Klan leaders made the necessary adjustments and flirted with a number of American fascist organizations throughout the 1930s. If the Canadian Klan had done the same, it might have continued through the decade; it is significant that it lasted the longest in Alberta, where it turned its fire on labor and communists. But the Canadian Klan had neither the leadership capability nor the organizational strength to fine tune its ideology to the conditions of the 1930s. Many of its members probably joined the fascist movement of the period, groups which made the brown shirt their uniform and Adolf Hitler's rising Third Reich their model. It was these organizations — Adrien Arcand's anti-semitic movement in Quebec and various Nazi parties in Ontario and the west — and not the Klan that dominated Canada's extreme right during the depression. The fascists in Canada seized on people's insecurity during the crisis to sell their simplistic solutions. They blamed democracy, communism and the Jews for all of Canada's woes and offered as an alternative the stability and order of Mussolini's Italy and Hitler's Germany. Though never a major political force, Canada's fascist groups did have thousands of members.

Adrien Arcand was a journalist who used his literary talents to fill newspapers like Le Goglu and Le Miroir with vile attacks on Jews. Indeed, a 1932 article by Arcand entitled "Drinkers of Blood" sparked two Jewish members of the provincial legislature to introduce a group libel bill.[2] It was an early attempt to control hate propaganda through legislation. But, in a harbinger for the debates in the 1980s on banning the Klan, the bill was successfully opposed by politicians and the press in the name of "freedom of speech". Arcand's influence continued to grow. He maintained direct contacts with the Nazi movement in Germany and in 1934 created the Parti Nationale Social Chretien. In other parts of Canada, fascist groups also flourished: the Swastika Clubs in Ontario, the Canadian Nationalist Party in Manitoba, and the Canadian Union of Fascists. When Arcand sought to expand his

National Social Christian Party into Ontario in 1937, a young fascist named John Ross Taylor — only 24 at the time — was chosen as its leader. Taylor, the son of a lawyer and grandson of a prosperous manufacturer, went on to become one of the leading Canadian Nazis of the 1930s. At a meeting with Arcand, it was decided that Taylor should run in the upcoming provincial elections in a largely-Jewish Toronto riding. The eager candidate, sporting a swastika on his lapel and flashing the Nazi salute, flooded the district with pro-Hitler leaflets.[3] As it turned out, a squabble within the ranks of the fascists prevented Taylor's official nomination, but he continued to distribute his hate literature before and after voting day. In another harbinger for the future, his opponents discovered, much to their dismay, that the laws at the time were not strong enough to stop Taylor's activities. Taylor went on to form the Canadian Union of Fascists and became a national organizer for the group as it extended into western Canada. The second world war put a temporary halt to Taylor's political career. But he would reappear in the 1960s and 1970s with connections to the new Klan and neo-Nazi groups, just as surviving followers of Arcand in Quebec would be sought after by modern-day Klan leaders.

The right-wing extremists of the 1930s, like the Klan before them in the 1920s, benefitted from some direct and indirect assistance from more respectable quarters. Prime minister Bennett and the federal Conservatives were not above using Arcand's political machine and influence in the hope of weakening the ruling provincial Liberal government (not unlike the Tory co-operation with the Klan in Saskatchewan a decade earlier). The Tories funnelled about $18,000 to Arcand in 1930 and another $27,000 to his newspapers in 1936; Arcand was even hired as publicity director for one of Bennett's electoral campaigns in Quebec.[4] The major newspapers lent respectability to fascist leaders and their ideas. The *Globe and Mail*, which had described Arcand as "the brilliant young French Canadian," wrote in one editorial: "Although it cannot be said that a majority of Jews are communists, the indications are that a large percentage and probably a majority of communists are Jews."[5]

The fascists' message did not sit too well, however, with large sections of the population. When Norman Bethune, the Canadian doctor, returned from the Spanish Civil War, some 30,000 citizens crowded into stadiums and theatres across the country to hear him decry the evils of fascism. Meetings and marches of fascist groups in Toronto, Winnipeg and other cities were frequently disrupted by large demonstrations by trade unionists, communists, Jewish groups and others. This kind of sustained public pressure, along with the outbreak of the war, forced governments in Canada to ban various fascist groups, halt the spread of their propaganda, and imprison some of their leaders. It would be three decades before the fascists, or the Klan, returned publicly to Canada.

Part II   The Modern Klan

"I am a true Nazi — and that is the most beautiful and the most noble philosophy of all the political philosophies that have existed on this earth."

— Armand Siksna,
Canadian Klan treasurer

6. The fascist connection

AFTER ITS DISAPPEARANCE in the early 1930s the Canadian Klan did not formally reappear until 1980. The rebirth was the product of two trends of the 1970s: the revival in the United States of a modern-day Klan with links to the neo-Nazi movement, and the prominence of fascist groups and activities in Toronto.

Unlike the Canadian KKK, the American Klan did not die out completely in the 1930s. As the depression years turned into the war years, Klan activities declined but the organization never formally disbanded. Shortly after the war the KKK resumed the terrorist activities that are its trademark, though at first on a smaller scale than in the 1920s. It bombed a multiracial housing project in Miami, as well as several Jewish synagogues and Catholic churches. In 1951, a Klan dynamite blast killed Harry Moore, the Florida leader of the National Association for the Advancement of Colored People, and his wife. But it was the historic 1954 U.S. supreme court decision against school segregation which sparked the full revival of the modern-day Klan. Over the next decade, the fight for school segregation, the Montgomery bus boycott, the voter registration campaigns and the civil rights marches marked an upsurge in the black people's fight for equality similar to the Reconstruction period of a century before. And again, the night riders of the KKK were called out to protect "the American way of life" in the South.

In 1959 alone, the National Council of Churches listed 530 cases of Klan-inspired racial violence, reprisals and intimidation. According to the U.S. justice department, between 1954 and 1965 the Klan was responsible for 70 bombings in Georgia and Mississippi; the burning of 30 churches used by blacks in Mississippi; and ten murders in Alabama. On September 15, 1963, a dynamite bomb demolished the Sixteenth Street Baptist Church in Birmingham, killing four black girls. The FBI had many informants in the Klan circles which had planned the bombing, but in part because of obstruction by an unco-operative FBI chief J. Edgar Hoover, the investigations were botched and delayed. Not until 1977, fourteen years after the killings, was one of the Klansmen convicted — the only conviction.

One of the most shocking and celebrated Klan murders occurred in June, 1964. The summer of 1964 was an explosive one, as the civil rights campaign to register black voters met with fear and resistance from southern white communities. When James Earl Chaney, a 21-year-old black, and his two white fellow civil rights workers, Michael Henry Schwerner, 24, and Andrew Goodman, 20, arrived in Mississippi's Neshoba County, the local White Knights of the Ku Klux Klan plotted to deal with the "invaders". A local church frequented by black Methodists was burned in order to lure the three youths to the area, Klansmen later testified. Chaney, Schwerner and Goodman were arrested and jailed on trumped-up speeding charges by deputy sheriff Cecil Price, himself a KKK member. The Klansmen were informed immediately of the arrest and made preparations for their execution scheme. After several hours in jail, Chaney, Schwerner and Goodman were released. But on a dark highway in the dead of night, Price and other Klansmen in several cars caught up with the three youths, took them to a remote area, shot them and then used a bulldozer to bury their bodies. The disappearance of the three created a national uproar and from the start the FBI suspected the Klan was involved. But, as in the Birmingham bombing, justice proved to be slow and incomplete. It was two months before the three bodies were unearthed and, in the eyes of black critics like Martin Luther King, Jr., the FBI seemed to be painstakingly slow in building its case. Meanwhile, the Klan gloated. Imperial Wizard Sam Bowers, in a reference to the murdered Schwerner, said: "This is the first time in history that Christians have carried out the execution of a Jew."[1] Klan membership soared. In September, a county grand jury in the small town of Philadelphia, Miss., concluded a three-day inquiry into the murder cases without returning any indictments. By December, the FBI — aided by confessions of two Klansmen — charged nineteen men, including the sheriff and deputy Price, with conspiring "to injure, oppress, threaten and intimidate" the three civil rights workers. But at a preliminary hearing, the presiding commissioner took the unprecedented step of dismissing the charges. It was not until February, 1965, that a federal grand jury returned two indictments against the accused men — and then a U.S. district court judge, William Cox, ruled they could be tried under federal law for nothing more serious than a misdemeanor and a felony. The Klan was exultant, and the accused police officers were featured speakers at local rallies organized by national Klan leader Robert Shelton. A year later, the supreme court overturned Cox's ruling, but, amazingly, in September, 1966, the U.S. department of justice agreed with appeals by defence attorneys and threw out the indictments on a technicality. Finally, in February, 1967, another grand jury reinstated the murder conspiracy indictment and added local Klan chieftain Sam Bowers to the list of the accused. In October, 1967 — more than three years after the bodies had been discovered — eighteen men went to trial in a federal court. Only seven were convicted by the all-white jury; Bowers was sentenced to a ten-year prison term, deputy sheriff Cecil Price got six years. (Another Klansman who pleaded guilty in a separate trial was given a four-year term.) The defendants appealed their convictions to the supreme court, but in February, 1970, the court refused to hear their case. Almost six years after the murder of Chaney, Schwerner and Goodman, their killers were in prison at last.

The murder of the three youths in 1964 was not the last incidence of Klan terror. In March, 1965, a white civil rights worker, Mrs. Viola Liuzzo, was shot and killed by Klansmen in Alabama. Other fatal shootings, beatings and bombings marked the decade. Years later, reminiscing about the violence of the 1960s, Klan leader Robert Shelton would remark: "It's unfortunate, really, that there wasn't more than what it was."[2]

As always, the Klan had its benefactors among the rich and powerful. In the "long hot summer" of 1964, the Republican national convention was held in San Francisco. A platform amendment which condemned extremism and the Klan was voted down, as conservative delegates saw it as an attempt to split their forces and deny Senator Barry Goldwater the party nomination for president. Goldwater, well known for his espousal of right-wing causes, was cheered by the convention when he said in his speech that extremism in the defense of liberty was no crime. While he later distanced himself from the KKK, both Dean Burch, the new Republican party chairman, and William Miller, the vice-presidential candidate, stated publicly their willingness to accept the votes of the Klan.[3] The hooded terrorists of the KKK found another ally in Alabama governor George Wallace, a staunch opponent of desegregation and black rights. Shelton's Klan played a big role in helping Wallace win office in 1962 and the governor generously rewarded his friends. He pressured a Mobile construction company to do business with Shelton's father and had Shelton placed on the payroll of an engineering firm responsible for highway contracts. In return, Klan members backed Wallace's successive bids for governor and president. One of the speechwriters in the 1964 Wallace presidential campaign team was Asa Carter, who was the leader of a Birmingham Klan group which in 1957 had castrated a black handyman (the KKK assailants had been sentenced to 20 years in prison, but Wallace paroled them when he became governor). Wallace would never apologize for his support of the Klan. "At least a Klansman will fight for his country," he told a reporter in 1967.[4]

In its heyday in the 1960s, Klan membership peaked at around 15,000. It declined as the traditional Klan bickering arose and the organizations splintered into various factions, but by the late

1970s, a resurgence began.

Between 1975 and 1978, Klan membership across the United States rose to 8,000 from 5,000 and its activities became much more open and widespread. Much of the growth of the new Klan was attributed to the Louisiana-based Knights of the Ku Klux Klan, led by the charismatic David Duke. Duke's group began to outshine Shelton's powerful United Klans of America, at least in the media's eyes. Six-foot-two, with a neatly-trimmed mustache and wavy hair, Duke was not your ordinary Klansman. "David Duke epitomizes the new look of the Klan," said his newspaper *The Crusader* in gushing tones. "His tall, trim physical presence and sandy-haired Nordic appearance complete the portrait of a man moving millions." The son of an engineer who worked for the American state department, Duke attended a private military college before earning a history degree at Louisiana State University. He was "about 13" when he rejected what he calls his liberal upbringing and turned to white supremacy. When he was 17, Duke joined the Knights of the Ku Klux Klan, a small group funded and led by wealthy New Orleans real estate executive Jim Lindsay.[5] While attending LSU, the eager Duke formed the White Youth Alliance, which soon spread to 40 other universities. He went on to found the National Party, a neo-fascist organization that quickly ran into trouble with the law. Duke and fellow National Party members were charged with making Molotov cocktails, theft, fraud, contributing to the delinquency of a minor, and inflaming race relations in New Orleans high schools. Duke also picketed a campus speech by radical lawyer William Kunstler dressed in a storm-trooper uniform adorned with a swastika, earning himself the name "the Nazi of Louisiana State University."[6] In the Klan, Duke progressed rapidly from Grand Dragon of Louisiana and national information director; in 1975 he became national director, or Grand Wizard, of the fastest-growing Klan group in the U.S. Duke combined shrewd politics with a clever use of the media to "sell" the Klan in much the same way he used to sell vacuum cleaners during the summer to put himself through school. Duke's skilful manipulation of the media set him apart from other Klan leaders, and Canadian Klansmen would learn to copy him. "The Klan was an organization worthy of publicity," Duke said. "People knew it existed. People knew it was sizeable. It had a lot of interesting characteristics — from a news person's point of view. The fiery cross. The robes make good copy. Good pictures."[7] Attired in neat business suits, Duke appeared on radio and television shows across the country: *The Crusader*'s profile of him boasted that he had appeared on more than 800 shows worldwide. He took out newspaper and radio advertisements and hired rock bands to attract young people. "We're the Klan with sex appeal," Duke once remarked. To help the sales pitch, Duke consciously tried to clean up the Klan's image. "I never really say things that are radical and I try to refrain from 'nigger'," he told Patsy Sims, author of a book on the American Klan. Off camera, of course, Duke's speeches *were* punctuated with derogatory references to "niggers".[8]

Duke also pushed the Klan directly into the political arena, a terrain where the KKK previously had ventured only indirectly, when they supported other political parties. "We want political power in our country for our philosophy of life," said Duke, who polled 11,000 votes — an impressive 35 per cent — in a 1975 Louisiana state senate race.

The fascist sympathies of Duke's Klan were no secret. Nazi salutes were common at Duke rallies. He had close links with the American Nazi Lincoln Rockwell. His newspaper regularly promoted Hitler's autobiography *Mein Kampf* and Nazi paraphernalia. Indeed, Duke's Nazi leanings led many rival Klansmen to charge that he was not a true Klan devotee, but a political opportunist who was building a fortune from the money collected by his expanding empire. His former lieutenant, Bill Wilkinson, leveled these accusations when he quit Duke's organization to set up his own Klan in 1975. Other Klan groups were also critical of Duke's untraditional policy of accepting membership by mail (a method of building up "associate" membership which the Canadian Klan would copy). In July, 1981, Duke finally left the Knights of the Ku Klux Klan to set up and lead the National Association for the Advancement of White People, an organization designed to give his white power ideas more political mileage. Duke apparently thought there was only so much soft-selling one could do for a discredited organization such as the Klan and that a new vehicle was better suited to his political ambitions. He insisted that his departure from the Klan was voluntary, but rivals say it was forced after they videotaped a meeting at which Duke offered to sell his membership lists to other Klan groups for $35,000.[9]

Despite this infighting, Klan forces continued to grow. By 1979, total membership in the various American Klan organizations was estimated to be about 10,000 — a 25 per cent increase since 1978. The Klan was active in 22 states and had an additional 100,000 supporters outside its active members. The largest group remained Robert Shelton's United Klans of America, with 3,500 to 4,000 members. The two factions of Duke's Klan came next: Duke's own group (which was taken over by Duke information director Don Black when Duke left) had about 1,500 to 2,000 Klansmen. The Invisible Empire, Bill Wilkinson's split-off from Duke's Klan, had at least 2,000 to 2,500 members.

The late 1970s and early 1980s also saw an increase in Klan violence in the United States. The most violent Klan group was the Invisible Empire; Wilkinson would appear at Klan rallies flanked by machine gun-toting bodyguards. "These guns ain't for killing rabbits; they're to waste people," he would boast.[10] In seven states Wilkinson's Klan set up a Youth Corps to train white teenagers to use firearms, baseball bats and other weapons of "self defence". "We don't teach our kids to hate niggers," Wilkinson told a newspaper reporter. "Most of them do that already. We teach them that they are superior to them."[11] In one "survival camp" in Texas, young KKKers were taught how to handle guns and strangle and decapitate people. In the summer of 1978, Klansmen from Wilkinson's organization, wearing hoods and carrying arms, attacked a peaceful protest march by blacks in Mississippi. In 1979, Youth Corps members participated in the burning of a school bus. In May of that year, 150 club-carrying Invisible Empire Klansmen broke up a quiet civil rights march in Decatur, Alabama; two marchers were wounded by gunshots. Between 1979 and 1981, more than 250 of Wilkinson's members were arrested on charges ranging from illegal parading to murder.

Duke's Klan, meanwhile, was not exactly well-behaved and tranquil during the same period. In May, 1979, two California members of his group were convicted of murdering a fellow Klansman. Duke himself was found guilty of inciting to riot. A Texas leader of Duke's Klan told a 1979 Klan convention: "The government is murdering our people, busing our children... There are penalties for murder: death. Prepare for what is coming!"

On November 3, 1979, in Greensboro, North Carolina, several heavily-armed Klansmen and American Nazis — in full view of television cameras — fired into a crowd of about 100 marchers at a "Death to the Klan" rally sponsored by a group called the Communist Workers Party. A TV reporter on the scene recalled: "As the marchers were getting ready to move out, two vehicles pulled up and about a dozen men jumped out and commenced firing automatic weapons and shotguns." Shots were fired by some of the marchers who were armed, but the battle was one-sided. Television cameras recorded the Klansmen and Nazis methodically unloading their weapons from their vehicles, stalking their victims and opening fire, in one case pumping shot after shot into a victim's body. Four whites and one black were slain. The incident grabbed American and international headlines; four Klansmen and two Nazis were arrested on five counts of first-degree murder. During the trial, excerpts of the television news film were shown, including frames which seemed to show that the Klansmen and Nazis had fired first. But on November 17, 1980, an all-white jury acquitted the six accused, apparently accepting their story that they acted in self defence. George Simkins, president of the Greensboro chapter of the National Association for the Advancement of Colored People, said: "I think the verdict is tantamount to giving the Klan and Nazis a licence to kill." Indeed, the six acquitted men were heroes to their peers. One of them, Klansman Jerry Paul Smith, was rewarded with a promotion in the White Knights of North Carolina. Said a leader of Smith's Klan: "We've got the fire power and the artillery and if a race war breaks out, the organization will hold its own." In the following year, at least 300 incidents involving violence, harassment and intimidation were committed by Klan members across the U.S., according to the civil rights group Klanwatch.

Three months after the Greensboro killing, more than 10,000

people marched through the streets of that city in a protest demonstration sponsored by 300 organizations. The march was indicative of a burgeoning anti-Klan movement in the U.S. in two ways. First, its size reflected the movement's strength; it was becoming more common across the U.S. to see Klan rallies matched by much larger counter-demonstrations. Second, the broad sponsorship of the Greensboro protest was a sign of growing unity among diverse anti-Klan forces. The KKK had faced opposition in every period of its existence, from anti-slavery abolitionists in the nineteenth century to labor unions in the 1930s and the massive civil rights marches of the 1960s. What distinguished the anti-Klan movement of the late 1970s was a greater organizational cohesion. In August, 1979, in response to the resurgence of Klan violence and particularly the Klan attack on peaceful marchers in Decatur, Alabama, the Southern Christian Leadership Conference called a meeting of more than 30 organizations, and the National Anti-Klan Network was established. The network was designed to help various church, community, labor and political groups co-ordinate their activities and pool their resources in countering the Klan. In 1979 as well, the Southern Poverty Law Center, a civil rights group located in Montgomery, Alabama, began its Klanwatch project. Klanwatch was set up to identify and keep track of Klan members and Nazis across the U.S., recording their involvement in crime and violence, and regularly disseminating this information to the media, law enforcement agencies and politicians. Klanwatch's legal division won a permanent injunction in Texas against Klan harassment of Vietnamese fishermen, a favorite new target of the KKK. Klanwatch also won a major legal victory in that state when a federal judge banned Klan paramilitary activity there. One of Klanwatch's fundraising letters was written by Maria von Trapp, whose flight from Nazism was made famous by the film *The Sound of Music*. She drew the connection between the resurgence of the Klan and fascism: "It *is* happening here, right now. The Ku Klux Klan and their brothers in hate, the American neo-Nazis, are growing in strength and belligerence across the country. Klansmen in their robes may look ridiculous, but the threat they pose is deadly serious. Hitler started out with just a handful of followers. Today, the Klan boasts thousands of members."

While David Duke and other U.S. Klan leaders were mustering their troops for battle, plans were also brewing among their ideological breathren to the north. In Canada, the Ku Klux Klan — and for that matter similar groups on the extreme right — had been largely dormant for three decades. What provided the bridge of continuity was the fascist movement. Just as many Klan members of the 1920s probably went on to become Canada's fascists of the depression years, so too did a good number of the Nazis who emerged in Toronto in the late 1960s and 1970s lay the groundwork for the rebirth of the Klan in that city.

There were scattered spurts of KKK activity outside of Toronto during this period. On August 9, 1965, a cross was burned at the main intersection of Amherstburg, a small town near Windsor, Ontario. The message "Niggers Beware" was scrawled on one side of a local Baptist church and "The Klan is coming" on the other. The words "Home of the KKK" were added to the population sign at the entrance to the community.[12] In what was later to become a familiar pattern in the 1980s, the authorities did not take the incidents very seriously. Mayor Murray Smith said it was the work of childish pranksters, and seemed more worried about the bad publicity the town was getting as a result. A police report was prepared for the Ontario attorney general's office, but no further action was taken. Said deputy attorney general A. Rendall Dick: "It appears there has been a disturbance but it has been purely young hoodlums. It was very crude and there was no organized racial disturbances." Police chief George Hannah confidently declared: "There is no Klan or hint of the Klan." But many of the black residents of Amherstburg — which had been the terminus of the "underground railway" for slaves escaping from the U.S. in the nineteenth century — were not willing to take the incidents so lightly. "What joker and what teenager is going to take the trouble to build a 10-foot cross and bind it carefully with gasoline-soaked rags and set fire to it?" asked George McCurdy, president of the South Essex Citizens Advancement Association. They were convinced there was something more serious behind the event. Some local commercial establishments had recently been barring blacks. McCurdy's own grandson had been physically ejected from an amusement centre, and his brother was struck when he came to his defence. Two other boys reported that a white resident had fired over their heads with a rifle; the father of one of the children complained that the police did not take the charge seriously. Several black residents also reported receiving obscene calls from people identifying themselves as members of the KKK. The South Essex Citizens Advancement Association submitted a brief to the government pointing to failures by local police to enfore the law.

These incidents occured at the same time as the newspapers were full of stories of the bloody race riots in America. It is possible that local racists in Amherstburg who were either secret members of the Klan or were inspired by its hate message had decided it was time to try and terrorize the black citizens of their town. In an interview at the time, Robert Shelton of the United Klans of America admitted that some Windsor-area Canadians had recently joined the Klan.

In Alberta, the Klan made a more official appearance. In May, 1972, Ivan Ross Macpherson (who Celticized his name to Tearlach Mac a' Phearsoin) and four other people incorporated the Klan under the Societies Act of Alberta.[13] Their Confederate Klans of Alberta originally had three members in Calgary and two from Banff. They were dedicated, as their charter put it, "to preserve the traditions and ideals of the White races." By August, Mac a' Phearsoin was claiming to have five "klaverns" or chapters in Calgary, four in Edmonton and one each in Red Deer and Lethbridge. The following month, the Alberta Klan came out in support of the Conservative party in the federal election, an interesting throwback to the Klan's politics on the prairies five decades earlier. Not much else was heard from Mac a' Phearsoin and his group for some time. He gave press interviews in which he said he was devoted to promote Protestantism, the British monarchy, and the fight against drug use, abortion and communism. He claimed to draw a salary of $300 a month as Imperial Wizard. Then, in September, 1974, the Alberta Klan leader was charged with criminal negligence in a bizarre shooting in his home. Apparently Mac a' Phearsoin had brought a 22-year-old man from Mexico to be a companion for his ailing father. "We were arguing. The gun went off," Mac a' Phearsoin said as he was led away by police. The Alberta Klan quickly fell apart. In July, 1975, the provincial registrar gave notice that among the societies considered dissolved was the Confederate Klan of Alberta. And after a week-long trial in December of that year, Mac a' Phearsoin was convicted of criminal negligence and dangerous use of a firearm and fined $2,000. "The operations of the Klan are irrelevant to his case," said judge W.K. Moore.[14]

Aside from these isolated outbreaks of Klan activity in Amherstburg and Alberta, though, it was in Toronto that the solid roots were laid for what would become Alexander McQuirter's Ku Klux Klan. From the late 1960s to the mid-1970s a number of extreme right-wing groups popped up. They bore different names but shared a virulent racism, a strident opposition to liberal or progressive causes, an appetite for violence and, often, the same leaders. A direct line could be traced from the Canadian Nazi Party to the Canadian National Socialist Party to the Edmund Burke Society, the Western Guard, the Nationalist Party, and finally to the Ku Klux Klan.

In the mid-sixties, William John Beattie made headlines as the noisy leader of the Canadian Nazi Party. A six-foot-tall man who wore his dark, straight hair across his forehead in imitation of Hitler, Beattie maintained that the Nazi dictator was the best thing to come along in the world since Jesus Christ.[15] His party caused a riot in 1965 at Toronto's Allan Gardens when about 5,000 people came out to protest a Nazi rally. Beattie was later arrested and convicted of public mischief for his attempt to paint swastikas on selected homes and sites in the Toronto area. Beattie was "constantly getting material from the American Klan," according to Max Chikofsky, an Ontario private investigator who followed the fascist movement closely at the time. A lot of Beattie's money came from European Nazis and fascists now living in Canada and from right-wing emigre Hungarians, Latvians, Serbians and others. "Some of these people have been fascists for 25 to 30 years; why should they stop now?" says the private investigator. "Many of the younger people from these families and organizations went on to become active in the extreme right-wing groups of the 1970s." After Beattie's jailing, a German immigrant named Martin Weiche took over the party in 1967 and renamed it the Canadian National Socialist Party. But the organization soon lost what influence it had and continued to exist in name only.

Leadership of the fascist movement fell to the Edmund Burke Society, created in the fall of 1968 by two young Torontonians, Donald Andrews and Paul Fromm. Fromm, a teacher, would later become prominent in the city's Progressive Conservative Party. Other active members of the Edmund Burke Society included Martin Weiche, the National Socialist Party leader, and two Torontonians sympathetic to Nazism, Jacob Prins and Armand Siksna.

The Edmund Burke Society, named in honor of the British conservative thinker, was ostensibly a more cerebral right-wing group than its overtly Nazi predecessors. But it did not take long for it to prove itself true to fascist form. In 1971, the group violently disrupted a meeting at the University of Toronto where Quebec labor leader Michel Chartrand and lawyer Robert Lemieux were speaking in the aftermath of the 1970 imposition of the War Measures Act. Society members beat, clubbed and kicked several members of the audience, spraying some people with a Mace-like irritant which caused temporary blindness. Three attackers were arrested. In November, 1971, Edmund Burke Society members attacked an anti-Vietnam war march; two more were arrested.

In 1972, Andrews replaced the Edmund Burke Society with a more openly racialist — and more violent — group called the Western Guard. For most of the rest of the decade, the Guard gained notoriety for vandalizing synagogues, the homes of prominent blacks and progressive bookstores by painting swastikas or smashing windows. Sometimes the Guard's violence was directed at people. In April, 1974, for example, a Western Guard member attacked two people at a film showing sponsored by the Toronto Committee for the Liberation of Portuguese African Colonies. The Guard member was sentenced to 28 days in jail for common assault. In June, 1975, 30 Guard members started a fight in a Toronto television studio where a black musical group was performing. The band leader was struck by a metal pipe and other musicians were severely beaten, while Guard members flashed the Nazi salute for the television cameras. Andrews and one of his cohorts from his Edmund Burke days, Jacob Prins, were charged with assault, but Andrews was acquitted because of lack of positive identification during the brawl. In November, 1977, Andrews and two other Guard members went on trial for arson and mischief after more Guard activities. In February, 1978, he was convicted of possessing explosives, and conspiring to commit arson. He was also banned from associating with the Guard.

The impact of the Western Guard experience on the Canadian extreme-right was immeasurable. From 1972 to 1978, it dominated that political fringe and received wide media coverage for its numerous acts of vandalism and violence. Its internal mailing list contained the names of 104 members. The Guard's influence on the future Canadian Klan was twofold. Ideologically, the creation of the Western Guard was significant because, while previous extreme right-wing organizations had been primarily anti-semitic and anti-communist, the Guard combined these standard Nazi fares with a strong dose of white supremacist, anti-black ideology. It was upon this marriage of ideas that the new Klan would be built. As one extreme right-wing publication later put it: "In 1972, the Western Guard Party developed the ideology of White Nationalism in a dramatic breakaway from its previous conservative ideology, which was far from what anyone could call 'racism' but was rather anti-communist only, in word and in deed."[16] Organizationally, the Western Guard was important to the Klan as a breeding ground for fascists, a training school for many people who would go on to have connections with, or top leadership posts in, the Canadian Ku Klux Klan. Klan officials would later boast that 25 per cent of its members came from the Western Guard. Among the key players on the 1970s Toronto fascist scene:

• **Don Andrews**, through the Edmund Burke Society and the Western Guard, dominated the extreme right-wing stage in Toronto for most of the decade and became a sort of godfather to many of the present-day organizers of the Klan. "Many of them were my lieutenants in the Guard," he boasted. Of Serbian descent, Andrews came to Canada as a child with his mother after the second world war. "I'm not upset if you call me a fascist," he once told a reporter. He worked in the Scarborough public health department and later at Toronto East General Hospital. Andrews, by his own admission, received money from right-wing sympathizers in the Serbian and other Eastern European immigrant communities. Neatly attired in business suits, Andrews was intelligent, well-read and eloquent. In his six years as Guard leader, his penchant for violence seemed to be matched only by his political and organizational cunning. As a candidate in Toronto's mayoralty race in 1972, he polled 1,916 votes. Running again in 1974 on a white power ticket with his name on posters plastered across the city, he came in second in a field of eleven, with close to 6,000 votes. Andrews's political career did not come to an end when he was sentenced in 1978 to a brief jail term and forbidden to associate with the Guard. He went on to found the Nationalist Party of Canada and, in 1980, would attempt a merger with the newly-formed Canadian Ku Klux Klan.

• **John Ross Taylor**, the veteran Nazi from the 1930s, was a Guard leader with official responsibility for propaganda. (Taylor was involved in other political formations before signing up with the Western Guard. He had earlier set up the National Order Party, but in 1965 the government terminated his use of the mail for distribution of American neo-nazi and other anti-semitic literature.) Taylor ran for the Western Guard in the 1972 Toronto elections, an interesting rerun of his 1937 bid for municipal office. Along with Andrews and other Canadian fascists, Taylor attended a 1972 banquet in Michigan organized by the American Ku Klux Klan, and Taylor maintained friendly links with U.S. racists. He spoke at the 1973 convention of the National States Rights Party, a right-wing group allied with the Klan and similar groups.* In 1976, Taylor attended an "international congress"

---

*The connections between the NSRP and the Western Guard have led to speculation that Canadian fascists may have given assistance to James Earl Ray, the assassin of black civil rights leader Martin Luther King. American Klan chronicler Patsy Sims has pointed out that Ray was in Toronto a year before the slaying. He fled there four days after killing King in April, 1968, organized by David Duke's Klan in New Orleans. When Don Andrews was forced by the courts to dissociate himself from the Guard in 1978, Taylor assumed complete control of what was left of the organization. Despite repeated legal proceedings against him, Taylor and his Western Guard group refused to disconnect a white power telephone "hotline" which played tape-recorded messages of anti-semitic and anti-black hate propaganda. In 1980, Taylor was finally sentenced to one year in jail and the Western Guard was fined $5,000 for preaching race hatred over the telephone. Taylor appealed, but lost his case in February, 1981. He spent two months in hiding before turning himself in to begin a one-year sentence in Toronto's Don Jail.

• **Wolfgang Droege**, another Western Guard activist, played a much more crucial role in the reborn Klan. Born in 1949 in Forchheim, Bavaria, Droege became a committed Nazi while still a boy. His father was in the German air force during the second world war and even after Hitler's defeat "his sympathies always remained true" to the Third Reich, Droege recalls.[18] Droege's grandfather, with whom he spent much of his childhood, was a close friend of Julius Streicher, a Nazi and confidant of Hitler who was hanged for war crimes in 1946 after the Nuremburg trials. ("It was a kangaroo court," Droege says bitterly today. "Streicher's only crime was that he stirred up anti-semitic hatred throughout Germany.") Droege remembers that while at Nuremburg Streicher and "other top leaders in Germany" frequented his grandfather's hotel. "Meetings were held there often [and] it had a tremendous impact on my personal development." The young Droege was fired up by his grandfather's tales of racial pride and "the great ideals" of the Third Reich. Droege came to Canada when he was 13, though he once returned briefly to Germany and tried unsuccessfully to join the army there ("I disliked having to leave the fatherland"). While in Germany in 1967, he attended meetings of the neo-Nazi National Party, led by Adolf van Thadden. Once back in Canada,

---

and remained in hiding for a month. J.B. Stoner, a leader of the NSRP, was a friend of and lawyer for Ray's brother. Stoner also addressed a Western Guard dinner in 1974. These and other links led Sims to suggest that Canadian fascists "could. . . have aided James Earl Ray."[17]

Droege drifted from job to job as a copper smelter worker and printing apprentice. In 1974, he met Don Andrews and joined the Western Guard. "I decided to take my part in reshaping and saving my racial destiny. Like a misplaced warrior, seeking to find a place in a...decadent environment, I felt I had finally found my true calling." In any event, Droege quickly became, in his words, "an active promoter" and "vigorous activist" in the Guard. He accumulated the usual Guard credentials. In May, 1975, he painted white power slogans along the route of an African Liberation Day march in Toronto; he was subsequently convicted of mischief and damage to private property, for which he was sentenced to fourteen days in jail, and assault against a Toronto newspaper reporter, for which he was fined $100.

• **Jacob Prins**, like Droege, was a long-standing fascist sympathizer from Europe. He originally fought against Hitler's army when it invaded his native Holland, but soon became a collaborator. He regrets his brief anti-Nazi activity: "I betrayed myself and my country. I had killed Germans. I regretted it ever since and maybe that's why subconsciously I try to make up for it." If Hitler had won the war, "we would have had a much better world," he says.[19] Prins, a former professional wrestler who stands over six feet tall, was a bodyguard for Canadian Nazi leader William Beattie. Though over 50 years of age, Prins went on to be an active (and arrested) member of the Edmund Burke Society and the Western Guard. A fanatical anti-semite, Prins once wrote a letter to newspaper columnist Douglas Fisher insisting that the Nazi extermination of six million Jews during the war was a hoax. Prins was one of those fined in 1969 for the telephone "hotline" transmitting anti-semitic messages. Over the years he also accumulated charges of violence, theft and break and entry.

• **Martin Weiche**, another man in his fifties during the Western Guard's heydays, shared Droege's and Prins's enthusiasm for the Third Reich but in addition was able to make a direct contribution to Hitler's rule, as a pilot in the German air force. "Today, I like being called a Nazi," he says. "You get used to things." After he came to Canada in 1951, Weiche made a small fortune in real estate and comfortably installed himself on a large estate on the outskirts of London, Ontario. He took over the Canadian Nazi party from Beattie in the late 1960s, but confessed that there were "just some remnants left, a loose connection of people." In 1974, Weiche, though not a lawyer, conducted the court defence for a Western Guard member named Thomas Reade who was charged with a violent assault. Weiche had befriended Reade, a 240-pound ex-motorcycle gang member, when the latter was released from prison in 1970 and made him his personal bodyguard. He provided Reade and his wife with an apartment and helped them get back to what Weiche called "normal society" by getting Reade involved in the Guard. Weiche would go on to become a friend of the Klan and it was on his lawn in 1980 that the first modern-day cross burning would take place.

• **Armand Siksna** was another Western Guard member who would move on to the Klan. Born in 1944 in Riga, Latvia, Siksna was raised by parents he described as "anti-communist conservatives". His father owned two turpentine refineries and supplied the Germans during the war; Siksna's uncle had a stake in two banks and belonged "to a right-wing fascist-inclined organization," according to Siksna. Siksna moved to Canada in 1957 where he worked in numerous jobs. A confirmed anti-communist, he joined the Progressive Conservative party but soon found it "was not really right-wing enough for me." He eventually joined the Edmund Burke Society and then the Guard when he "started to realize the importance of racism — the preservation of our race." Siksna recalls: "I had come to the conclusion that I am a true Nazi — and that is the most beautiful and the most noble philosophy of all the political philosophies that have ever existed on this earth."[20] Siksna was on the executive of the Western Guard and he ran in several municipal and provincial elections. His main contribution seemed to be constant run-ins with the law. As a Guard member, he faced charges for the defacement of property by affixing hate posters. He was accused of the theft of a typewriter when he worked as a security guard at a warehouse, and when police raided his apartment for evidence he was charged with violating the propaganda law because Nazi and Klan material was found there. (Some of Siksna's confrontations with the law were more comical. In 1980, he was convicted of fraudulent misuse of a credit card and received a suspended sentence of eighteen months. The card, which he had found on the floor of a store and attempted to use, was a demonstration card made out to "Mrs. Happy Shopper".) He handled the Klan's finances during McQuirter's reign.

• **James Alexander McQuirter** was attracted to Don Andrews's organization while still in his teens. His background was different from that of his fellow Guard members, many of whom seemed to have inherited their fascist leanings from their European families or experiences. The eldest of five children, McQuirter was born in May, 1958 and grew up in what he described as a "liberal, middle class" home in the Toronto borough of North York. At "about 14 or 15" years of age McQuirter, through his own readings, became convinced of the inferiority of blacks and Jews and started to try and win his friends at York Mills Collegiate over to his beliefs: "I was always a conservationist. When I was going to high school, I was interested in the whales and seals. Then I started reading about some of the population statistics of the white race. We're a dying species. I used to talk to other conversationists about this, but they weren't interested — it was all racist stuff to them. But at the time, I wasn't a racist. I just thought, well, gee, everything should be protected.* So I was forced to look at different groups, so-called right-wing fanatical groups. I was interested in what they had to offer, what their solutions were." McQuirter's parents apparently did not take too kindly to their son's new ideological bent, and he was told by his parents not to talk about the race question at home. "Today, I don't see any of [my parents] very much," he said in one newspaper interview. "Let's say they don't agree with me." After he graduated from high school, McQuirter spent four years in the Canadian militia. In 1976, when he was 18, McQuirter joined up with Don Andrews. "At that

---

*It is debatable how much of McQuirter's story about being a child conservationist is fact and how much is an attempt to give a scientific gloss to his conversion to racism. His "endangered species" line is a favorite argument of the American Klan; one issue of the U.S. Klan newspaper *The Crusader* complained that the U.S. government protects species like the snail darter, a breed of tiny fish, but at the same time "pushed programs that threaten the continued existence of our unique and beautiful White race. Hopefully, we are as important as the snail darter."

time, really, the Western Guard was the only game in town,"
McQuirter explains. Andrews was instrumental in fleshing out the
style and substance of the young McQuirter's right-wing politics.
"I remember McQuirter coming to my house in the early days
when he was about 18," recalls Andrews. "He used to come into
my back yard and we would discuss organizational and political
things. McQuirter didn't really know how to speak to the press all
that much because he didn't have much background knowledge
on political, international and other racial matters. So we would
chit-chat and I would give him some pointers on how to answer
some questions."[21]

The Edmund Burke Society, the Western Guard, the Canadian
Nazi Party, the Nationalist Party of Canada; Taylor, Andrews,
Droege, Prins, Siksna, Weiche and McQuirter: the foundations
had been sunk, the builders assembled, for the latest reincarnation
of Canada's Klan.

"The news media really blew it up and did all our work for us."

—Alexander McQuirter

7. Rebirth of the Klan

THROUGHOUT THE 1970s, WHEN the future leaders of Canada's Klan were building up their organizing skills (and criminal records) in the various extreme right-wing movements, they remained in touch with their American counterparts. In March, 1971, David Duke of the Louisiana-based Knights of the Ku Klux Klan visited Toronto to recruit new members. (On that trip he also tried to meet with Ontario attorney general Roy McMurtry, but was refused.[1]) On February 19, 1972, Western Guardsmen John Ross Taylor, Jacob Prins, Don Andrews and his wife, along with four other Canadians, attended a meeting at the Roma Hall in east Detroit, Michigan. The audience accorded a standing ovation to these "friends from Canada" when they were introduced. A newspaper account of the meeting referred to Prins as a "former cohort of Nazi John Beattie and now Canadian Dragon of the Klan;" Taylor was described as "a longtime Canadian fascist."[2]

Three months later, the Klan made a more direct appearance in Toronto itself. "KU KLUX KLAN HERE," was the banner headline on the front page of the May 1, 1972 Toronto *Sun*. "The Ku Klux Klan is in Canada," the article reported, revealing that it had announced its presence at a Western Guard banquet two nights earlier. A Rev. Robert Miles, described as a leader of the U.S. Klan (and one of the Klansmen charged with bombing schools in Pontiac, Michigan), told the gathering of 130 that Canada was the "last stronghold of white, Christian supremacist culture and a place for white Americans to come if the struggle against the Jewish-inspired mongrelization of white and black is allowed to continue." Paul Fromm of the Western Guard gave the opening address; Jacob Prins was also on hand. So was Martin Weiche of the Canadian National Socialist Party, along with his bodyguard Reade, who was selling Nazi symbols and bumper stickers. The meeting announced an international alliance of the extreme right, including the KKK, the Western Guard and some American neo-Nazi groups.

Still, the Klan in Canada remained little more than a social group for those already involved in extreme right politics and who wanted the extra thrill of belonging to the renowned American organization. Said Don Andrews, recalling that many Western Guard members were also members of the Klan at the time:* "There was a little Klan going on and they had a few meetings. They would meet socially and discuss things." The Klan was so unstructured at the time that not all its Canadian members belonged to the same branch of the American Klan. Prins, for example, held the nominal title of "Grand Dragon" in an organization called the Invisible Empire, Knights of the Ku Klux Klan, led by Dale Reusch from Ohio. Armand Siksna got in touch in 1974 with Klan leader David Duke from Louisiana, and helped set up a "quite small den" of Klansmen in Toronto.

But by the mid-1970s American Klansmen were eager to organize something more serious in Canada; contacts increased between them and their Toronto admirers. The aging Taylor, the veteran Droege and a youthful McQuirter all attended David Duke's international congress of white supremacist groups in New Orleans in 1976. It was a spellbinding affair. "The white people have to unite if we are to save ourselves," Duke told the wildly enthusiastic crowd of 600. "There is no other organization. There is no other hope...We want a constitutional amendment *against* niggers...The American white people are searching, are reaching

---

*McQuirter notes that "I originally got the address of Klansmen in Toronto at Western Guard meetings."

out, for a movement to carry forth their ideals, their values, the dreams they carry in their hearts. And the Ku Klux Klan is their movement!" "Nigger, Nigger! White power!" the crowd chanted in response. After the speeches, the mob gathered for a cross-burning ceremony on the outskirts of New Orleans. As flames engulfed the cross and Klansmen extended their arms in Nazi-style salutes, Duke proclaimed: "May we be victorious in this struggle for our race and our freedom! White power!"[3]

All this hysteria, the crowd, the demagoguery of Duke, left a mark on the impressionable young racist McQuirter, fresh out of high school. But the older and more experienced Droege was also moved. Though he declined Duke's offer to link up with the Klan directly ("at the time I felt that the Klan wouldn't go over well in Canada"), Droege was clearly swayed by the potential of the Klan's attraction: "I felt uplifted by the attendance, the atmosphere, and the patriotic energies that prevailed throughout the congress. There was a march, a rally and a cross-lighting. I felt renewed strength and vigor, inspired by the tremendous oratories and the vibrant setting. I will never forget this event."

The momentum for setting up a genuine Canadian Klan organization was slowly building. In the early spring of 1977, Droege took advantage of a visit by Duke to Buffalo, New York, to convince him to hop across the border and make a tour of Toronto. "Duke's media appearances* created a storm of letters and requests for memberships in the Klan," says Droege. "By this time, James McQuirter and I had become close friends and we both shared great respect for Duke's ability." Duke told the Toronto press that within a year the Ku Klux Klan would rise in Canada.

McQuirter and Droege would prove their idol right. They began to work together, contacting members of Duke's organization in Canada and creating, in Droege's words, "a solidified, cohesive group from what had been a loosely grouped band of individual members." In January, 1978, the reborn Canadian Klan garnered newspaper headlines for its first major public appearance. That month, a furor erupted in the Toronto

---

*Including a very high-profile television debate with media personality and political commentator Morton Shulman.

media when a teacher at Cardinal Newman high school invited Canadian Klansman "Jim Alexander" — a nervous McQuirter decided to use only his first two names publicly — to speak to his class studying the American civil war. The teacher was given permission by a member of the school administration to invite a spokesperson from the KKK. But when news of the planned talk was publicized, the school principal cancelled the visit. Still, the incident put the Canadian Klan's name in the headlines for the first time in years; McQuirter had begun his media career. "You can't take them [blacks] from the jungle and expect them to work out in the civilized culture of the whites," he said in one press interview. McQuirter told the press there were "more than three" Klan chapters in the city. "Until we develop a grass roots backing, we just want the people to know we're here, that we've arrived."[4]

Looking back on the incident a few years later, McQuirter was modest about his debut as public spokesman for the Klan. "That was just a one-shot deal," he said. "At that time, as far as I was concerned, that would be the last public thing I ever did for the Klan." Droege also felt the young McQuirter was still a little green. "The basic talents were there, but he needed cultivation when I first met him; his views needed to be somewhat refined and his reactions tempered." The Klan's first steps, it appeared, had been shaky ones.

McQuirter continued to dabble in various right-wing activities. He set up companies with names like Positive Products and Victory Books to distribute white nationalist literature. But those ventures came to an end when he and Siksna were charged with violating Canada's hate propaganda laws in March, 1978.* McQuirter and Droege soon left Toronto for Vancouver ("The people we left in charge in Toronto preferred to organize quietly and remain secretive for the time being," said Droege). Droege decided to stay on the west coast to organize there, but McQuirter was soon back in Toronto. While still active in the Klan, both organizers flirted with other rightist formations. When their close associate Don Andrews set up the Nationalist Party of Canada in 1978 to carry on the Western Guard's traditions, McQuirter and Droege joined. Their collaboration with Andrews was marked by

*The case did not come to trial until March, 1980. See pages 192-193.

less than complete enthusiasm, perhaps because, having experienced the thrill and media publicity of running their own Klan show, they chafed at what Droege called Andrews's "tight-fisted" leadership. Nonetheless, Droege became the NPC's western organizer and McQuirter sat on the executive of the Nationalist Party for a while, and it was he who signed the party's official application for registration as a legal political party in Ontario in 1978. But within a year, McQuirter and Droege obviously came to the conclusion that a brighter political future lay in building their Klan in Canada independent of Andrews's NPC (though there would be an attempt to merge the Klan with Andrews's party in the fall of 1980).* McQuirter resigned from the Nationalist Party executive and let his membership lapse, as did Droege. Other Guard members, like Armand Siksna and Jacob Prins, already had links to the Klan. In B.C., thanks largely to the tour by David Duke, Droege and others "were able to form a number of units." They corresponded with people across Canada who had asked for information on the Klan and, according to Droege, began "to acquire members in all major Canadian centres." By October, 1979, Droege felt confident enough to quit his job in a printing plant "to pursue full time the affairs of the movement." By December, McQuirter was boasting to the Toronto *Sun* that membership in the KKK in Toronto had tripled over the past three years.[5] He noted, however, that the Canadian Klan still kept a low profile, content primarily to meet with other extreme right-wing groups and discuss ways to get their message out.

Throughout 1980 McQuirter and his fellow Klansmen gained in confidence. They started distributing KKK literature and listed the Canadian Knights of the Ku Klux Klan in the Toronto telephone directory. A *Globe and Mail* story in June about the Klan's public activities was picked up by the media across the country; politicians, police and citizens' groups heatedly debated what to do about the reborn Klan.

"It was nothing planned, really," said McQuirter. "We had the phone installed so we could print up some literature. The news media really blew it up and did all our work for us."

*See pages 157-158.

McQuirter was the obvious choice to be spokesman and leader for the suddenly publicity-hungry Klan. "By default, he became leader because there was no one else who wanted to put themselves forward," said Don Andrews. McQuirter had the youthful image and good media presence lacking in any of the other right-wing veterans such as Droege and Prins. The modern Canadian Klan was off and running.

From the start, the Canadian Klan owed much to its American namesake; it was born and remains in many ways a branch plant of the bigger American operation.

McQuirter always played down his dependence on the American Klan. "We're not under their leadership," he told reporters when the Canadian Klan was launched. "We're interested in Canada, they're interested in the States. If we can help each other, fine." In fact, though, the links between the Klansmen in the two countries went far beyond that.

In the early 1970s, Canada was considered merely a "realm", or territory, the equivalent of an American state; hence Jacob Prins's designation as a "Grand Dragon" and not a "Grand Wizard", the title accorded a national leader in the U.S. When McQuirter and others were signing up with the Klan, they were joining a branch of the American Klan (usually Duke's); it was not until later that there was a real "Canadian" Klan as such to join. It was only when the KKK went public in 1980 and McQuirter was named national director that the Klan here obtained a distinct Canadian identity. Even then, it was more like a growing subsidiary that had been given the franchise for the country by its parent company, than a fully independent operation.

David Duke, the dynamic leader of one of the fastest-growing American Klan groups, was instrumental in building the Klan in Canada. On the simplest level, Duke had an important inspirational effect on Canadian Klansmen. It was his September, 1976, "International Patriotic Congress" in New Orleans that was the turning point for some of them. "I was impressed with David Duke," McQuirter recounted. "Many times you have right-wing leaders who were misfits or inarticulate people that people can't identify with. David Duke wasn't like that. He was a good speaker; he discussed issues at the level of the common man. He was young, a college graduate, and good looking." McQuirter, predictably, tried to fashion his own image after Duke's successful style. Droege also credited Duke with inspiring him to foresake the Western Guard for the Klan. "David Duke is the most dynamic white supremacist leader in America," he said in 1978. Other members of the new Canadian Klan also got a taste of Duke's oratory: tapes of his speeches were regularly played at Klan meetings in Toronto.

Duke's influence extended beyond inspiration, into the concrete areas of building up the Canadian Klan's membership. Duke's visits to Toronto in 1971 and 1977 helped spur interest in the Klan. When Droege and McQuirter went to B.C. in 1978, they first approached people who had acquired membership through the mail in Duke's Klan. In April, 1979, the B.C. Klansmen sponsored a media tour of the province by David Duke "for the purpose of raising membership and attention." Duke appeared on a number of programs, including Vancouver television station CKVU's prime time talk show. He told viewers they would be contacted by a local organizer if they forwarded their names to his Louisiana address; Droege reported a "tremendous response." Interestingly, Duke had been let into Canada despite the fact that he had been deported from Britain a year earlier for inciting race hatred. B.C.'s deputy attorney general Richard Vogel, and Jack McKinstry, the federal immigration director for Vancouver, both said that Duke would be allowed into Canada as long as he behaved himself. When Duke returned to Vancouver for another organizing drive in the spring of 1980, public outcry and protests forced his arrest and cut short his visit — but not before he appeared on at least fifteen radio and television shows to deliver what publicity manager Droege called "a valuable message on a large scale."

Duke also helped put together the Canadian Klan's political platform. "The interest in the Klan has really grown in Canada over the past two years," he said in a November, 1979, newspaper interview, "primarily because of the massive non-white immigration. Our plans for Canada are simple. We are 100 per cent for stopping the non-white immigration into Canada. And then we believe that the government should pay to send the blacks back to their own countries." McQuirter would repeat this statement almost word for word in his own media interviews, making it the Canadian Klan's central demand on the issue of immigration. Duke's anti-semitism and pro-Nazi bent — characteristics of his group more so than of competing Klans — also influenced McQuirter.

The American Klan took pains to train its new Canadian leaders. Droege attended a September, 1979 leadership conference of the Knights of the Ku Klux Klan in Louisiana, and stayed there for two weeks to help Duke in one of his senatorial election campaigns. The following year, McQuirter attended a national leadership convention of the Klan in Birmingham, Alabama.

The American influence over the Canadian Klan extended to the finer details of organization. McQuirter admitted in one newspaper interview that his decision to go public in mid-1980 may have been prompted by orders upstairs: "We were around for years, but our phone number was never listed. Headquarters in Louisiana were getting so many phone calls from Toronto they said it was time we went public."

Even much of the literature which the Canadian Klan used initially came from south of the border. The letters which the Canadian Klan gave to prospective members to explain the group's ideology were written and printed in the U.S. for an American audience. The two-page, typeset flyer was entitled, "An Introduction to the Knights of the Ku Klux Klan." Under the section headed "What the Klan stands for," one line was added to give the pamphlet Canadian content: "CANADA FIRST — First before any foreign influence or interest." Admitted one B.C. Klansman: "Yes, you might say that's an American introduction, but, you know, we just use it, made it over as best we could."[6]

But despite the undeniable inspirational, political and organizational influence of the American KKK, the reborn Canadian Klan was distinctly Canadian. Its members and leaders were Canadian citizens, in contrast to the Klan on the prairies in the 1920s, which had been organized by Americans. The new Canadian Klan emerged out of Toronto's indigenous hotbed of fascist groups in the 1970s, giving the Canadian KKK its distinct blend of white supremacy and a Nazi-like anti-semitism. Perhaps most importantly, the Klan fed on local conditions and a racism that was as "made in Canada" as maple syrup.

The situation was ripe for a group like the Klan. By 1977, the Ontario Human Rights Commission was warning that the "number of reported incidents of racial violence in public places has increased dramatically recently." Explained the commission: "As was the case during the great depression, severe job shortages and economic constraint provide the climate for hostility against members of visible minorities who are seen as illegitimate competition for economic and social rewards."[7] By the time the Ku Klux Klan went public in 1980, Canada's most troubled post-war decade had come to a close and a difficult new one was beginning. The economy was stagnating under the crushing burden of record inflation and mounting unemployment. The "Just Society" had become the society of restraint, of cutbacks in social services, of layoffs, of "belt-tightening". Immigrants and minorities became some of the first victims of these changing times. The screws had begun to tighten on them from the very start of the economic crisis. The 1960s had seen an influx of third world immigrants to Canada, in part to meet the needs for a cheaper labor force; in the 1970s, the flow continued but the doors were starting to close. In 1972, it became impossible to apply for permanent resident staus from within Canada. Deportation rules were toughened; between 1971 and 1973, for example, more than 1,500 Haitians were deported. In 1974-75, fears of immigrants stealing jobs and overburdening social services were cultivated by public hearings for Ottawa's proposed "Green Paper" on immigration. The paper, which set the tone for subsequent immigration policy, adopted a strong anti-immigrant bias and warned of "the consequences for national identity that might follow any significant change in the ethnic composition of the population." In 1978, Bud Cullen, the federal immigration minister, charged that immigrants were worsening "the already serious job situation" and that they are a "social and economic burden" in difficult times. That same year, the new Immigration Act — introduced as Bill C-24 two years earlier amidst protests in the immigrant communities — became law. It enshrined a point system with built-in racial biases favoring the education and skills usually possessed by white Europeans or Americans.[8] The National Citizens' Coalition, a lobby group funded by business, ran full-page advertisements in major newspapers warning that the massive influx of Indochinese refugees — the "boat people" — into Canada would wreak havoc on the country. Racism in the job market, certainly nothing new in Canada, also intensified as the economic crisis worsened. The Social Planning Council of Metro Toronto reported "widespread discrimination" toward racial minorities, with West Indians in the city earning between $2,400 and $3,500 a year less than whites with the same qualifications. The council concluded that high unemployment allowed employers to pit workers of different nationalities against one another.[9]

Government and business policies were not the only factors aggravating racism in Canada. Police forces in large metropolitan centres like Toronto and Vancouver appeared to take little or no action against the alarming number of attacks on blacks, East Indians and immigrants. Indeed, in some cases, the *victims* were often arrested when they defended themselves against racial harassment. Racial tensions reached boiling point in Toronto when police shot and killed two black men — Buddy Evans, an 18-year-old Canadian citizen, in 1978, and Albert Johnson, a Jamaican-born father of four, in 1979. The police claimed both shootings were in self defence, but witnesses in both cases insisted the police officers made disparaging remarks about "niggers" before firing the fatal shots. The Johnson shooting brought thousands of Toronto's blacks into the streets in protest against what they saw as the institutionalized racism of the police and justice system. The two separate inquests into these shootings, during which the black men's character and not the policemen's conduct often seemed to be the main focus, only inflamed the situation. When the two policemen involved in the Johnson death were cleared, black community leader Dudley Laws called it "an endorsement of continuing police brutality and harassment." Despite the public outcry against police racism, governments and the authorities seemed to move very slowly, if at all, to meet the calls for reform. Commissions of inquiry were set up, psychologists hired to study police staff, an ombudsman was eventually named, but little appeared really to change.

The commercial media also did its share in nurturing racism. One particularly glaring example was a sensationalist report in 1979 on the alleged "invasion" of Canada's universities by Chinese immigrant students, featured on CTV's widely-watched public affairs program, *W5*. In this modern version of the yellow peril story, entitled "Campus Giveaway", faces of Chinese students filled the television screen as worrisome statistics on the overcrowding of Canada's educational facilities were presented. An outraged Chinese Canadian community mounted a nation-wide series of marches, protests and educational campaigns. They pointed out that not only had *W5* grossly mispresented many statistics, it also neglected to mention that the majority of "Chinese" students in Canadian schools were Canadian-born citizens, not immigrants. CTV was finally forced to take the unprecedented move of apologizing on the air for the racist overtones of the program. But the damage had been done.

For various reasons, then, the Ku Klux Klan found the Canadian terrain in 1980 to be fertile for its seeds of hate. It would not be too difficult for the organization to sprout across the country.

*"White people are sitting here waiting for
someone to organize them. The potential is
fantastic."*

— Alexander McQuirter

8. Spreading the flames

IN JUNE, 1980, THE KU KLUX KLAN opened its first public headquarters in Canada. It wasn't a lavish beginning. The office was
located in the Toronto east end community of Riverdale, in
McQuirter's home at 1439 Dundas Street East. The KKK shared a
run-down room with a company McQuirter was running called
Arcon Mail Forwarding. "This is the first office in the province,"
Klan organizer Wolfgang Droege told the local media, which gave
the opening wide coverage. "People don't know what we stand
for, so we're going public to try and wake them up and educate
them."

It was to be expected that the Klan would choose Toronto for
its public unveiling. After all, McQuirter, Droege, Prins and most
of the other early activists in the Klan were from Toronto, where
there had already been a decade of fascist activity. Toronto, the
preferred home of 25 per cent of all immigrants to Canada, also
had the target the Klan needed for its hate propaganda: the largest
black community of any city in the country, estimated at about
150,000 and made up mainly of Caribbean immigrants and black
Canadians. East Indians and Chinese Canadians were also
numerous. And Toronto had seen mounting racial tensions over
the previous few years. Klan leaders insisted the public reaction to

97

their setting up shop was favorable. "People are seeking us out and we've been encouraged by the response so far," said Droege. Added McQuirter: "The response in Ontario has been terrific."

Unlike most new political formations, the Canadian KKK never issued a founding statement of principles or a public platform. Instead the Klan's policies on immigration, blacks, Jews and other issues took shape through the public pronouncements of its leaders and the statements made in Klan publications. From the start, though, the Klansmen were intent on presenting their organization in as positive a light as possible. It was the Canadian version of Duke's successful Madison Avenue approach: the "new" Klan was not anti-black, it was pro-white; it was not violent, it was law-abiding. "We're not anti-anybody. We're just pro-white," McQuirter said in one early press interview. "I'm not a hate monger. I'm not out to belittle people, I just want to improve the quality of life for the people that built this country, the white people." Sometimes the Klan chieftain tried to pass off his organization as a harmless pressure group: "We don't go around in the night with hoods, lynching Negroes. We want to protect the white man's heritage by creating a lobby group which can influence the decision makers." Wolfgang Droege was equally adamant about the Klan's peaceful nature, an ironic assertion considering his own violent past and criminal record from his Western Guard days: "Most people think we're a violent group but that's not true. We're against violence. It's one of our oaths not to commit illegal acts. Although I'm sure some Klansmen have committed illegal acts, they're not condoned by the Klan."

From its Toronto base, the modern Klan expanded quickly into southern Ontario, built up its presence in B.C. and to some extent penetrated the prairies and Atlantic provinces. Everywhere the response was the same: from politicians and the authorities, tough words but little action; from the concerned voices in the community, outcry and opposition.

"I want to slam the door of Toronto in their faces," said Paul Godfrey, Toronto Metro Chairman and member of the board of police commissioners. He pledged to do everything in his power to prevent the Klan from being set up "anywhere in the Metro area." Roy McMurtry, Ontario's attorney general, was equally adamant: "They're bloody well not welcome in this province," he stormed. Federal politicians too joined the chorus of condemnation, passing unanimously the following resolution:

> That this House reaffirms its commitment to Canada as a multicultural and multiracial society, whose foundations are political, racial and religious tolerance, places on record its opposition to everything the Ku Klux Klan stands for, and its conviction that this organization is not welcome anywhere in Canada, and calls upon all levels of government to ensure that all Canadians are protected from racial attack, harassment and intimidation wherever and whenever they occur, and prosecute the perpetuation of these attacks with the full force of the law.

Despite the talk, no direct moves were taken by either municipal, provincial or federal authorities when the Klan opened its Dundas office. Indeed, over the next two years, as the Klan occupied a series of offices and continued to be listed in the Toronto phone directory, not a single measure was taken by any official to restrict their activities.

Fortunately, some members of the public were less reluctant to act. Despite Droege's and McQuirter's boasts not everyone in Toronto's Riverdale community was favorably disposed toward their new Klan neighbors. The South Riverdale Community Health Centre called on municipal, provincial and federal authorities to "take action to remove the KKK from the Riverdale community and anywhere in Ontario and Canada." The Innstead Housing Co-Operative called the KKK "a disruptive and dangerous force in our community." A multi-ethnic working class area, Riverdale had obvious potential for the Canadian Klansmen. Walking the streets or riding the streetcars that ramble through the main arteries of the neighborhood, one sees and hears East Indians, Chinese, Greek and other ethnic groups and nationalities. "There are a number of immigrant groups here, as well as blue collar, Anglo-Saxon workers," explained Dierdre Power, a teacher. "There is also high unemployment. As unemployment and inflation rise, young workers and students become increasingly frustrated and look for solutions. Riverdale is just the type of community where the Klan is active." Said Rev. John Robson of the Queen Street Presbyterian Church: "Where there's unemployment and fear because of people from different cultures moving into an old community, the Klan knows that people are frightened and angry and looking for people to dump on. It's a good way for the Klan to organize a political base — by capitalizing on those feelings and trying to fan that into a flame."

Resolutions against the Klan and concern about its activities were voiced by community centres, church groups and legal aid clinics. They contacted the Riverdale Inter-Cultural Council (RICC), an organization promoting awareness and understanding between the different ethnic groups in the neighborhood. "All these groups were stirred up and started passing resolutions and RICC was the group that brought them together," recalled RICC chairman Robson. In the summer of 1980, a meeting was held and RACAR — the Riverdale Action Committee Against Racism — was founded. "We got together and set out to build a community-based organization," said Deirdre Power, who became a RACAR co-ordinator. "Its focus was simple: to get rid of the Klan."

While the battle lines were being drawn in Riverdale, the Klan was spreading its tentacles throughout southern Ontario. McQuirter traveled to Windsor — which has a large indigenous black population whose roots date to the last century — where he told an open line radio show that the Klan already had twenty members in the area. In August, the Klan announced plans to set up an office in Kitchener. That same month, McQuirter said that Klan dens had been established in the smaller communities of Clifford and Walkerton. Previous white supremacist groups had concentrated their activities almost exclusively in Toronto, so the Klan's penetration into rural western Ontario was novel. Droege remarked that the KKK "unlike the other white nationalist groups in Canada, moved out of the cities and launched literature distribution drives in smaller, rural communities. This move was very effective." Droege felt there was a "healthier racial element" in the rural areas — in other words, fewer non-whites — and that people were more receptive to the Klan's views.

In the fall of 1980, McQuirter flew out to Vancouver to drum up some media attention to supplement the organizing work Droege had been doing there for the past year. With the largest East Indian community in the country and the second largest Chinese population, Vancouver was a choice spot for the merchants of hate. "There is potential because of dissatisfaction with the Pakistani and East Indian population," McQuirter said in one interview. He said his initial reception in B.C. was a lot better than it had been in Toronto. "We had to work at being accepted in Toronto, but here it didn't take that long at all. Vancouver on the whole has been ripe for a long time for a white man's organization. White people are sitting here waiting for someone to organize them. The potential is fantastic." In his media interviews, McQuirter warned that other races "breed faster" and were making "the white race an endangered species;" insisted that the "Oriental contribution" to society consisted of the illegal drug trade; decried the "multiracial crap" in Canada and proposed that non-whites be paid "$30,000 to $35,000 per family to go back to [their] land of origin."

Evan Wolfe, the provincial secretary in B.C.'s Social Credit government, replied that "the Klan and its goals are repugnant" to British Columbians, and branded Klan tactics as "similar to those of Nazi Germany." But like the B.C. government of the 1920s, the B.C. government of the 1980s seemed hesitant to move beyond words; indeed, at times it even displayed a fear of words themselves. In July, 1980, the opposition New Democratic Party proposed a resolution against the Klan, a motion that was basically toothless; the NDP itself admitted it "does not call for the outlawing of the Klan, nor even restricting its members' civil rights to belong to it."[1] Still, it would have put the provincial parliament on record as being "in opposition to the Ku Klux Klan." But the Socreds refused to allow the motion onto the floor of the legislature for debate.

When, that fall, several citizens voiced concern over the Klan's preaching of white superiority through the media, they found the government reluctant to act. Delicia Crump of the B.C. Association for the Advancement of Colored People, Paul Winn of the Black Solidarity Association and Aziz Khaki of the Committee for Racial Justice all lodged separate complaints about the Klan's use of the media with the various government branches and the provincial human rights commission. They particularly objected to McQuirter's public call to ship non-whites in Canada "back to where they came from." But the complainants were told by the provincial attorney general's office and the human rights body that the authorities had "no power" to move against the Klan.[2]

Opposition to the Klan in B.C. was soon taken up by the many groups in the province fighting racism. The Committee for Racial Justice brought together such groups as the B.C. Teachers Federation and the Black Solidarity Association, and the Coalition to Fight Racism united union and community activists.

November, 1980, saw the creation of an organization that was to spearhead the campaign against the Klan in the province — the British Columbia Organization to Fight Racism. Set up as "a permanent organization which can provide resistance to racism," the BCOFR quickly made fighting the Klan one of its major activities. As one of the early BCOFR pamphlets put it:

> Over much of the world, extreme right wing and racist violence is growing. In Canada, we face hard times — unemployment, housing shortages, inflation, cutbacks in social services.
> People are suffering. They are angry.
> Who is responsible?
> Some people look for an easy target such as immigrants to blame for these hard times. The Klan...takes this a step further. They are actively pushing their program of lies, violence and expulsion against various ethnic and religious groups.

Headed by Charan Gill, a social worker with the B.C. Ministry of Human Resources and secretary of the Canadian Farmworkers Union, the BCOFR drew most of its membership from the East Indian community. But it quickly gathered support from a wide range of nationalities and organizations.

The BCOFR established a goal that was to become controversial for governments and within the anti-racism movement itself: to ban the Klan. "Freedom of speech is definitely a fundamental right," explained Gill. "But the Klan should not be allowed to infringe on the rights of others, to propagate hate towards national and ethnic minorities."

From Vancouver, meanwhile, the Klan tried to expand into the prairies. "We're big in Alberta," Droege claimed, a plausible boast considering the Klan's roots in the province in the 1920s. But there was as yet little public Klan activity in Alberta. Most of the Klan noises in the province came from another KKK sect run by Tearlach Mac a' Phearsoin.*

The Klan also moved into Saskatchewan. McQuirter said there were several Klan members in "some rural areas of Saskatchewan" — perhaps in some of the small towns where the Klan had exercised considerable political clout a few decades earlier. But most of the KKK's work was concentrated in Regina. In November, Klansmen began distributing membership cards, leaflets and posters in the north central part of the city. Klan literature appeared in residential areas with a high concentration of native people (about one fifth of the city's population is native), in bars, schools and at the Regina Correctional Centre. Public reaction to the Klan's inroads in Regina was swift. That same month a Native Rights Coalition, which included non-native individuals and organizations, was formed. At its founding meeting, the coalition established a special committee to "take action against the KKK resurgence in Regina." This committee later distributed an educational pamphlet and "Ban the Klan" buttons throughout the city.

As 1980 drew to a close and the new Klan continued to expand across the country, two ominous characteristics of the new KKK emerged. The first was the Klan's eagerness to recruit teenagers. The Canadian Klansmen no doubt got the idea from their mentor David Duke, who pioneered the penetration of the American Klan organizations into the schools ("White students! Fight for White

---

*Mac a' Phearsoin had reappeared in 1980 as director of the newly-incorporated Invisible Empire Association of Alberta. He denounced McQuirter's Klan as "a bunch of neo-Nazis" and insisted that only he had the true franchise for the Klan in Canada. He claimed 325 members in the revived Alberta Klan. When two "lawn burnings" took place at the homes of East Indians and Japanese Canadians in Red Deer — the shape of a cross was burned into their lawns — Mac a' Phearsoin denied his group had anything to do with the incident.[3]

Power by becoming a member of the Klan Youth Corps!" urged one leaflet widely distributed by Duke's squads in high schools in a number of American cities). The Canadians caught on. "During the fall, one of our main projects had been to organize high school students," said Wolfgang Droege. Skeptics said it was a move born of desperation because the Klan was failing to recruit many adults. More likely the Klan's youth campaign was based on the expectation that the frustrations of young people could be easily exploited. "Some of the young people had become disillusioned with the older generation," Droege noted. "They recognized that their job prospects were not the same as their ancestors." The Klan's analysis of the cause of young people's woes was simple: they had been forced "to take a back seat to minorities who had been receiving special privileges."

The campaign soon began in earnest in schools in British Columbia and Ontario. Klan recruiters handed out business cards which talked about "racial purity" at schools in the Vancouver area. Several high schools as well as the University of British Columbia and the B.C. Institute of Technology were canvassed, according to the B.C. Teachers Federation. One high school which followed up on the orange business cards and asked for information on the Klan received, from Louisiana, a package containing Klan newspapers and application forms for the Klan Youth Corps. A member of the Ontario Secondary School Teachers Federation complained that Klan material was filtering into some schools in the Durham region. The next month, Klansmen were handing out business cards at Monarch Park Secondary School in Toronto. "Racial purity is Canada's security," the cards said, blaming "blacks, East Indians and minorities" for everything from higher taxes to "an ever increasing rate of brutal crime." The cards gave a local address and phone number to contact the Klan. Similar cards were also handed out to boys playing after-school ball hockey on the grounds of D.A. Morrison Junior High School in East York.

The authorities' reaction to these Klan incursions was sluggish. Just one week before the Klan business cards hit the Toronto schools, Toronto school board member Susan Hunter-Harvey failed in a bid to persuade her fellow trustees to pass a motion against the Klan. Several trustees walked out of a board meeting before the proposal was discussed because "they didn't want to waste time on yet another issue that doesn't relate to our schools." Two weeks later, perhaps somewhat chastised by the outburst of Klan activity that suddenly made the issue more relevant, the board passed a motion to "emphatically denounce the presence of the Ku Klux Klan in Toronto and make it clear that the Ku Klux Klan is not welcome in this community." The board also called on Ontario's attorney general Roy McMurtry and Toronto's police chief to "closely monitor the activities of this organization."[4] Public outrage also forced McMurtry to warn the province's other school boards about the recruitment drive. But little else was done. In October, McMurtry told an angry provincial legislature that police were examining the material the Klan was distributing to see if it violated sections of the Criminal Code concerning hate literature. Outside the legislature, McMurtry admitted that his ministry's legal officials had studied the Klan propaganda and had concluded that "in their judgment, it violates the hate literature sections of the law." Yet no action was taken.

The second worrisome trend in the KKK's renaissance was the vandalism and violence which, if not always committed by the Klan itself, was doubtless inspired by it. In October, 1979, a black man was temporarily blinded when a white couple sprayed tear gas in his face in an attack in a Toronto subway station. The assailants punched their victim and called a white woman accompanying him "white trash". When arrested the attackers were carrying KKK cards bearing the slogan "Racial purity is America's security." They were convicted of assault and possession of a prohibited weapon. On January 24, 1980, Winnipeg police arrested two 17-year-olds and one adult for burning crosses into the front lawns of five homes, mostly belonging to East Indian families. "I'm so afraid, I slept in my clothes last night," said Surinder Singh, a mother of four. After a fiery cross burned on her front lawn, she received a terrifying midnight call: "We're not finished with you. We're going to kidnap your kids. . . .We're going to burn your yard tonight."[5] Outside another home in the same neighborhood, a six-foot cross was soaked in gasoline and set ablaze. In the same city in July, a gang of whites wearing KKK T-shirts attacked four black youths, slashing one of them in the face with a knife. The following month, in Red Deer, Alberta, two non-white families had cross shapes burned into their lawns. In November, Nigerian students attending the B.C. Institute of Technology got a taste of Klan hospitality. The students' homes in New Westminster and Burnaby were spray painted with racist slogans ("Go home niggers — KKK") and garbage was dumped on their porches and lawns. The students also reported four other incidents of racial harassment in the previous ten days, including threatening and obscene phone calls.[6]

By the end of 1980 — just six months after it went public — the Canadian Knights of the Ku Klux Klan had been heard of in nearly all corners of the country. A year-end bulletin entitled *KKK Canada Action Report*, which served as the organization's newsletter, drew an encouraging picture of the Klan's expansion. It noted that "the Klan in B.C. has grown considerably." In Ontario, Ottawa and Kingston were said to have "increased membership," the Kitchener, Waterloo, Hanover, and Walkerton units "reported a small, but steady increase" in numbers, and "Sarnia and London have now been added to the growing list in southern Ontario to start Klan dens." Klan groups were sprouting up in the cities of Hamilton and Dundas "with the help of Toronto organizers." The *Action Report* also recorded "the new formation of the Maritime units" after McQuirter's widely-publicized tour there and announced the naming of organizers for Nova Scotia and New Brunswick. "The Ku Klux Klan does have plans to move into New Brunswick," McQuirter told one local newspaper. "The time is ripe to develop in the Atlantic region." There was a report in late 1980 that the Klan was trying to establish a northern beachhead in Whitehorse, but not much came of that. As for Quebec, McQuirter claimed to have supporters in Montreal — "old followers of Adrien Arcand" — but he never visited the province for the same kind of public membership drive as he had undertaken in B.C., Ontario or the Atlantic provinces.

To celebrate — or perhaps flaunt — its newfound strength, the Canadian Ku Klux Klan held its first large cross-burning ceremony in decades. It was a chilly November 8 evening, near London, Ont. Twenty-five Klansmen met at the twelve and a half acres estate of Martin Weiche, who was not a Klan member. "They needed a place," said Weiche. "A friend of mine asked if they could use my lawn, and I didn't see anything wrong with that. They're welcome anytime." The KKK crowd gathered around the cross, held hands and swore to protect the white race. The cross was set ablaze and the Klansmen gave the fascist salute.[7]

The Klan was confident, almost cocky, about its future. And why not? The past year had seen people in responsible positions in police forces, the government and the media turn a blind eye to the threat of the Klan when not actually lending it a hand. McQuirter claimed that active Klan members and supporters included "highly placed Ontario civil servants, Metro [Toronto] cops and big names in the news media."[8] He had told the Ottawa *Citizen* that some of the Klan's major boosters were Toronto policemen: "We talk to the man on the beat and he supports what we're doing," the Klan leader said. "He may not do so openly and publicly not admit it if asked, but inside he agrees with us."[9] Such statements may have been wishful boasts. But in the U.S., many policemen, sheriffs and law officers have been known to be Klan members and some have even been arrested for their Klan activities. Could not the same situation, on a reduced scale, exist in Canada? In any case, one thing was indisputable: throughout 1980, in no city across Canada did any police officials take measures to curb the Klan's activities and growth. The reaction from politicians and government authorities, aside from the occasional anti-Klan pronouncement, had been equally permissive. The flippant attitude of Robert Kaplan, the federal solicitor general, was typical of the reluctance of governments to put their muscle where their mouth was. When asked in November, 1980, if Ottawa was keeping an eye on the Klan, Kaplan responded: "What's to monitor? There's no evidence that they're making headway."[10] Kaplan's remark came after a year which saw the Klan open its first public office, expand to many centres across southern Ontario, B.C. and the rest of the country, and distribute hate literature in high schools in Toronto and

Vancouver.

Perhaps no single factor helped the Klan more in its first year than the widespread, usually uncritical and at times flattering, coverage it received in the media. Said Klan leader McQuirter: "It's the key to our success. It's up to us to grab it." The media itself seemed aware of its own role in boosting the Klan's fortunes. One Canadian Press story at the end of 1980 drew this accurate comparison between the Klan of the 1920s and the modern KKK:

> Unlike its predecessor, which packed meeting halls to raucous overflowing 50 years ago, the 1980 version [of the Klan] capitalizes on media attention.
>
> McQuirter has been on numerous radio talk shows, appeared on television and has had his name mentioned in most print media. Rarely does a day go by that some newspaper in Canada doesn't mention the Klan. And McQuirter loves it.[11]

The Canadian Klan learned how to use the media from its American counterpart which, according to a study published by the *Columbia Journalism Review*, has a long history of getting "help from the press in achieving its nefarious goals."[12] David Duke developed this tactic into a fine art, presenting a prime time media image to soft sell racism. He told his Klansmen at a national convention in September, 1979, that only designated spokesmen should deal with the media: "Not everyone is to get on the soapbox. Some say the wrong things. 'Why did you join the Klan?' 'Well, I want to hang some niggers, you know.' Yeah, that may sound good, but that's not exactly what we're trying to get over to the American public...There should be a 'media line' that everyone adheres to."[13]

McQuirter applied the teachings of his American idol well. "We learned some of the lessons the U.S. Klan has learned about combatting the media blackout," he said proudly. He points out that the key was to effectively make use of the contradiction between the media's "generally negative image" of the Klan and the good-looking, eloquent impression projected by Duke and himself. McQuirter's scheme worked. Typically enthralled with form rather than substance, the media played into the hands of his slick salesmanship. McQuirter was described as "fresh-faced, polite, articulate" and as "an idealistic young man." Said one wire service story which appeared in many newspapers across the country: "He speaks with the lofty ideals of a Boy Scout counsellor." Another wire service story began this way: "Fresh from his mid-day jog, Alexander McQuirter pumps the visitor's hand with a neighborly grip and with calm, meticulous action sets out to explain his cause." The article went on to describe the reporter's meeting with the Klan leader "in his book-lined living room." One paragraph read: "Hate-monger, racist rabble rouser, nut — he's been called every name in the book, but shrugs them off with the equanamity of a crusading do-gooder, a man who has his answer to the world's problems."

Sometimes the media went beyond simply giving complimentary descriptions of the Klan leader. A CBC radio producer in Toronto once admitted to Riverdale anti-Klan activists that he had to edit a taped interview with McQuirter to make it presentable for the audience. "That's horrendous," commented RACAR's Dierdre Power. "They didn't say on the air that they had to leave out stuff to make McQuirter come off as a decent young man." Of course, the reverse — not editing McQuirter's comments and giving him free rein on the airwaves — was hardly better. On a CFUN radio show in Vancouver, McQuirter complained that non-whites "breed at a fantastic rate...We don't want them to work here. We don't want them to live here." On CBC television's *Pacific Report*, the Klan leader, after elaborating his policy of deporting all non-whites to their "home" country, went on to say:

> I think that intelligence tests are testing the person's ability to live, breathe and work in a North American environment and if he can't come up to those standards for whatever reason, you know it could be the climate, then he should not be allowed to enjoy the same rights, in fact not even be in the same country...[14]

Such statements were arguably in violation of the Broadcasting Act in Canada, which states that "no station or network operation shall broadcast any abusive comment or abusive pictorial representation on any race, religion or creed."

The kind of coverage that the Klan was getting in the media

helped its cause immeasurably; the KKK itself certainly felt so —
and boasted about it. At the end of 1980, the Klan's *Action Report*
gleefully recounted its media successes. Commenting on a
Vancouver rally, it stressed that "the appearance of a CBC camera
crew showed the effectiveness of the meeting which was broadcast
on nationwide T.V." The newsletter went on to report that
"during the last month, over 23 interviews were granted to press
by Director McQuirter...Ottawa and Kingston have also
increased membership, as a result of local publicity." A vicious
circle was beginning to set in: the Klan was expanding its
influence, attracting the attention of uncritical media; the
subsequent mass exposure fueled the Klan's work even more and
encouraged the Klan to seek more media publicity. McQuirter
privately admitted that he sometimes egged on the media with
exaggerated claims about the Klan's operations, and that
cross-burning ceremonies were staged for the media's benefit.
"Sure I was able to lead them on in some ways," he said, adding
that he was grateful that the Klan had "the opportunity to 'use' the
media for our propaganda."

Particularly noteworthy in the media's handling of the Klan
were some of the comments made by Toronto *Sun* columnists.
Like most of the other papers, the *Sun* featured the standard fare
of interviews with McQuirter and pictures of the Klan leader. But
Sun columnist Claire Hoy went further. During the furor over the
Klan's activities in Ontario schools, Hoy wrote that the
authorities should "leave them alone," at least "until they bust
somebody's head or commit other crimes." The Klan "shouldn't
be unduly harassed by officialdom and unfairly labelled as
criminals," he argued. "Surely, it's not illegal to hate people, and
until that hate is translated into concrete actions, these guys are as
entitled as the Knights of Columbus or the Shriners to recruit
members." In an editorial, the *Sun* curiously deplored the undue
media publicity for the KKK since "the KKK has done nothing in
Canada except indulge in mildly provocative rhetoric."[15] Hoy's
comments were not out of place in a tabloid newspaper renowned
for its own provocative rhetoric and espousal of right-wing
causes. The *Sun* was often criticized by the city's minorities for its
excesses. One typical column by regular contributor Mackenzie

Porter, for example, stated that the people in the third world were "like the people of India and Pakistan, not of this century...they belong to the 14th century as surely as the masses of sub-Sahara Africa belong to the Stone Age." Porter insisted that the "mawkish appeal that the people of Asia and Africa are equal politically, intellectually, morally and artistically to people of Western European ancestry is invalid." Could the Klan have said it any better?

Of course, neither Porter nor Hoy were in any way connected with the Klan. (Wrote Hoy: "It should be clear I do not support the Klan.") But the influence of their comments could not be easily discounted, considering the *Sun's* daily circulation of about a quarter of a million readers.* The *Sun's* treatment of the Klan and racism in general was a far cry from the outright editorial support which the Klan of the 1920s received from some newspapers in western Canada. But it was unsettling just the same, if only as a reflection of how the media — along with the politicians and the police — did not appear very resolute in countering the Klan.

If by the end of 1980 the Klan's fortunes were riding high, there were indications that popular opposition to the KKK was gathering strength. In western Canada, groups like the BCOFR and the Regina Native Rights Coalition were beginning their anti-Klan campaigns. In Toronto, an organization called the Committee for Racial Equality held a successful demonstration against the Klan. About 550 people marched down Yonge Street and listened to speeches decrying the Klan's mounting violence. "They have committed enough crimes and they should be banned," Dudley Laws, a black community activist, told the crowd. The rally also received a message of support from John Sewell, then Toronto's mayor. In Riverdale, meanwhile, the newly-formed RACAR held its first major community event in November. A day-long seminar on how to fight the Klan drew more than 200 people. A documentary on the American Klan was shown and workshops discussed the Klan's attitudes toward the community, trade unions, women and gays.

---

*The *Sun* empire also included papers in Edmonton and Calgary and the United Press Canada news service. In 1981, it controlled 8.3 per cent of the English-language circulation in the country.

The closing months of 1980 also saw the first two setbacks in the Klan's expansion drive — each minor victories in their own right, but significant for the precedents they set. In Sudbury, a two-day phone campaign in October forced a local television station to cancel an appearance by Alexander McQuirter. The area labor council, supported by the Sudbury Committee for Human Rights, had threatened a demonstration if the show went ahead. "It was a broad-based operation, not a fraction of the community, so they had to relent," said labor council secretary Peter Desilets. In Toronto, the KKK had been discreetly occupying a Yonge Street office, which they had used as a mailing address and a sort of private national headquarters. But when they got wind of the Klan's presence in November, the tenants of the six offices and thirty apartments in the building circulated a petition demanding the KKK's eviction. The landlord, who charged that the Klan had rented the premises under false pretenses, told them to move. (The lease had been signed under the name of the "National Association for the Advancement of White People.") Incensed, Klan officials made some bitter comments to the press about "Jewish landlords". But they were obliged to pack their bags and move back to McQuirter's house in Riverdale.

The Klansmen had been given the boot. It was a sign of things to come.

"We see this as a race war, a struggle between whites and non-whites."

— Alexander McQuirter

9. Inside the invisible empire

By THE WINTER OF 1981, the Canadian Ku Klux Klan had spread its message of white power to most of the country. Worried observers were beginning to ask questions about the "invisible empire," as the Klan liked to call itself. How many members and supporters did the Canadian KKK really have? Where did the Klan get its money? How well was it organized?

The Canadian Klan officially refuses to release membership statistics. "We never give figures," McQuirter once said. "I don't think numbers are important." But individual Klan officials are not always tight-lipped. In December, 1979, McQuirter told the Toronto *Sun* the Klan had 500 members in Toronto, Vancouver and Alberta and that there were 2,000 Canadian subscibers to the KKK newspaper *The Crusader*, an American publication. Several months later, he repeated the figure of 2,000 subscribers in an Ottawa *Citizen* interview and also claimed that 120 people had sought membership information in the few months since the Klan had gone public.[1] In April, 1980, Wolfgang Droege said B.C. membership had risen to 200 from 50.

The Klan's boasts about its size were impossible to verify, but the figures it did give were almost certainly exaggerated. In one interview, for example, B.C. Klan official Dave Cook admitted that 200 members was the figure that his superiors told him "is the number that you must use."[2] The largest recorded number of people at a public Klan event was 45, at a KKK cross burning in British Columbia in the summer of 1981; about 25 had attended a similar function in Ontario in late 1980. Assuming there were not many Klansmen who attended both ceremonies (McQuirter was one who did), that would mean there were at most 70 people who were willing to be publicly associated with the Klan. That figure corresponds roughly to the estimates by police and human rights authorities of the "hard core" strength of the Klan in Toronto and Vancouver: between 25 and 50 people in each city. These were the public, most active Klansmen who, in the words of a secret internal guide called the *Canadian Knights of the Ku Klux Klan Handbook*, "provide the backbone of the Movement. These members do the brunt of Klan work." Around this core of activists were other Klan supporters, more discreet and probably more numerous. "Associate Members," as the *Handbook* called them, "are essential — they make up the largest element of Klan membership in Canada. An Associate Member is one who is not active in most Klan activities. They are Klansmen who have most contact with the Movement by use of the mails and telephone." By calling subscribers or sympathizers "members," the Klan was of course boosting its ranks. Still, these "associates" were part of the Klan's forces. Neil Louttit, a Toronto *Star* reporter who infiltrated the Klan for several months in 1981, put the total number of Klan members in Canada at about 300, based on the press run of Klan literature he handled. A far cry from McQuirter's claim of 2,000 subscribers, but a not insignificant number just the same.

What kind of people did the Klan attract? The Klan *Handbook*, needless to say, insists that only the cream of the white race joined the Klan: "Our decision to become a citizen of the Invisible Empire is the beginning of a whole new attitude toward life. We are the new elite, men and women of Race and honour." While there was no detailed analysis of the characteristics of Canadian Klan membership, the conclusions of a study of David Duke's Klan — with which McQuirter's organization was affiliated — probably applied to Canada as well.[3] The study found that American Klan members tended to be young. At a typical Klan rally, 15 per cent of the crowd were teenagers (three Klan members arrested in Toronto in 1981 were aged 17 and 18 years old). About 60 to 80 per cent of U.S. Klan members were in their early twenties to mid-thirties (like McQuirter and Droege) and only about 15 per cent were older (like Jacob Prins). The sexual breakdown was found to be one-quarter to one-third female, with most of the women being wives and girlfriends of Klansmen. The Canadian Klan appeared to have fewer women (only a handful of female names have ever appeared in the press in connection with the KKK), but they did tend to be associated with a male Klan member. B.C. Klan spokesperson Ann Farmer, for example, was described as Droege's girlfriend and his common law wife; Jean MacGarry, the woman who helped run the Klan's Toronto office, had the same relationship with Klan security chief Gary MacFarlane. The American study also showed that the class composition of the Klan was mainly blue collar, with a small number of lower middle class members. The average KKK member had three years of high school education, Klan leaders often having somewhat more schooling.

In Canada, the active Klan members appeared to fall into one of three general categories. The first type of Klansmen could be described as "losers" — frustrated, down-and-out young whites. *Star* reporter Louttit observed that a good number of KKK members he met were simply "down-and-out WASP losers, trying to blame their own failures on anybody but themselves." That assessment was echoed by an Ontario police officer who followed the Klan: "They're a bunch of losers. The Klan is just a vehicle for these guys, it's highly visible for young people who have nothing. It's a place for them to go, to be somebody." Even Klan leader McQuirter conceded he had attracted plenty of "misfits" and Don Andrews dismissed most Klan members as "knee-jerk reactionaries" with little education who "are just looking around to kick some niggers." The average age of six Klansmen arrested in Toronto on different occasions for various charges of mischief was 20 years; most were either unemployed or had no steady job. Typical among them was Derek Edward Saunders. Raised by his grandparents in a poor, run-down section of east Toronto, Saunders was 17 when he was drawn to the KKK. He had frequent run-ins with the police. According to one neighbor whose teenage son was brought to Klan meetings by Saunders, a major attraction for youths at Klan meetings was the heavy consumption of alcohol at the Klan's Dundas Street headquarters. Included in this category of Klan "losers" were some small-time criminals. In British Columbia, for example, the Klan began to flirt with biker organizations; some members of a Surrey motorcycle gang were reported to have joined the KKK. One B.C. Klan organizer, Al Hooper, conceded "a lot of bikers" came to Klan meetings.

These younger members were the Klan's arms and legs, carrying out some of the organization's dirty work, but remaining essentially the foot soldiers. Less numerous but more influential in the Klan were the older fascists, like Wolfgang Droege and Jacob Prins — "the throwback to World War II types," as Louttit called them. These were men born in Europe who were sympathetic or active in the Nazi movement there long before they encountered the Klan. They exerted an ideological influence over the Canadian Klan and helped give it its decidedly anti-semitic bent.

The third, smallest category of Klan members consisted of those who came to the KKK not as frustrated losers or longtime Nazis, but as middle class Canadians intellectually attracted to the Klan's racism. McQuirter fit into this category. So did Ann Farmer, a student at the University of B.C. who became a provincial KKK leader. Proud of her Christian upbringing, she said she was "concerned about the increasing number of non-whites in Canadian society" and decided to join the Klan "because I am impressed by the Klan's spectacular history of fighting for white rights." These young, articulate leaders provided the public image for the Klan, the sanitized facade behind which the confused "losers" and the committed Nazis could hide.

In addition to these Klan members, there were also the secret supporters of the KKK, the sympathetic financiers. "The Supporter provides the monies needed and is a mainstay of the organization," the Klan *Handbook* stated. Running a country-wide operation such as the Klan was not cheap. Never formally registered as a legal entity or political party, the Klan was not required to provide a public budget or a list of contributors. But its annual spending must have run into the thousands of dollars. McQuirter made a cross-Canada media tour in 1980; the following year he made frequent trips between Toronto and Vancouver to check on Klan activities. The KKK printed business cards, leaflets and a newsletter and it would eventually publish a tabloid newspaper. Membership dues presumably paid for part of these expenses (according to the *Handbook*, there was a one-time $15 initiation fee, annual dues of $30 and lifetime memberships available for $300). But there also had to be outside sources of money. McQuirter claimed that well-placed people in business and government gave money to his Klan, but secretly, in order to protect their jobs.[4] Wolfgang Droege made a similar boast about "more prominent members of the nation" clandestinely backing the KKK: "Such parties preferred to stay in the background. . . Their motives [for secrecy] were well-founded and proved obvious: they couldn't compromise their positions of standing, but their deepest convictions were that of a Canada overrun with race mixing, mongrels, breakdown of morals."[5]

Needless to say, such Klan claims were difficult to confirm. Martin Weiche, the Nazi who lent his London estate to the Klan for cross burnings, said he was sympathetic to the KKK: "I'm not a member. They're just friends. There's a potential for them. They have a number of young people who all want to go out and have some action." Weiche, who made his money in real estate, admitted he gave cash to the Klan but wouldn't say how much. "Sometimes, when I attend their meetings, I'll put some money in the collection box."[6] When asked by *Star* reporter Louttit how much Weiche contributed to the Klan, McQuirter replied obliquely, "Put it this way, he was a millionaire."

Another wealthy Klan backer was Ian V. Macdonald, a senior civil servant in the construction and consulting services branch of the federal department of Industry, Trade and Commerce. McQuirter, who made frequent trips to Ottawa, boasted of his acquaintance with Macdonald,* who admits his Klan sympathies

---

*Later, in one of McQuirter's trials, an undercover OPP constable testified that the Klan chieftain told him "his friend in Ottawa is high up in the federal government. The friend owns buildings in Ottawa. He has an important government job."

but says he is not a member. "Sympathetic? In a way," Macdonald said in an interview. "I was with the Klan in the sense that they were a minority and they are discriminated against. They are harassed to a certain extent and I think they should be allowed to have freedom of expression." He shares the Klan's views on immigration. "Some people just get off the boat and they are more or less calling the tune in our country for those of us who have been here for generations. If you define racism as having a preference for your own kind, I'm a racist, though I have no antipathy to other races," he said. At one point Klan treasurer Siksna wrote that Macdonald "has given money" to the Klan. But in a later letter — apparently written after consulting with McQuirter — Siksna recanted, insisting that "I have never issued any receipts in his name, nor have I any knowledge of him ever contributing anything to our organization."[7] For his part Macdonald stated he had made "no financial contributions" to the KKK. "I provided only hospitality to McQuirter," he said without elaborating. "Some of his points of view have merit. The Klan tends to clear the air; it puts things right out in public."*

The Canadian Klan apparently also relied heavily on financing from an international web of fascist organizations and movements. "We get money coming in from different parts of the world — England, Germany, France, Spain, Mexico and other parts of South America," claimed Jacob Prins, one of the founding members of the Canadian KKK.[9] Prins, who made several trips abroad, frequently boasted about his connections with the National Front in England and neo-Nazi groups in Germany. His boasts were probably not without foundation. During a murder trial involving members of the pro-Nazi German Action Group in Stuttgart, West Germany, it was reported that "new evidence of the existence of a world-wide neo-Nazi organization has been uncovered," and German Action Group leaders testified they were "in constant touch" with like-minded organizations in

---

*Another name mentioned in connection with the Klan is that of John Stifel, a Toronto real estate agent and avowed right-wing extremist who has run as an independent candidate for parliament. *Star* reporter Louttit wrote that McQuirter confided to him that Stifel had made "small donations" to the Klan; on another occasion McQuirter said he "gave $30".[8] Certainly there is no evidence that Stifel provided the Klan with any substantial backing.

Canada.[10]

Aside from its actual size and its secret financiers, there was another disturbing aspect of the invisible empire: a number of Klan members appeared to be connected with various law enforcement agencies. It was widely suspected by anti-racism activists that the Klan was heavily infiltrated by the police. Certainly, the American experience supported such suspicions. In the mid-sixties, for example, it was estimated that the FBI had informers in the top levels of seven of the fourteen different Klans then in existence; of the estimated 10,000 active Klansmen, 2,000 were reportedly relaying information to the government. The morality, let alone the legality, of the actions of FBI informers within the Klan was highly questionable. A suspect involved in the 1964 Birmingham church bombings that killed four girls was hired two months after the murders as a paid informer. Another Klansman, Gary Thomas Rowe, Jr., the FBI's chief informer inside the Birmingham Klan in the 1960s, was indicted in the 1965 slaying of civil rights worker Viola Liuzzo. Rowe received $22,000 from the FBI for his work as an informer. A suit filed by the Liuzzo family in 1977 charged the U.S. federal government with negligence and wrongdoing in the recruitment, training and supervision of Rowe.* The Greensboro killings of 1979 also revealed a crop of informers: Edward Dawson, a former FBI informer and a local police contact, helped to organize the disruption of the ill-fated anti-Klan march by recruiting Klan participants and riding in the lead attack vehicle; Bernard Butkovich, an agent for the Bureau of Alcohol, Tobacco and Firearms, was identified as one of the members of the Nazis who advised bringing guns to the demonstration. Neither man was charged. In 1981, Bill Wilkinson, the leader of the best-armed and most violent Klan group in the U.S., was revealed by the

---

*When the case was finally heard, in May, 1983, Liuzzo's family argued that Rowe fired the shot which killed her, and that he had warned the FBI of the Klan's plan to attack the demonstration, but that the FBI had done nothing. The defence said Rowe feigned shooting his weapon so as not to arouse suspicion among his fellow Klansmen. The judge ruled that the Liuzzos had failed to prove the FBI was negligent in its direction of its agent Rowe.

Nashville *Tennessean* to be an FBI informer.[11]*

Was the same pattern occuring in Canada? Certainly, authorities here have shown little reluctance to hire and pay informers who commit racial crimes while on the police payroll. The best documented case of this was revealed during the 1977 trial of Western Guard leader Don Andrews. One of the chief witnesses at the trial was Robert Toope, who in May, 1975, had been approached by a Corporal George Duggan of the RCMP to join the Western Guard. Over the next year, Toope went out "a couple of hundred times" on Western Guard raids, which included postering, spray painting swastikas and anti-semitic slogans on homes and buildings, and throwing bricks through the windows of black and Jewish religious establishments and homes. Toope testified that at times he "would go to any extent to help the [Western Guard] Party" in order "to gain their confidence." He eventually became a "group leader" and sat in on their executive meetings. Toope said he usually met with his RCMP supervisor a few times a month: "On every incident that I did go out, on most incidents, I did phone my — the boss that I was working for then, Mr. George Duggan." Toope was paid "between $300 and $500 a month."[13] He was never prosecuted for his participation in the Guard's illegal actions. His RCMP handlers were also let off the hook. The trial judge at the time concluded that the RCMP learned of the illegal acts only after the fact. But four years later the McDonald Royal Commission into RCMP activities, which studied the Toope case, concluded otherwise: "We find it hard to reconcile the findings of the trial judge with the testimony" since the RCMP officer and his superiors were aware that Toope "was being paid by the RCMP at the time he was committing the

*David Duke, Wilkinson's rival and Alexander McQuirter's friend, was possibly also an informer, according to Patsy Sims, whose reasons for suspecting Duke include that fact that he travelled extensively and spent more money than he appeared to have; he slipped past British customs in 1978 after he had been banned from entering the country; he would have been useful to authorities since he met with international and national extremist leaders; and that his father worked for the State Department in Vietnam, Laos and Cambodia. Duke himself claimed to have worked in areas where the CIA was known to be active and where at least a government security clearance was required: "During the later part of the Viet Nam war," one of his newspapers said, "he taught military English to high-ranking, anti-communist Laotian army officers in Vientiane, Laos."[12]

offences" over a fourteen-month period. The commission concluded unequivocably: "Many of the acts of vandalism carried out by the informer were performed with the full knowledge of the handler and his supervisors."[14]

How many Toopes were there in the Klan working for the police? One likely candidate was a KKK official named William Lau Richardson. Police informants usually "are chosen because of an existing personal history which allows them to approach a target without arousing suspicion," according to the McDonald inquiry. "For example, the source might 'espouse' a philosophy similar to that of the target." Toope became known to the RCMP because of his anti-union and anti-communist work during a stormy strike at Artistic Woodworkers. Richardson came with similar credentials. In the latter half of the 1970s, he worked for Centurion Investigations Ltd. under Daniel McGarry, a former Toronto policeman. Centurion specialized in union-busting. In 1976, one of Richardson's assignments was to work in a clothing company's warehouse to help set up the firing of two union organizers. Three years later, Richardson built a bomb which was planted in the car of union activists at McDonnell Douglas of Canada Ltd. He was put on probation after pleading guilty to public mischief. Testimony at trials focusing on Centurion's activities revealed that Richardson had previously worked for the Central Intelligence Agency and U.S. Army Intelligence before coming to Canada in 1970. Richardson was quoted as saying he had a "professional relationship" with the RCMP. *Star* reporter Louttit said Richardson's experiences included spying on left-wing groups, Chilean exiles and American draft dodgers.[15]

Once he joined the Canadian Klan, it did not take long for Richardson to rise quickly. A tall man in his forties, usually sporting dark sunglasses, a brown leather jacket, jeans and black boots, Richardson exuded the kind of confidence and toughness that must have appealed to the Klansmen. He was named to head the Klan Intelligence Agency* (KIA), which was supposed to spy

*In later court testimony by an undercover policeman (see page 179), McQuirter was quoted as saying that a good friend of his, obviously Richardson, "had worked as a civilian employee of the Central Intelligence Agency...then resigned from the CIA and tried to join the Canadian Klan, but because the Klan didn't trust him at the time, he was given the

on left-wing and anti-racist groups for the Klan (and, through Richardson, perhaps for the police as well?). The KIA's effectiveness — in fact its very existence apart from Richardson himself — was difficult to gauge, shrouded as the KIA was in secrecy. Klan leader McQuirter did have high praise for "my Intelligence Advisor, Lau Richardson, and his very useful Intelligence Network." Asked once how he rated the Klan's counter-intelligence unit, McQuirter said "it was the best individual segment of the Canadian KKK." (Added Richardson modestly: "Praise is always nice; McQuirter is a truthful individual.") B.C. Klan chief Al Hooper, who told reporters that the RCMP had approached his members to become paid informers, claimed the KIA had "infiltrated several left-wing organizations in Canada." Richardson did succeed briefly in joining the Riverdale Action Committee Against Racism. Offering to help with the security for a major anti-Klan rally set for the spring of 1981, he even managed to secure a partial list of RACAR members and supporters before he was shut out of the group when his background was discovered.[17]

Was Richardson still on the RCMP payroll, sent in to join the Klan with the promise of immunity from prosecution, much like Robert Toope's infiltration of the Western Guard? Or did Richardson sign up with the Klan on his own initiative, hoping to later offer his information to his police contacts? The answers will probably never be known for certain. Richardson himself, naturally, declines to confirm or deny his association with the police. "Why should I? Print what you want," he said from his Toronto home. Klan boss McQuirter was less tight-lipped about his intelligence advisor's role. "Lau was up front that he had been reporting to the RCMP in the past," McQuirter said, adding he was not concerned if Richardson continued his work for the police. "There is nothing that he knows that I would be worried about his passing on." The RCMP officer who supervised Richardson's work (his "handler" as the position is known in the trade) told one Toronto journalist that Richardson had been put in a "cool-off" period after the bad publicity around the Centurion

---

opportunity to prove himself by establishing for the Klan a counter-intelligence unit."[16]

trials. Still, old informers never die, they just hang around until they are needed again. There were indications that Richardson had been reactivated — either by his police supervisors or on his own initiative — in the hope that his data on the Klan would be marketable to the RCMP or other police forces. In the spring of 1981, for example, Richardson was told that the Klan was expanding in the west, about the same time that police officials independently obtained a list of Klan leaders in B.C.; doubtless, a more on-the-spot investigation of the B.C. scene would have been helpful. By coincidence, Richardson managed to convince Klan leaders to send him off to Vancouver at the end of the summer to check on KIA work there. The partial RACAR membership list which Richardson had obtained would also have been of interest to the RCMP, traditionally much more curious about left-wing organizations than about the extreme right.

Police officials, needless to say, refuse to divulge the names of their informers inside the Klan, though they indirectly conceded they have them. "We know what McQuirter is going to do before he does," boasted one Ontario Provincial Police official who watched the Klan. The inch-thick file he had on the KKK included many color photographs of Klan members taken at their meetings. The RCMP admitted to the McDonald Commission that the use of informers was "the bread and butter" of its security service. For the authorities, the employment of informers within groups like the KKK was justified by the fact that it allowed them to keep tabs on the organization and to catch criminal elements it attracted.

Such reasoning might have been acceptable had the police forces' inside information on the Klan led to prosecutions, but the law enforcement bodies proved to be extremely slow in moving against the Klan in any way. More importantly, the use of police informers within the Klan posed serious legal and ethical questions. "A paid informant may think he has a license to commit any offense in order to gain the desired result," warned the McDonald Commission. "The nature of his task and the environment in which he must work often create considerable pressure on him to commit unlawful acts."[18] The nagging questions remained: how many Klansmen were getting paid by the police while they were carrying out various activities of racial harassment and violence?

The Ku Klux Klan was as secretive about its internal structures as it was about its membership and financing. Nevertheless, from public and private Klan documents, a picture could be painted of a highly-centralized organization. "Our Movement," said the Klan's internal *Handbook*, "must be strong, viable and capable of instant mobilization." As national director, or Grand Wizard, Alexander McQuirter ran a tight ship. He generally worked out of the Klan's national headquarters in Toronto, but frequently made trips to the Maritimes, southern Ontario, the prairies and especially British Columbia to promote the organization's media image and keep the troops in line. McQuirter's right-hand man was Wolfgang Droege, chief Klan organizer. Droege, who had helped to build the Klan on the west coast and in Ontario, was probably the only person in the Canadian Klan whom McQuirter respected as his equal. Certainly he was the only other person who, as a Klan national organizer, made as many official statements to the press as McQuirter did. Directly beneath McQuirter was Gary MacFarlane, a former U.S. Marine and security guard who headed the Klan's White Security Force. The security force included the Klan Intelligence Agency led by William Lau Richardson.

Below this national level were the Klan structures in individual provinces, called "realms". Provincial leaders were called Grand Dragons. Jacob Prins held that post in Ontario for several years. In the Maritimes, a man named Tom Zink was named in a Klan newsletter as a regional director. In B.C., the Klan chief initially was Dave Cook, a fisherman from Vancouver, until he was kicked out of the KKK for publicly criticizing Klan policy.* He was replaced by Al Hooper, a burly former truck driver and construction worker who ran the Klan's activities in the Vancouver area, along with Klan media spokesperson Ann Farmer and another Klan official named Dan Wray. ("I've always been right-wing politically," explained Hooper, "and so when the Klan emerged here I jumped on the bandwagon." Hooper made his

*See page 141.

living running Patriot Press, a distribution outlet for Klan and Nazi T-shirts, badges and related paraphernalia.)

Ordinary Klan members were part of small groups or cells called dens, containing six to 30 members each. In a region where there were several dens, a local chapter was formed, led by a Giant. The Giant for northwestern Metro Toronto, for example, was John Gilroy, a truck driver in his thirties. Each den was supposed to be led by a Den Commander. In Rexdale, Ontario, for instance, a young Klansman named Kenneth Whalen had that responsibility. Each den, according to the *Handbook*, was to hold three official functions per month. A regular business meeting was supposed to be scheduled in the first week of every month; there was supposed to be "at least one Klan social activity" such as a party or picnic per month, and every den was "required to conduct some sort of activity each month that will spread the Klan message and build membership" such as distributing literature, holding a demonstration or calling a public meeting. The Klan also claimed to operate a Youth Corps "composed of boys and girls aged 14 through 17 who believe in the principles of the Ku Klux Klan."

What was particularly worrisome about the Klan's structure was its paramilitary overtones. The Klan, after all, had a mission to accomplish, a war to win. "We see this as a race war, a struggle between whites and non-whites," McQuirter allowed in one of his less guarded moments during a cross burning in B.C. The "elite troops" of the Klan, as the *Handbook* described them, were selected for the White Security Force. "Preference will be given to those having military or police background." The force ostensibly was divided into three sections: a Defensive Security Branch trained in defence, crowd and riot control, the handling of attack dogs and military conduct; Richardson's KIA, specializing in the infiltration and disruption of opposition groups; and the Klokan, or secret police. It is doubtful that the White Security Force actually operated effectively; the *Handbook*'s description of it appears for the most part to be Klan bravado and fiction.

It was undeniable, however, that Klan officials took the question of violence seriously. MacFarlane, head of the security force, was reported by the Toronto *Star* to wear a pistol and carry a blackjack in his hip pocket. "You never argue with a man with a gun," he was quoted as saying. MacFarlane should know: he shot and killed a man in an argument; in April, 1973, he was found not guilty by reason of insanity. He was committed to the maximum security mental health centre in Penentanguishene, where he stayed until June, 1979.[19] Jacob Prins, the Ontario Klan leader and former professional wrestler, said the .22 calibre magnum handgun was his favorite gun because "it packs a good wallop." To ensure other Klan members developed an appreciation for guns and military training, the Klan organized "survival" camps which included arms instruction. McQuirter claimed there were four such camps in southern Ontario, but there is no direct evidence of their existence. In B.C., on the other hand, Klan leader Cook announced the KKK was preparing for "unavoidable race war" by arming its members with rifles, handguns, and survival equipment. "We recommend that our members buy guns and learn how to use them," he said.[20] Klan member Dave Harris, who claimed five years experience in the army, conducted arms training for his fellow Klansmen. Al Hooper admitted he and other KKK members took a "lot of weapons training," usually in the form of exercises lasting one or two days or, occasionally, longer. "A lot of people use their own hunting rifles, semi-automatic assault rifles, M14s, AR15s," he said. A reporter for the New Westminster *Columbian*, Terry Glavin, was able to confirm that at least one day-long training course was given to 30 to 40 people by an arms expert who charged $100 an hour. "They're arming themselves and they're quite serious," he reported.

The "invisible empire" of the Ku Klux Klan in Canada was deadly serious about its race war. With a small but devoted band of members, access to outside funds and a paramilitary structure, it was prepared. Warned Charan Gill of the B.C. Organization to Fight Racism: "I think it's only a matter of time before someone gets killed."

"Less than 47 per cent of the people in Canada today are of British descent... Then do you wonder why the Klan has been called into being?" Klan leader J.H. Hawkins asked a crowd in Moose Jaw, Saskatchewan, in 1928.

Saskatchewan Archives

The Western Guard's headquarters were in this house in Toronto. Martin Weiche is at the far left in this 1973 photo; the man talking to him is Don Andrews.

Toronto's Riverdale and Parkdale neighborhoods rid themselves of the Klan by organizing. Above, the RACAR demonstration. Below, the PACAR demonstration. Left, the defiant Klan — Armand Siksna is at the far right — watch the PACAR demonstration. But they soon left Parkdale.

Elinor Mahoney

Elinor Mahoney

In the summer of 1982 McQuirter suddenly "retired" and was succeeded as Klan leader by Ann Farmer. At a September, 1982 Klan leadership training seminar she posed for this snapshot with James Venable, 76, honorary Imperial Emperor of the Confederation of the Klans, and Don Black, who succeeded David Duke as head of the largest U.S. Klan. At the time Black was free while appealing his Dominica conviction.

BCOFR leader Charan Gill at an October, 1981 anti-Klan rally in Vancouver. The BCOFR favors banning the Klan.

Canada Wide / Mike Peake

Todd Harris

Alexander McQuirter used his good looks and charm to seduce the media. In March, 1980, he was "Jim", the Toronto *Sun*'s Sunshine Boy. "He'd like to find himself a seat on Parliament Hill one day," said the caption. He's currently serving a ten-year prison sentence.

William Lau Richardson, head of the "Klan Intelligence Agency" during McQuirter's reign, was a former CIA agent and boasted of his "professional relationship" with the RCMP.

Toronto *Star*

Armand Siksna and Wolfgang Droege in the Klan's Toronto office, June, 1980. Upon his release from jail in May, 1983, Droege moved to B.C. to rebuild the Klan there.

Pacific Tribune

With McQuirter's imprisonment the B.C. Klan became the country's most active. Al Hooper is second from left in this photo taken at a May, 1983 KKK picket at the Communist Party of Canada's Vancouver bookstore.

"We made the community aware. The Klan is here, we said. We don't want them. And we're prepared to work against them."

— Dierdre Power, Riverdale
Action Committee Against Racism

10. Standing up to the Klan

IT WAS TWENTY TO FOUR IN THE MORNING on January 3, 1981. Balwinder Singh Sidhu, 20, was awake in her home in the Vancouver suburb of Delta while the other seven members of her family slept.

Suddenly a lighted five-gallon can of gasoline crashed through the living room window. Balwinder quickly threw the burning cannister back outside and hastily awoke the other members of her family while the flames spread. Because Balwinder happened to be awake nobody was hurt, but the main floor of Sidhu's home was gutted.

Delta police declined to regard the incident as a racial attack. Delta police chief Doug MacLeod stated that racism was not a problem in the area and that there was "no pattern of violence" against minorities. The Sidhu family was not so sure. "People are saying that there is no racism here, but they have been doing things to us ever since we moved here seven years ago," Balwinder said. "We have had to put in plexiglass windows because the glass was broken so many times." Stones and eggs had been thrown at the house and the family endured verbal threats. Several neighbors, including a former tenant of the Sidhus, reported being approached by local Klansmen to join the KKK.

To protest the firebombings and what they saw as police foot-dragging, the two-month-old B.C. Organization to Fight Racism organized a demonstration which saw 500 people march from the charred home of the Sidhus to the Delta police station. The action had some effect: the local city council offered a $1,000 reward for information leading to the arrest of the attackers, and the provincial attorney general launched a special investigation of the incident.

Later that month, the BCOFR held its first public meeting, attracting more than 400 people. Held in the Vancouver suburb of Surrey, where the KKK was active, the meeting was billed as a "Take a Stand, Ban the Klan" rally. It was jointly sponsored by the B.C. Teachers Federation, the International Woodworkers of America and the Union of B.C. Indian Chiefs. "By educating people and warning them against the Klan, by mobilizing to demand a ban on the Klan, we'll build a strong force not just against the Klan, but against all forms of racism," Charan Gill told the gathering.

The racial attacks — and the BCOFR's counter-offensive — continued unabated for the next few months. On February 11, in Ladner, four Molotov cocktails were thrown at the home of Kuldip Gill, a sawmill worker. No one was hurt. But the Gill family began sleeping in shifts out of fear for their lives. Around the same time, a young East Indian sitting in his car with a friend outside a Vancouver high school was attacked by a gang of youths who smashed the car's windows with an iron bar and baseball bats. These and many other racial incidents could not all be traced directly to the Klan, but as a Vancouver *Sun* report on racism said in March: "It is noteworthy that racist incidents have taken place in the areas where the Klan has been active."[1]

Against this backdrop of escalating racial violence, the BCOFR was uniting a wide array of ethnic, political and religious forces. "One of the major successes we've had is in uniting the various communities and groups together," leader Charan Gill noted. "We have a united front against the Ku Klux Klan." Most of the BCOFR's members and militants came, like Gill himself, from B.C.'s large East Indian community. The BCOFR was the only political organization in the Vancouver area granted permission to use the Sikh temples as platforms to speak to and organize East Indians. The BCOFR also succeeded in garnering support from other nationalities. Its actions were endorsed by the Union of B.C. Indian Chiefs and the Tribal Council of British Columbia. (For a while, an administrator with the Council was the BCOFR's treasurer.) The Chinese Benevolent Association also lent its support. An umbrella organization of churches in the Vancouver area, too, backed the BCOFR. A variety of trade unions — even rival groups such as the Confederation of Canadian Unions and the B.C. Federation of Labour—came out together behind the BCOFR. The Canadian Association of Industrial, Mechanical and Allied Workers agreed to circulate BCOFR literature among its members. The B.C. Telecommunications Workers Union endorsed the BCOFR and invited a representative to speak at its annual convention. The B.C. Teachers Federation, the Vancouver and District Labour Council and the Provincial New Democratic Party added their voices to the chorus of support. The BCOFR also worked with the Committee for Racial Justice, a Vancouver-based coalition of 25 organizations.[2]

Angered by government inaction toward the Klan, the BCOFR launched a province-wide petition demanding the Klan be banned. The petition found its way into various ethnic and national communities and was circulated within trade union and student circles. In a few months, 16,000 people signed it. Despite a torrential downpour, 750 marchers took part in a "Ban the Klan" march on April 4, the largest anti-racism demonstration Vancouver had seen for years. In Chinatown, the demonstrators met up with a contingent from the Chinese Benevolent Association. Together, the crowd marched to the B.C. government offices in downtown Vancouver to hand over the petition. B.C. attorney general Allan Williams had been invited to accept the petitions. He declined.

In the winter and spring of 1981 the Klan and its opponents were also busy in Toronto. In February, a couple of teenage Klan members pleaded guilty to public mischief arising out of the destruction of several Liberal Party campaign posters in a recent provincial election. Seventeen-year-old Derek Edward Saunders was fined $100 and put on 18 months probation and his 18-year-old companion, Christopher Somerville, received a suspended sentence with the same probation period. That same month, five members of the Toronto Klan were charged with public mischief. Using spray bombs and plywood stencils, they had painted "KKK" and the Klan's phone number on construction hoardings in downtown Toronto. They also had a stencil which read "White Victory" but apparently did not get a chance to use it before police nabbed them. The five arrested included Derek Saunders again, Steven Allan Bolt, 17; Keith Cabot, 28; Brad Love, 22; and an American neo-Nazi from Chicago named Larry Raeder. (The Klan newsletter was proud of its members' exploits: "The telephone numbers that were painted and the ensuing publicity from the arrests resulted in more than 250 inquiries at Klan headquarters from interested citizens. Our telephone number was shown on at least two television channels.")

The Toronto Klan was also engaged in more serious ventures: they were stepping up their recruitment of students, this time from *inside* the schools, instead of just passing out their calling cards at the gates. Sometimes, Klan youth members distributed hate literature to their fellow students. In February, two students at Norman Bethune Collegiate Institute in the Toronto suburb of Scarborough distributed application forms and material calling on whites to band together in their own organization to defend themselves. The two became aggressive and violent when school officials confiscated the Klan material. One was suspended; the other left school for good. The other method which the Klan used to reach teenagers inside their schools was to get its representatives invited to speak in the classrooms. This was, after all, how McQuirter first made headlines for the Klan back in 1978. As a guest lecturer, a Klan spokesman had a captive audience and the added advantage of the credibility accorded a special speaker by young students. In March, 1981, two members of the Klan, including McQuirter, addressed a class at Don Mills Collegiate outside Toronto for 40 minutes. They were given permission by the teacher, who was approached a few minutes before the class by a student who requested that the Klansmen be allowed to make an appearance. In its news bulletin, *KKK Canada Action Report*, the Klan boasted that McQuirter "was well received by the student body and given much applause." The Klansmen talked of Toronto as a city that had become a "racial time bomb" because it was "overrun with racial minorities." "There are only a few years before a racial war in Toronto and the time to prepare is now," they told the 22 youngsters in the class, including several non-whites. The KKK members handed out their calling cards to interested students and told them where to pick up additional white supremacist literature. Said one student after the visit: "They sounded like they were trying to recruit a few people."[3]

The Klan's renewed penetration into Toronto area schools prompted a swifter response this time than it had the previous fall. The acting director of education of the Toronto school board sent a letter to all school principals reiterating the board's condemnation of the Klan. The race relations department of the board produced an educational pamphlet on the Klan which, after detailing its history of violence and hatred, concluded with these words: "The only way to beat the KKK's threat to our society is to state, loud and clear, your refusal of racism in all its forms. The schools are at the forefront of society, and we can't afford to sit by idly at this crucial time." The Klan was coming under fire elsewhere as well. In February, the Committee for Racial Equality held a press conference to announce it was presenting an anti-Klan petition, signed by 8,000, to attorney general Roy McMurtry. The petition, which was circulated in English, Chinese and Italian versions, condemned the Klan as a "racist, anti-semitic, fascist organization" and blamed the provincial government for allowing the Klan to "spread its racist influence."

In Riverdale, the battle to drive out the Klan was gaining momentum. The Riverdale Action Committee Against Racism set up groups to produce a regular newsletter, to do research on the Klan, to counter the KKK's youth organizing and to begin circulating an anti-Klan petition. The newsletter reported Klan actions and what was being done to stop them. It talked of "documented instances of harassment, vandalism, death threats, racist sign paintings and attempts to recruit kids into paramilitary training groups." It also criticized "government inaction and the media's game of sensationalism" concerning the KKK. The newsletter kept Riverdale residents informed of other forms of racism, such as disparaging comments made in a police association magazine about blacks, South Asians and Jews, and the harassment by police of a popular black musical group. RACAR also wanted to reach Riverdale's youth, since the Klan was known to have canvassed local schools and playgrounds. "We started handing out brochures and meeting the kids on their own territory — near the schools, on street corners — to counter the Klan," said RACAR's Dierdre Power. When the Ku Klux Klan was able to get its message into some of the schools, some of the teachers invited RACAR people to talk to the students. Much of RACAR's efforts went into an intense petition drive to sensitize people in the neighborhood to the dangers of the Klan. The drive was concentrated on streets near the Klan headquarters. "It was a great chance to talk to people and we always left our material — in English, Greek, Punjabi and some Spanish and Portuguese," said Power. "We got a very favorable reaction. And the reaction was just as good among whites as among immigrants." Throughout the winter until May, more than 3,000 Riverdale residents signed the anti-Klan petition.

RACAR's efforts reached a peak on May 31 when 1,000 people took part in what was by far the largest anti-Klan rally Canada had ever seen. It was sunny for the Riverdale Community Festival Against the Klan, as the all-day affair was called. The event was endorsed by 60 trade unions, community groups and organizations such as the Native-American Prisoners' Rights Committee and the Chinese-Canadian National Council for Equality. People gathered at Greenwood Park for opening speeches. "In reality, no one is safe from the Klan's attack," Power told the rally, noting that the Klan's targets included Jews, Catholics, blacks, Chinese, trade unionists, social reformers, homosexuals and women fighting for their rights. The crowd then marched through the streets. Hundreds of people gathered on the corners and in the doorways as the procession made its way through the community and past the Ku Klux Klan's headquarters. "When we marched right past the Klan office, going through that stretch I felt like we were liberating Paris," Power said. "The people who lived around the Klan office or on the opposite side of the street were out on their porches, cheering us on." Half a dozen Klansmen stood in their robes outside their office, bravely giving the fascist salute for the television cameras. But the demonstrators filed past the Klan headquarters without incident and returned to the park for an afternoon of picnicking and music. The Gayap Rhythm Drummers, West Indian and African musicians, performed several anti-racist songs. Backed by pulsating drums, they chanted:

> Racism is not a sickness
> it's an ideology
> that starts at the top
> and moves to the bottom of
> society
> a tactic
> to divide the black and white worker
> a tactic
> to get us fighting each other
> and distract us from the real problems
> it's easy to see
> who are the culprits
> it's not just the Klan
> racism is a ploy
> racism is a crime
> racism is a capitalistic lie

Less than a month after this show of force, McQuirter and his followers moved out of Riverdale. RACAR had accomplished its goal. The Klan claimed it was planning to move anyway and that it had not been intimidated by the opposition to its activities in the neighborhood. But a better indication of the Klansmen's real appreciation of their opponents came from the harassment they used in their vain effort to stop RACAR. "I would walk into my house and suddenly the phone would ring, just like that; it was constantly happening," said Power. One RACAR militant received death threats over the phone; a menacing and obscene call was also received during a RACAR meeting at a local church. But RACAR activists held firm until they succeeded in driving the Klan from their community. Concluded Power: "We made the community aware. The Klan is here, we said. We don't want them. And we're prepared to work against them. There were challenges to the state and its structures — to McMurtry, who said only he was keeping an eye on the Klan, to the police, who said they were keeping the KKK under surveillance, and to the media, which was used by the Klan."

British Columbia and Ontario were not the only places where the Klan was running into opposition. In Nova Scotia, members of the large black community, some Jewish residents and other citizens banded together when the Klan announced its plans to set up a Maritimes office in early 1981. In March, the Nova Scotia Coalition Against the KKK called a meeting; the 80 people who attended decided to campaign for a ban on the Klan while conducting education on the dangers of racism. A month later, 250 people came out to the coalition's first public rally in Halifax. Black actor Walter Borden attacked "the assholes in government who refuse to lift a finger against the Klan." Messages of support were read from the Chinese Cultural Centre, the East Indian community, the African Students Association, the Workers Communist Party and the Cape Breton Labour Council.

As if mounting opposition to its activities across the country was not enough, in the spring of 1981 the Canadian Klan was struck by another blow from which it never fully recovered: on April 27, ten mercenaries, including Droege and another Canadian Klansman, were arrested in New Orleans during a bizarre bid to invade the small Caribbean island nation of Dominica. The incident gave the Klan a less welcome brand of widespread publicity. McQuirter initially denied any official Klan involvement, but details of McQuirter's key role in the plot quickly leaked out.* Another Klan member from Toronto was jailed in Dominica for her role in the planned invasion; eleven months later, the Klan leader himself was arrested on conspiracy charges connected with the coup.

The Dominica fiasco had several effects on the Canadian Klan, not the least of which was a lot of bad publicity for an organization that tried to cultivate a "new" non-violent image. It

*See chapter 13.

also put Droege, the national organizer and probably the hardest working Klan official, behind American bars and out of the picture for a while. Klan activities in Toronto took a nosedive as McQuirter apparently sought to stay out of the limelight in the hope that the Dominica storm would blow over. Indeed, a paralysis seemed to have gripped the Toronto Klan: little was heard from them after the coup attempt was revealed.

Adding to the confusion within the ranks of the Toronto KKK was the strange death of Kenneth David Whalen, 25, the Rexdale Den Commander, and his lover, Carole Miller, 36, in a house fire. The blaze broke out in the early hours of May 24 in Miller's home in Etobicoke. Whalen and Miller were trapped in an upstairs bedroom. Both had been drinking heavily. Although a coroner's jury ruled "the cause of the fire was undetermined, but the results are consistent with the effects of a cigarette smouldering among household objects,"⁴ there were many unanswered questions. During the inquest, arson investigators testified they had suspected foul play because of the fire's intensity and the irregular burn area in the living room and hallway. No traces of gasoline or flammable liquid were found, but one fire investigator insisted the fire was "unusual to say the least."

Internal Klan intrigue surrounded the incident. Carole Miller was at the time of her death apparently trying to wrest her son Stephen away from the Klan. "She wanted nothing to do with them [the Klan] or have her son doing anything with them," said a neighbor. Stephen, 17 at the time, was the second-in-command in the Rexdale den. The basement of the Miller home had been used for Klan meetings; after the fire, it was found to be strewn with Klan paraphernalia, and Klan slogans were written on the walls. Stephen told the press that his mother had kicked him out of her home because of his association with the Klan. He also said Whalen was a frequent visitor and often spent the night. According to press reports, Whalen was at the Miller home the night of the fire because he had received threats that his own house would be burned. To complicate matters, Whalen had been suspended for two weeks by the Klan shortly before he died (McQuirter insisted the Klan wanted him back because he was a good organizer).

Some Klan members accused "fanatical" opponents to the Klan of murdering Whalen and Miller, but there is no evidence this is so. On the other hand, some anti-Klan activists believe the fatal fire may have been the settling of accounts within the Klan. Whatever the case, the unsavory incident sapped the already ailing morale of Klan forces in Toronto.

Not much was heard from the Klan in most other parts of the country, although during the week of July 12, KKK symbols were painted on the road to Preston, Nova Scotia, a local junior high school and the Colored Children's Home in Cherrybrook, N.S. But in British Columbia, the Klan appeared to be in better shape. Summer, 1981, saw no noticeable decline in Klan activities there. Indeed, the continued activity of the Vancouver-area Klansmen contrasting with the stagnation of their Toronto counterparts would cause tension between the west coast Klan and the national headquarters in Toronto.

The fallout from the Dominica scandal did claim its west coast victims. David Cook, the B.C. Klan leader, publicly called the plot "a dumb stunt" and said it meant "the Klan is dead." He was promptly booted out of the organization and McQuirter flew to Vancouver to clean up shop. Except for this minor setback, though, the Klan in B.C. maintained a relatively high profile. "Cross-burning B.C. Klan holds rally behind armed guards," read the headline in the Vancouver *Sun* when the first public cross lighting in the province took place in late May. Forty Klansmen burned an eight-metre cross at Stave Lake near Mission. At least two of the KKK members carried rifles and shots were fired into the air. "Let us offer a prayer of thanks to God for creating us in his image, for giving us white skin and superior intellect," said KKK leader Ann Farmer as she opened the ceremony with a prayer. The Klan crowd gave Nazi-style salutes and chanted "white power!"[5] Three months later, the same scene was repeated at the side of the Fraser River in Surrey, as 45 Klansmen — several of them carrying weapons — held a cross burning. The proceedings were seen on television, thanks to a BCTV film crew which had been invited to the event.

The Klan did not limit itself to cross burnings; it also tried to intimidate its opponents. BCOFR president Gill received threatening phone calls. "They have called my wife when I am not at home and told her I would be dead," he reported. "She got quite scared about it. 'We'll get you,' they have told me."

Sometimes the KKK went further. On May 28, 1981, the offices of Rape Relief House in Vancouver were ransacked, the files destroyed and papers scattered everywhere. The same day, Rape Relief received some Klan hate literature in the mail. A spokesperson for the group said the timing was no coincidence; Rape Relief had been supportive of the BCOFR and had a contingent in a recent anti-KKK demonstration. "We envision a society which is safe for women, people of all color and workers to walk the streets and live in peace," said a member of the group. "The KKK represents the extreme of people who disagree with this vision."

The Norman Bethune Bookstore in Vancouver, run by the Workers Communist Party, also received Klan hate literature. A copy of a special anti-Klan supplement of the WCP's newspaper was scrawled with threats of violence and sent to the bookstore. The Klan warned the bookstore to stop distributing anti-Klan literature.

The summer of 1981 also saw a rash of racial violence in B.C. which, if not committed by the Klan, was probably inspired by its propaganda and presence. In May, four white men set fire to an unoccupied home and two cars belonging to an East Indian farmer in the Fraser Valley community of Matsqui. In August, in the Vancouver suburb of Richmond, three Fijian Indians were chased by whites armed with baseball bats who smashed the Fijians' car and dragged them out, beating them severely and leaving them with serious internal and external injuries. At least they survived. That same month, an East Indian restaurant worker in Vancouver was not so lucky. Khuspal Singh Gill, 21, finished his late night shift and started to walk home, but he never made it. Witnesses said Gill was attacked by three whites who beat and kicked him mercilessly. He died from his injuries. A few weeks later, on September 9, as Ajit Singh Phunal was waiting for a bus a pellet gun was fired from a passing car and a three-inch needle pierced his stomach. The needle carried a label with the message: "With the compliments of the KKK." The needle missed his heart by two inches.

To counter the Klan and the increasing incidence of racial attacks, the BCOFR and others kept up their campaigns. By now, the BCOFR had 850 members in all parts of B.C. In May, about 400 people came out to a meeting in Clearbrook, co-sponsored by the Mennonite Church and the BCOFR, to protest the Matsqui firebombing. The BCOFR combined educational and political activities with legal work and on-the-street organizing and demonstrating. It set up a research and publications committee to prepare and distribute educational material. A speakers bureau was charged with informing the public about the problems of racism and the need to fight the Klan. An investigations and support committee pursued known cases of racial attacks, pressured the law enforcement agencies to do their job, and provided moral, material and legal support to the victims of racial incidents.

Perhaps the most innovative BCOFR program was its Neighborhood Support Units, designed to organize people in their own communities to protect themselves from racist violence. Three such units began operating, in Surrey, Burnaby and Vancouver. "We go block by block in certain areas, talking to people," Gill explained. "It's hard work but that's the only way we feel we can do the job — by going to the community at the grass roots level and organizing. These units give confidence to the people. We make up a standard letter that we distribute when something happens, like some windows get smashed. We explain that we are people from the community and we need everybody's support. We unite all the people in the area — black, brown, white."

As the summer gave way to fall, the Klan's problems continued to mount. Back in Toronto, finding a new home proved difficult. When it left the Riverdale community, the Klan moved its headquarters to 15 Springhurst Avenue in Toronto's west end, a house owned by Jean MacGarry, the wife of Klan security chief Gary MacFarlane. McQuirter denied that the house, on a quiet tree-lined street in the Parkdale community, was the KKK's new headquarters, but the home did house the public Klan phone number and McQuirter himself started living there.

Parkdale was in many ways similar to Riverdale. It had a mainly working class population derived from more than 25 different nationalities and ethnic groups. It did not take long for the Klan to find it was no more welcome there than in Riverdale. In mid-August, a demonstration was organized at the initiative of local New Democratic Party and community activists. A noisy crowd of 350 marched past the Klan home carrying signs which read "No Nazis, kick the Klan out." The protest laid the basis for the creation shortly thereafter of the Parkdale Action Committee Against Racism, a community coalition modeled after RACAR. "We wanted to make it quite clear that RACAR's work was not isolated, that opposition was going to follow the Klan wherever they went and that communities were not going to tolerate the KKK," said John Meyers, one of PACAR's founders. PACAR brought together Filipino, Caribbean, Chinese, Japanese, Latin American and other members of the community. Committees were set up to encourage the participation of a wide number of nationalities. A public education group helped produce a leaflet on the danger of the Klan. A petition campaign against the KKK and racism in general was undertaken in the neighborhood around the Klan headquarters; over the next few months, 4,000 names were collected. PACAR also organized a letter-writing campaign criticizing Bell Canada for its policy of allowing the Klan a phone listing; Bell received more than 500 protest letters. Protests were also delivered to the Canadian Radio-television and Telecommunications Commission, which regulates Bell, but both the company and the CRTC said the Klan's use of the phones was a question for the courts and not themselves to settle. PACAR also distributed educational material produced by the Ontario Federation of Labour for its own anti-racism campaign. To end 1981, PACAR held a fund-raising Rock Against Racism dance attended by 500 people.

PACAR was so effective that the Klan never achieved the level of activity in Parkdale it had in Riverdale. Not a single Parkdale school was visited by the KKK; not a single street was hit by Klan literature distribution. "The cumulative effect of work by the

OFL, church groups, PACAR and others means the Klan just can't get a foothold because the community is healthy," noted Meyers.

Indeed, as 1981 ended, the Klan was finding it harder and harder to establish a foothold anywhere in Canada. A story out of the Yukon in late November reflected how bad a year it had been. James Mcdonald, a 490-pound Whitehorse resident, did not take kindly to the news that two local teenagers, Terry Smith and Kerry Anderson, were trying to recruit members for the KKK, and an ad Mcdonald placed in a local newspaper asking for support for anti-Klan activities elicited calls from more than 200 people. But to make sure the Klan got the message, the 490-pound Klanbuster used his own intimidation tactics. "I went over to Anderson's home with my gun in my belt and told them how people felt about their group," he said. "I think they were scared, because they signed a statement saying they'd shut down."[6] Some Whitehorse citizens formed a group to take on the Klan. "We'll beat them up if they bother anyone," said one organizer. Mcdonald also circulated a petition calling on the Yukon territorial council to outlaw racism. "We're sending a petition to the legislature to have any racist groups banned," said Mcdonald.

It was ironic. The Ku Klux Klan's avowed goal was the separation of the races and the incitement of race hatred, yet its appearance in Canada sparked a vigorous anti-racism movement extending from Whitehorse to Halifax and uniting diverse national, ethnic and political forces. A speaker at an early anti-Klan rally in Toronto summed it up best: "By its own presence the Klan has sown the seed of its own destruction," said Norman Kwon, a Chinese Canadian who had been active in the protests against the CTV's *W5* show alleging abuse of Canadian schools by Chinese. "They think they can divide us, but they have actually brought us together." Indeed, people were drawn to the anti-Klan movement from all walks of life — church people like Rev. John Robson, teachers like Dierdre Power, ethnic leaders and trade unionists like Charan Gill, and hundreds of others. The voices raised against the Klan were those of various nationalities and ethnic groups, trade unions and progressive organizations. In Nova Scotia, the African Baptist Church, representing more than

80 per cent of the province's 20,000 to 30,000 blacks, asked other Baptist churches in the region, black and white, to take "appropriate action against the Klan." The Black United Front in Halifax also called for preventative action against the KKK. Wilson Head, chairman of the National Black Coalition of Canada, criticized the media for the publicity it gave the racist organization. In Montreal, Roy States, president of the local NBCC chapter, delivered a stinging rebuke to the Klan's proposal to deport Canada's blacks to their "home" countries. States, whose family had been in North America since 1778, pointed out that many of the blacks in this country trace their roots here back several centuries, farther than many whites can. Denouncing the Klan as "a cancer that must be removed," States said "there have been lots of movements to try and uproot blacks over time, but blacks have always resisted them, despite discrimination and social repression." In Vancouver, the NBCC tried unsuccessfully to persuade B.C.'s attorney general to prosecute the Klan for inciting race hatred. In Edmonton, NBCC leaders spoke out against local Klan organizing attempts.

East Indians, another frequent target of Klan hate propaganda, were especially active in the anti-Klan movement in Vancouver and Toronto. Organizations such as the Indian Peoples Association of North America and the Canadian Farmworkers Association, which has a high East Indian membership, took part in numerous anti-Klan marches and activities. Chinese Canadians, through such groups as the Chinese Benevolent Association and the Chinese Canadian National Council for Equality, spoke up against the Klan's diatribes against "Orientals." In Vancouver, the CBA passed a resolution calling upon the provincial government "to pass and/or enforce legislation...to ban the Ku Klux Klan, to prohibit its registration under the Societies Act and to prohibit...the distribution of literature inciting race hatred against ethnic groups and minority groups or their removal from Canada." Native people in Regina, Vancouver and other cities added their voices to the anti-Klan chorus. Debbie Mearns, president of the Vancouver Indian Centre, said, "My people face racism all the time at different levels of society, but they are outraged by the blatant nature of the Klan's presence and its overt racism."

Jewish and Catholic groups also stood up to the Klan. The
Canadian Jewish Congress and B'nai Brith joined with the
National Black Coalition of Canada to complain to the CRTC
about media coverage of the Klan. Rabbi Jordon Pearlson,
national chairman of the joint community relations committee of
the CJC and B'nai Brith, said the KKK was "using the media as a
podium." The United Jewish Peoples Order, in a public statement
against the Klan, pointed out that "we cannot afford to be silent
observers . . . We have not forgotten the days when Hitler and his
followers were laughed at, were not taken seriously — until it was
too late." The Roman Catholic Archdiocese of Toronto
condemned the opening of the first KKK office in Toronto as
"totally unwelcome." Said Father Bard H. Massman, director of
the archdiocese communications office, "Racism is an evil that
cannot be tolerated under any circumstances."

The labor movement in Canada made its antipathy toward the
Klan abundantly clear. "The Klan is against everything we stand
for," said Michael Lyons, executive secretary of the Toronto
Labour Council. "The labor movement in Toronto will undertake
any legal means in its power to see that the Klan is frustrated in its
organizing efforts and goals." The labor movement was all too
aware of how the Klan's racism could be used to divide workers in
the employers' interests. In the southern Ontario town of
Walkerton, where Union Carbide Ltd. was planning to build a
plant, the Klan tried to stir up fears that many of the jobs would
go to non-whites. A conscious effort at splitting workers along
racial lines also occurred at a small metal works factory in Toronto
in March, 1981. The Canadian Union of Industrial Employees had
been trying for some time to unionize the workers at Anderson
Metal Industries but was meeting with stiff resistance from the
employer. One day, a copy of the Klan's newsletter *Action Report*
appeared on a company notice board. The pamphlet boasted of
the KKK's success in Vancouver and about the need for whites to
counter groups organized by non-whites. The Klan literature was
left on the board for three weeks; the owner denied knowing who
put it up but said he did not have time to be bothered with taking it
down. "Leaving this racist sheet up three weeks is an anti-union

ploy to scare our non-white members," charged union president Peter Dorfman. "There are nine East Indians at the plant, two Filipinos and a black out of nineteen workers." Domingo Ramos, a 40-year-old Filipino worker, said the KKK hate literature was posted "to intimidate workers. It's an insult to the workers. I couldn't sleep at nights knowing that kind of thing was up on the board. It scared me."[7]

It was to stop this kind of divide-and-rule tactic that organized labor took a stand against the Klan, and many trade unions advocated banning the Klan. "They have already crossed the line of 'free speech'. We believe the KKK must be outlawed and strongly urge...such legislation in Parliament," read one resolution passed by Local 303 of the United Auto Workers. The Ottawa and Toronto Councils of the Canadian Union of Public Employees passed resolutions calling on their union's Ontario division to help mobilize to "ban all Klan activities in this province." The ban-the-Klan demand was also endorsed by labor councils in Vancouver, Regina, Windsor, Sudbury and Cape Breton. Jack Haley, president of the Cape Breton Labour Council, called on the government to take whatever measures were needed to keep the KKK out of his province, noting that the Klan had always shown a keen interest in establishing itself in economically-depressed regions. In October, the Ontario Federation of Labour launched a $100,000 campaign against racism. A three-week blitz, with 400,000 leaflets, 5,000 posters and a television advertisement, emphasized the theme "Racism hurts everyone." OFL leader Cliff Pilkey said the fact that white supremacist groups such as the Klan were "rearing their ugly heads in Ontario" compelled labor "to do something about it." "Racism runs contrary to what we believe in as a movement — unity," he told a press conference. "We do not have a strong labor movement when there are forces at play causing dissent...and racism does just that."

Student organizations, too, called for action against the Klan. "The Klan is a vile, criminal organization and it should be banned," said Doug Fleming, student society officer at Simon Fraser University in Burnaby. The SFU student society, along with the B.C. Students Federation, sent telegrams to the provincial attorney general demanding that the Klan be prosecuted for inciting race hatred. In Ontario, the provincial students federation also came out in favor of banning the Klan.

Progressive and left-wing groups made a contribution to the anti-Klan movement. Women's groups such as Rape Relief in Vancouver and the International Women's Day Committee in Toronto participated in anti-Klan demonstrations. Left-wing publications including *Leftwords* in B.C., *Briarpatch* in Saskatchewan, the Toronto *Clarion* and *The Forge* helped to counterbalance the often uncritical reporting on the Klan in the commercial media with regular exposures of the Klan's violence, history and motives. One of the earliest actions against the newly-emerging Canadian Klan was a picket line organized by the Workers Communist Party against American Klan organizer David Duke during his visit to Vancouver in April, 1980.

The Klan dismissed this vast opposition movement as inconsequential. After one demonstration outside his Toronto headquarters, a scornful Alexander McQuirter told reporters he did not take the protest seriously "because the only people involved in it are gays, Jews, socialists and other white trash."

But, McQuirter's opinion to the contrary, the anti-Klan movement did arouse the public to Klan activities. The constant protests, meetings and petitions had their effect on governments too. After the public uproar in Toronto over Klan recruitment in schools, Liberal MP D.M. Collenette, whose constituency included one of the targeted schools, introduced in the House of Commons a resolution — which passed unanimously — condemning the KKK. It went on to state that parliament

> urges all provincial departments of education and local school boards in Canada to take note of this condemnation, and reiterates its belief that the principle of freedom of speech does not give licence to preach hate against any racial minority group in this country.[8]

It was public pressure and the BCOFR's vociferous ban-the-Klan campaign that obliged the Socred government in British Columbia to take a few reluctant, timid steps. In March, 1981, it commissioned Vancouver lawyer John D. McAlpine to study the Klan in B.C. and the effectiveness of the province's existing human rights code. In July, it introduced a Civil Rights Protection Act in an attempt to appease its critics. "It's not a great act, because it lacks the teeth we would like the law to have," said the BCOFR's Gill. "But it did force the government to recognize that racism as a social evil does exist in B.C."

On a municipal level, the anti-Klan movement was even more effective. Vancouver City Council denied the Klan a business license, effectively preventing the Klan from opening an office in the city. In Toronto, the city council called on the provincial government and local police to "closely monitor the activities of this organization." In Windsor, after intense lobbying by a committee representing 30 groups and individuals, the city council urged the Ontario government to crack down on the KKK. Freedom of speech, the council insisted, should not include "slanderous and vicious attacks on certain groups of people." Chatham city council drafted a resolution seeking an amendment to the Criminal Code making it illegal "to be a member of an organization whose primary purpose is to harass or intimidate any person or groups on the grounds of race." The city of Kitchener also called for government action against the Klan. In Dartmouth, Nova Scotia, the council passed a resolution recommending "that amendments be made to the Criminal Code to provide that a person would be guilty of an offence for being a member of an organization where sole or primary purpose of such an organization was to harass or intimidate any person or groups on the grounds of race." And the Federation of Canadian Municipalities, at its annual conference in Calgary in June, 1981, called on all communities across Canada to condemn racist groups and to prevent them from recruiting supporters or distributing literature in schools.

School boards, too, were obliged to toughen their stands on the Klan. The Vancouver school board forbade the distribution of hate literature on school grounds, and the Toronto and Scarborough school boards urged teachers and staff to keep speakers from racist groups out of the classrooms.

The criticism directed at the media for its gratuitous and uncritical coverage of the Klan, too, had its effect. In May, the Ontario Human Rights Commission cautioned against "unwarranted publicity" for the Klan, as "one of the key strategies of the Klan is to create public awareness of its aims." Gordon Fairweather, the chief commissioner of the Canadian Human Rights Commission, said that Klan appearances on talk shows give the white supremacist group "a platform they're not entitled to... These people are elevated to a status I think is evil. Where else in the world would these people get this extraordinary amount of attention?" Wilson Head, president of the National Black Congress of Canada, said that most radio stations approached by the congress refused to give black spokesmen equal time with Klan members, "using only very lame excuses."[9] When the Vancouver *Sun* ran a front-page story and picture of a cross burning to which it had been invited by the publicity-hungry Klan, it received a flood of protest letters. The newspaper's "irresponsible action" was condemned by a University of B.C. professor who wrote: "By merely sending along a reporter and photographer, the *Sun* both condoned these activities and provided the publicity these people are seeking."

By the latter half of 1981, the uncritical reporting which had benefitted the Klan so much in its first year of expansion became less frequent. In July, the Toronto *Star* ran a two-part series by Neil Louttit, a reporter who had posed as a Klan member for three months. Louttit described the KKK as "little more than the Nazi party in nightriders' robes." Typical of the more critical line now being taken against the Klan was an editorial in the Vancouver *Sun* which criticized provincial politicians for keeping "their heads stuck in the sand like ostriches, hoping that if they ignore the KKK, it will quietly go away."[10] The editorial continued:

> It won't and it's time they woke up and did something about it... These people may be kooks, but they are dangerous kooks... It's time to take the gloves off.

Journalists themselves began to criticize the job their newspapers and radio or TV stations were doing. This concern was reflected at a conference held in January, 1982, in Vancouver, co-sponsored by the Newspaper Guild and the Centre for Investigative Journalism. "The main thing that came out of it was that people felt straight news stories were an inadequate way to cover the Klan," said Jan O'Brien, a reporter with the Vancouver *Province* who helped organize the seminar. "There was pretty much a consensus that to just report the Klan as one side of an argument and to report anti-racist groups or some ethnic groups as the other side was an inadequate way to deal with the situation — yet that really has been the extent of the coverage. It makes the Klan appear more legitimate than they are, treating them the way you would the Lions Club or something. There's a lot more to them than that."

The Klan itself sensed the changing winds. Admitted McQuirter: "Sooner or later, the media catches on and they will not allow you to tape or do radio and TV shows." Hounded in the communities in which it tried to set up shop, confronted by a multinational and diverse anti-racist movement, and increasingly shut out of the media, the Canadian Klan was finding it difficult to keep the flames burning. McQuirter would eventually have to admit that the Klan, at least in Toronto, was forced to keep its head low because of "so much pressure". If the Klan was going to survive, it appeared it would have to develop new tactics and strategies.

"When it comes to a point, drastic measures have to be taken. It's not going to matter if there is another Adolf Hitler figure coming along and people have to wear swastikas if it's going to eliminate their problems."
— Alexander McQuirter

11. Plotting new strategies

ON FEBRUARY 11, 1982, KKK national director Alexander McQuirter — along with Charles Yanover, described in newspapers as a small-time Toronto underworld figure — was arrested for conspiracy to overthrow the government of Dominica. Amost ten months after the abortive coup, it looked as if McQuirter might join his right-hand man, Wolfgang Droege, behind bars. McQuirter was released on bail and the trial date was set for early September. McQuirter's arrest further dampened the already quiescent Toronto Klan, though activities did continue throughout the year: Klan literature was distributed in various neighborhoods in Toronto; McQuirter tried to speak to a group of students at Humber College (but got a cool reception this time).

But in Vancouver, the Klan maintained a stronger presence. Klansmen were bold enough to march through the streets in their robes and distribute literature. They took to visiting restaurants and bars, especially those in the east end close to the docks, and driving out non-whites. Billy Bhopinder, 21, a student, was a victim of one such incident in early 1982. "I was in a pub with a friend and there was this group of people next to us," he said.

"One of them followed me to a washroom and started saying that he was from the KKK. I went back to my table and started drinking my beer, at which point they started to call me all sorts of names like 'You fucking Hindu' and things like that." Three of the heavy-set men, aged between about 20 and 45, were wearing T-shirts bearing the KKK emblem. "They came over and dropped a cigarette package on my table with "KKK" written over it. After that, two of them started walking around my table and shoving me. I decided it would be best to get out of there. As I got up to leave, they started to push me out of the pub. It was quite intimidating. I mean, it was ten of them to two of us. They were trying to get us outside where they could beat us without witnesses." Bhopinder was lucky: "Another patron, a white person, ran across the pub very fast to stop them." He said it was not the first time he was attacked and that the Klan did this kind of thing regularly. "I know that this type of incident often goes unchecked. I've had it happen to me twice before. It is very systematic."

Anti-Klan activity also continued. In March, the B.C. Organization to Fight Racism launched a new "Stop the Klan" campaign. The strategy — in addition to educational and cultural events designed to counter racism — was to limit the Klan's ability to function. The BCOFR hoped to pressure the post office and the B.C. Telephone Company into denying the Klan access to their services. In Toronto, PACAR met with Ontario attorney general McMurtry to urge him to toughen criminal and civil laws and their enforcement against the Klan. In March, the United Nations International Day for the Elimination of Racism was celebrated with a large festival in Toronto. In June, the Filipino community made anti-racism the theme of its National Day celebrations and 5,000 attended a picnic at which PACAR and similar groups publicized their activities. Anti-Klan sentiment was making itself felt in the higher circles of government, too. At a Vancouver symposium on race relations and the law organized by the multiculturalism branch of the federal government, delegates criticized Canada's hate literature laws as inadequate. Several of the speakers whom the government itself had invited called for tougher laws against the Klan.

Except for the outbursts by its B.C. branch, the Klan was so quiet in early 1982 that many thought it might be dying. But it was far from dead. The Klan leadership's response to its recent string of reverses was to direct the KKK's efforts into more orthodox political channels.

In an interview at the time, McQuirter admitted his organization was in a period of retrenchment. "Phase One of our operation is completed," he said, noting that wide media attention had given the Klan the publicity it wanted but also had its disadvantages: "Any group labelled as a fringe group by the media has its problems with oddballs; we attracted misfits. So we're stopping that and people who are just hangers-on are going away." McQuirter went on to explain his strategy for the future: "Phase Two is getting good quality people. That will go on until we've attracted the proper cadre that we want to launch Phase Three. Phase Three will be the launching of a new political party or another force, coinciding with six months before the next federal elections."

McQuirter's statements were partly bluster, an attempt to make a virtue out of necessity. His organization, battered by opposition and bad publicity, was in decline and disarray. But he did not invent his multi-phase strategy on the spur of the moment to cover up current problems; the official Klan *Handbook*, which he had written early in 1981, outlined a similar strategy in much the same language. "Stage One" of the Klan's development was identified as "the initial publicity stage." "The purpose of this stage is to break through the enemy-controlled media and get across our message to the White Majority," the *Handbook* said; it was a goal which McQuirter had accomplished by 1981. "This activity, if properly executed, attracts those Whites who are politically aware Racially, and are ready to join our movement. These people provide the manpower and organizational base for the next stage." Stage Two is one of consolidation, outlined in the internal *Handbook* this way: "This involves building the hard core of Klan structure; primarily a stage of internal organization, self-examination, leadership assessment and development. If we are to be effective then we must utilize, to advantage, the skills and experience of those in the Movement. We must weed out

those not suited for leadership roles, or those who, through lack
of ability and discretion, could damage the Klan movement."
Then, the *Handbook* revealed, comes Stage Three. "This is where
we go public and show our strength. It differs from Stage One in
that now we can impress with numbers and we can be legitimately
identified as a Political Movement. We are seen as an alternative
to the limp liberal system; we flex White political muscles. . . Stage
Three is aimed at attracting mass support and winning office for
our candidates. . .It is a step on our march to power."

The fourth and final stage is the Klan's ultimate goal: grabbing
power. "This is where the Klan, as a White Racialist Movement,
seizes power from the liberal left," the Klan *Handbook* stated. "At
this point, . . .protective forces, affiliate groups and other Klan
fronts will offer security. . .We will turn the democratic process
against itself, we will restore order and power through our White
Racialist Movement." The *Handbook*, under a section entitled
"Primary Objective", stated that "the ultimate goal is to assume
control of the municipal, provincial and federal governments." It
continued:

> We are not playing a game with only a few trinkets at stake
> — we are locked in a life and death struggle for the survival
> of the White Race. . .The objective of the Klan is to form not
> only an effective White Racialist political movement, but to
> grasp power.

The Klan's first moves in the direction of the electoral arena
actually came two years earlier, in the summer of 1980. At a press
conference in New York City, U.S. Klan leader David Duke
announced the establishment of the National Association for the
Advancement of White People. "McQuirter and myself helped set
up this press conference," Wolfgang Droege said. McQuirter
wanted to set up the NAAWP in Canada as a more respectable
alternative to the Klan, but couldn't because the black civil rights
group the NAAWP mimicked — the National Association for the
Advancement of Colored People — was not widely known in
Canada. But McQuirter did want to create a new group "with a
new name but the same philosophy," as one Klan leader candidly
admitted.

In September, 1980, it was announced that the Canadian KKK

would formally merge with the fascist Nationalist Party of Canada, led by McQuirter's old mentor Don Andrews. The Klan and the NPC signed a thirteen-point merger agreement on September 28, to "promote co-operation in the white nationalist ranks."[1] A council was created, with equal representation from both groups. For the Klan, the merger promised a vital political vehicle to sell its policies. Andrews, who had set up the NPC after his Western Guard party had fallen into disrepute, was an expert at making discredited movements appear respectable. Said Andrews of the Klan's motives for the merger: "They've come to the realization that if they operate under the Klan symbol, they're going to have problems at the political level." Wolfgang Droege, who announced the merger to the news media, agreed. "I feel we can politically get much farther this way," he said. McQuirter saw the merger as a way "to get the resources of both groups together." He noted that "it would be under the National Party name that our Klan members would run for political office."

The merger gave a tremendous boost to the NPC's membership. The NPC was no doubt jealous of the media coverage the Klan was getting ("They're very successful at advertising and in press appearances," a spokesman for the NPC said), and Andrews felt the merger would bring more people under his influence, though he didn't want many of the less sophisticated Klansmen the merger brought with it. "The original idea was that the Klan would recruit people on the basis of its name and we would educate them. We were going to get new recruits from an organization that was well-known. It does attract a certain element, so you pick the best from that element."

According to the details revealed by Droege, the Klan would not actually disband, but 60 to 70 per cent of its members and all its organizers would join the new party. McQuirter was to be the NPC's national director and Andrews was to become the head of the provincial party in Ontario and act as an international liaison officer with white supremacist groups in the U.S. and Europe. Fund-raising and a nationwide recruitment drive would begin immediately, in anticipation of a federal election expected three or four years later. "Hopefully, we'll be ready to run candidates across Canada," Droege boasted. Though the new party had not yet worked out a formal platform, Droege said the anti-third world immigration stand adopted by the NPC would suit the Klan (a 10-point program released by Andrews's party earlier pledged to "save Canada" by "prohibit[ing] all immigration into our country" and making all government, health, education and housing assistance available only to Canadian citizens).

But within a few weeks the merger collapsed. McQuirter blamed mistrust on the part of both groups. Andrews blamed the Klan for the failure of the merger, which was, he says, "discontinued and disallowed by our party because they didn't care for the methods of the Klan. Due to personal differences on method, the merger was quashed." Andrews said McQuirter never liked the idea that the NPC would absorb his Klan; the merger, he concluded, "was made impossible because of an ambivalent attitude by McQuirter." It is most likely that the NPC-KKK merger was hampered by the egos of McQuirter and Andrews. While they remained close friends, both were too arrogant and ambitious to play second fiddle to anybody. "It was a personality dispute between McQuirter and Andrews over who should be king," commented Toronto journalist Neil Louttit.

McQuirter's thirst for political prominence was not diminished by the abortive NPC merger attempt. If anything, it seemed to spur him on. Soon after the alliance collapsed, McQuirter told a newspaper reporter that the Klan planned to run "150 candidates in the next federal election. We hope to have just over half [the ridings contested] to become officially registered."[2] In November, 1980, the Klan's Armand Siksna ran in Toronto's mayoralty race "to promote the purity of the white race," as he put it. "We're not monsters like Hollywood makes us," candidate Siksna told the press. "We want to spread love, not hatred — love of the white race." Siksna finished sixth in a field of nine, with 867 votes. At the same time, two people who were living with Siksna were candidates in Toronto's school board elections. Christopher Greenland, who had been associated with the Western Guard, and his wife Brenda ran in Wards 8 and 9. Both denied belonging to the Klan, but Greenland was allowed to canvass a Klan meeting for campaign donations and Klansmen were urged to vote for him. He received 511 votes; his wife, 957.

The Klan made no new moves into the political arena in 1981, but by 1982 McQuirter was once again toying with a couple of options. He let on in February that he wasn't sure "if I am going to stay on with the Klan forever" and that he was "considering the creation of another political party for the federal elections." More concretely, he announced that he and his associates were "putting together a new tabloid newspaper, not necessarily linked but supportive of the Klan." This was to be the Klan's major political initiative of the year. The calculation was that a white supremacist newspaper, not identified as a Klan organ, would be able to reach a wider audience.

Not long after, the first issue of *The Spokesman* appeared on the streets of Toronto and Vancouver. Two thousand copies had been printed.* *The Spokesman* billed itself as "The Alternative Viewpoint of the Majority" and noted that "the very existence of the White Race and the Culture loved by White Canadians is being seriously threatened by overwhelmingly high non-White birth rates and by non-White immigration." It decried the "one man, one vote" principle which let "minority interests" run the country and proposed that "only the citizens of Canada, those of the common Racial bond" should have the right to vote and hold office. The front page of the first issue of *The Spokesman* headlined a statement by Conservative MP Dan McKenzie, upon his return from South Africa, that "the blacks are still quite primitive and uncivilized." The article congratulated McKenzie for letting "the cat out of the bag." Another article was devoted to "the falsehood about the six million Jews said to be gassed by Hitler." The following issues of *The Spokesman* kept up this barrage of racism and anti-semitism. Feature articles, usually printed from American or British fascist newspapers, purported to scientifically explain the dangers of race mixing, the "myth" of racial equality, the Jewish conspiracy against society, as well as

*The first issue was printed by an East European printer in Toronto who received the several hundred dollars to pay for the job in cash. By chance, the same printer also produced a black community paper and when people from that paper — one of his major clients — discovered *The Spokesman* was being done at the plant, they promptly told the printer they would take their business elsewhere if he continued printing any more *Spokesman* issues. The threat of a boycott worked.

frequent passing cracks against "Toronto's mongoloid area called Chinatown," East Indians and others.

The Spokesman differed from the many white supremacist publications that had preceded it in two ways. It was a much slicker production than anything the extreme right had put out in Canada in years. Published regularly (five eight-page issues came out in the first half of 1982), the newspaper had typeset articles, cartoons, photographs, and catchy news items designed to convince the reader of the inferiority and danger of blacks and Jews. *The Spokesman* represented a breakthrough for the extreme right in Canada in another sense. Not only had racialist groups in the past seldom been able to produce a regular, mass-oriented newspaper, *The Spokesman* was also the first publication that was more than a house organ of a single group. Of course, the paper's affinity with the Klan was apparent. Its premier issue contained a "special personal message" from McQuirter urging his supporters to help the cause by "subscribing [to], distributing and supporting" the paper. Klan member Armand Siksna was listed as the paper's "Latvian correspondent." And issues of *The Spokesman* gave prominent coverage to news and events of the Canadian Klan. At the same time, it was clear that *The Spokesman* was eager to be more than a Klan organ, that it was trying to be a tool for the entire white supremacist movement in Canada. One issue carried news that John Ross Taylor, the aging Western Guard leader, had been released from jail in March after serving his sentence for the tape-recorded telephone hate messages. *The Spokesman* noted that "the courageous Mr. Taylor is at it again" with a new recorded "message of truth."

Organizational unity between the Klan and like-minded organizations was not on the immediate agenda. Individual far-right groups continued to produce their own newsletters. Taylor's Western Guard published the *Aryan,** which contained

---

*After the Western Guard lost its mailing privileges in Canada, it began to operate out of a Buffalo post office box. Taylor's American operation (called the Committee for Free Speech in Canada) was run by Karl Hand, an American Nazi who was arrested along with three Western Guard members during a violent anti-black demonstration in Toronto in July, 1973. Hand was also a former national organizer for David Duke's Klan and headed the Buffalo chapter of the National Socialist Party of America.

articles about the Holocaust "hoax" and "Hitler's miracle in putting the German people back to work." In June, as *The Spokesman* had reported, the Western Guard resumed its "white power" recorded telephone messages after a two-year absence; Don Andrews and his Nationalist Party of Canada, meanwhile, published the *Nationalist Report*, which urged NPC members and supporters to "make 1982 the Year of White Nationalist Power" (for inspiration, NPC members attended private screenings of the Nazi propaganda film "Triumph of the Will"). Andrews said his organization was also gearing up for a run at the municipal elections, perhaps hoping to repeat his strong showing at the polls in 1974. But while there was still rivalry between the Guard, the NPC and the Klan, there was also contact among them. McQuirter kept in touch with his old friend Andrews, and from his prison cell in the United States, Wolfgang Droege kept in touch with the various movements and noted that the "broadening of full co-operation and unity between these various white nationalist organizations" was making "tremendous progress."

In the summer of 1982, McQuirter suddenly "retired" from the Klan. The fifth issue of *The Spokesman* carried the news that as of July 15 McQuirter was "retiring from my position as Wizard [national director], and, following tradition, from the Klan as well." McQuirter made it clear that he was leaving not "because of any dissatisfaction with the Klan, as I still believe there is a definite place for the KKK in Canada," but because he wanted to fight "through the Political Election process."

The departure of its prominent public leader seemed to drive the Toronto Klan deeper into obscurity, but boosted the fortunes of the Vancouver KKK. Ann Farmer, the Klan's able B.C. spokesperson, was chosen to succeed McQuirter as Grand Wizard. Farmer, a small blonde woman, was eloquent, educated and presentable if not as charismatic as McQuirter. She would be able to project the same youthful, articulate image which McQuirter had nurtured. It was also decided that she would continue to work out of the Vancouver area, where the national mailing address of the Klan had been transferred. The Klan was definitely heading west. Farmer immediately left Canada for a training tour "to learn the ropes," as McQuirter put it, under American Klan leader Don Black. The presence of the national director of the Klan on the west coast was a shot in the arm to the B.C. Klan. Enthused local Klan official Al Hooper: "We're going to get more and more in the public eye." In Toronto, on the other hand, the Klan seemed headed in the opposite direction, consciously keeping a lower profile. Jacob Prins continued to run things in Ontario and John Gilroy, a former Toronto leader, was named to a new post of organizer for eastern Canada. But the fallout from Dominica and other bad publicity along with popular opposition to the Klan seemed to have driven the Klan underground. Admitted McQuirter: "I think what pretty well everyone decided is that you can't make it as a public group, being above board, because there is so much pressure. They decided to revert back to the original idea of the Klan as an invisible empire." Ontario Klan leader Jacob Prins said bluntly: "You won't hear much from the Klan in the future, everything will be underground." Prins said *The Spokesman* would continue to be the Klan's main presence until the Ontario Klan would reappear prior to the federal election.

McQuirter's retirement from the Klan was a step toward fulfilling a long-held political ambition. Since at least the founding of the National Association for the Advancement of White People by his mentor David Duke, McQuirter had his eyes on wrapping his white supremacism in a more marketable, electable garb. The Klan had been useful because its name and notoriety had attracted publicity and people, but to McQuirter the KKK had also had its limits and he wanted a more effective political machine. "I want to go into more serious public politics. The Klan was a fraternity; you can't do very much with it except attract attention." (Droege, upon hearing in prison of McQuirter's departure from the Klan, said, "If nothing else . . . we have been able to get across a point of view, a message, to millions . . . We attracted a lot of attention to our cause, because of the name [of the Klan] in particular.") McQuirter ruled out joining an established political party, in part because "they wouldn't accept me anyways."* McQuirter was determined to create a new, white supremacist party. He calculated that, while he could use his experience and connections gained through the Klan, he could gain new supporters without the Klan name, in much the same way *The Spokesman* was designed to attract non-Klan readers. "I met a lot of people who didn't want to get involved with the Klan but wanted me to keep in touch if I ever left the Klan. I'm laying some groundwork; I have a lot of time until the next federal election — that's what I'm aiming for."

McQuirter was also shrewd enough to realize that a name change alone won't make his views more palatable to the electorate; he was also counting on a worsening economic crisis and increased social tensions to create better conditions for the spawning of a neo-Nazi movement in Canada. "It's not just a case of dropping the name that will help the white nationalist cause," he said. "What is really and truly going to help is the system breaking down — economically and socially. When it comes to a point, drastic measures have to be taken. People do not care what they call themselves. It's not going to matter if there is another Adolf Hitler figure coming along and people have to wear

*There was the case of Paul Fromm, the co-founder with Don Andrews of the Edmund Burke Society, who in 1981 became a treasurer of the federal Progressive Conservative Party's Metro Toronto organization. An English teacher, Fromm did not appear to shed any of his extreme racist views when he became a Tory official. He said in a newspaper interview that he believes in restricted immigration; that the Indochinese boat people should have been sent to desert islands because their influx into Canada will "upset the racial balance;" and that the belief of a supreme race "is a good idea."[3] The furor created by Fromm's public utterances obliged top Tory officials to fire him. What was revealing about the entire affair was not that an avowed racist like Fromm could obtain a prominent position in the Tory party, but that he should lose the post only after an embarrassing interview. Fromm did not leave the Conservative Party. In the summer of 1981, he was an active participant at the inaugural meeting of the New Right Coalition which attracted 300 people in Toronto. PC Metro officials were prominent in organizing the group, modelled after the right-wing political morality groups in the U.S. Fromm was not the only confirmed racist active in the major parties; Droege claimed that a federal MP (whom he would not name) was passed over for a cabinet post in the 1970s when his links with the Western Guard were discovered. And Jacob Prins claimed the Klan had secret members in political parties.

swastikas if it's going to eliminate their problems. It's as simple as that." McQuirter no doubt saw himself as that Hitler in Canada's future. (His fascination with Hitler was longstanding. Several copies of *Mein Kampf* and books on Hitler and Nazism were seized during a police raid on his apartment in 1978. In 1981, McQuirter's Klan office displayed a large Nazi flag and a bust of Adolf Hitler. In early 1982, McQuirter and the Klan held a meeting to celebrate the 49th anniversary of the Nazi dictator's ascension to power.) For the time being, though, McQuirter was content to bide his time and plan his new fascist movement quietly. "You have to walk softly and try to sneak in a big stick," he said.

By the middle of 1982, McQuirter's political strategy had been fleshed out, and it seemed the scuttling of the Klan in favor of another political vehicle to promote white supremacy was a key element in that strategy. But McQuirter still had a major hurdle to overcome: how could he lead a new political movement from inside a jail cell? Because in September, he was scheduled to go on trial on charges arising from the aborted invasion of Dominica. To make matters worse, even before his September trial, the ambitious McQuirter was struck by another blow that would put his political aspirations on hold for a while at least. On August 14, he, along with Klan members Jean MacGarry and Armand Siksna, were arrested and charged with conspiracy to commit murder. Their intended victim, police alleged, was none other than Klan security chief Gary MacFarlane.

"If you have a country and you control that country, you can make an awful lot of money...Our purpose was to make a lot of money for white nationalist circles."
— Alexander McQuirter

12. The trials

ON THE MORNING OF Friday, September 24, 1982, James Alexander McQuirter entered a Toronto courtroom to face charges arising from his involvement in an ill-fated plot to invade the Caribbean island nation of Dominica. Handcuffed and escorted by guards, McQuirter walked slowly to the defendant's box. He had grown a beard and lost some weight during the past month in jail, where he was being held without bail pending trial for conspiring to murder MacFarlane.

McQuirter looked around the large courtroom, perhaps hoping to find some friends or supporters. But all he saw were police officials or reporters, who had come to write about the fate of the ex-leader of Canada's Klan. Eventually, unnoticed by most of the media people, one of McQuirter's fellow Klansmen did make his way into the courtroom. He was William Lau Richardson, the Klan intelligence chief with a longstanding relationship with police and other law enforcement agencies. Richardson even managed to speak briefly to McQuirter before a court official separated them. It is ironic that when the leader of the KKK finally got his day in court, his only supporter in the courtroom was a police informer.

The court was declared in session and a clerk read the indictment, that McQuirter "in the years 1980 and 1981, did conspire one with the other and with Wolfgang Droege, Larry Jacklin, Marion McGuire, and Michael Perdue to effect an unlawful purpose in the Commonwealth of Dominica, West Indies, to wit, to use force or violence for the purpose of overthrowing the Government of Dominica..."* As the clerk read the charges, McQuirter nervously rolled his fingers, but otherwise he stood perfectly still. "How do you plead?" the clerk asked.

"Guilty," said McQuirter.

The complicated and at times confusing chain of events which had brought McQuirter to this Toronto courtroom had been set in motion more than two years earlier in the United States. The plot for the bungled invasion of Dominica — the news media dubbed it the Bayou of Pigs — was hatched by an American, Michael Eugene Perdue. Perdue seemed destined to fail at everything he attempted — except for racial terrorism. "He bragged about how he beat up blacks on Saturday nights," a high school teacher once reminisced to a reporter. A braggart, Perdue boasted and lied to his friends about having worked for the German government, being a mercenary in Uruguay and Nicaragua, and being a wounded and decorated Marine in Vietnam. In fact, Perdue did at one time enlist with the Marines but never made it; just prior to joining, he broke into a home and was sentenced to eleven months in a state prison. Perdue also flirted with various right-wing groups, including the American Ku Klux Klan.

Originally, Perdue's idea was to invade the Caribbean island of Grenada to help restore the ousted prime minister, Sir Eric Gairy, to power — with, of course, a handsome payoff for the mercenaries. Perdue had read an article about Gairy in May, 1979, and contacted him with the proposition. But, as Perdue

*Charles Yanover, arrested with McQuirter in February, 1981 as a co-conspirator, was tried separately. Described in press reports as an "international arms dealer," Yanover — nicknamed Chuck the Bike — was well known to police and had a ten-year criminal record which included numerous weapons charges.

later testified in court, "we never came to any agreements on it." Concluding that the government was "too entrenched in Grenada," Perdue was influenced instead by "the reports I got back from Dominica [that] the situation was ripe for a military coup in Dominica."[1]

Dominica, with a population of about 75,000 people, is an island in the Caribbean Sea about 500 miles southeast of Puerto Rico and 1,800 miles from New Orleans. An impoverished country which gained its sovereignty from Britain in November, 1978, Dominica had been ruled after independence by Patrick John and his Labour party. John, a demagogue and an ostensible leftist, steadily alienated the population with his harsh policies. He established links with apartheid South Africa, offered a Texas corporation virtual control of one fifth of the country, and planned a series of repressive laws against trade unions and the press. Ousted after a general strike, John was succeeded by Eugenia Charles whose Freedom Party won the general election in July, 1980. After her victory, Charles was able to secure some $10 million in aid from the U.S. and Britain.

Perdue saw in John what he had looked for in Gairy: a black politician to use as a front for a white mercenary coup. In the fall of 1980, he contacted John by telegram and then flew down to Dominica to meet with him for two days, there securing what he would call "a letter of intent." In December, Perdue returned to Dominica to finalize "the specifics of the coup" with John and some of his associates in the island's army; the conspirators met again the next month in neighboring Antigua and signed an agreement. "We offered weapons and manpower to reinstate him through a coup. . .to get Patrick John to sign a contract," Perdue testified later. In return for getting back in power, John promised Nordic Enterprises — set up by Perdue and his financial backers — $50,000 in cash, a free hand to exploit resources on the island, and a 20-year tax exemption. Perdue was also to get a high position in the government and responsibility for training the Dominican army. John and some of his associates would also receive a cut of Nordic's revenues.

The invasion scheme as such was simple enough. Through his contacts with white supremacist groups and advertisements in mercenary magazines, Perdue was able to recruit a force of ten mercenaries, most of them Klansmen and American Nazis (Perdue's band included two organizers for the Canadian Klan, Wolfgang Droege and Larry Jacklin, Don Black, the future leader of David Duke's Klan, and a Mississippi Klansman who had been convicted of 30 different acts of violence). Armed with 33 guns, 20 sticks of dynamite, 30 blasting caps, 5,000 bullets, fatigues, walkie-talkies, a rubber raft and Confederate and Nazi flags, the mercenaries were to land a few miles north of Dominica's capital, join up with local collaborators and quickly subdue the island's small police force.

The plot sounds harebrained but it might have worked. "The opinion of all parties who have been to Dominica, including Canadian and American law enforcement agents, is that the coup would have succeeded if it hadn't been uncovered," the prosecutor said at McQuirter's trial.[2] At the very least, in the words of prime minister Eugenia Charles, "many people would have died." But the Dominican government got wind of plans for a coup and jailed Patrick John and some of his associates in March, 1981. Perdue decided to go ahead with his coup anyway — adding to the plans the liberation of John from jail — but foolishly revealed the details of his plans to the owner of the boat he had rented to take the mercenaries from New Orleans to Dominica. American authorities were promptly informed of the scheme and planted an agent among the plotters. For the two months before their planned departure, much of what Perdue and his gang said or did was taped, filmed or photographed. On April 27, the ten mercenaries climbed aboard their van laden with guns and equipment and drove right into a police trap. In May, a U.S. federal grand jury indicted them on seven counts of conspiracy, alleging violations of various weapons and explosives laws as well as the U.S. Neutrality Act, which makes it a crime to launch a coup against a friendly nation. Seven conspirators, including both Canadians, pleaded guilty; most were sentenced to three-year terms in federal penitentiaries. Of the three who opted for trial, one was acquitted but the other two, Danny Hawkins and Klansman Don Black, were convicted.

Details about the financial backers of the coup attempt still remain murky, and none of them have been jailed. The scheme — with Perdue's frequent trips to the Caribbean and across North America, the purchase of arms and equipment — was obviously an expensive operation. Perdue reportedly raised about $63,000 from American sources. J.W. Kirkpatrick, a lawyer from Memphis, Tenn., committed suicide after Perdue testified in court that Kirkpatrick had donated $10,000 to finance the plot. Two other businessmen, James C. White of Texas and L.E. Matthews of Mississippi, were brought to trial on charges of allegedly taking part in the conspiracy. During their trial, Perdue claimed that he had met with Matthews on several occasions and had received $12,800 from him. He also alleged that White — with whom he had "a good relationship" for four years — had contributed $35,000 and that he allowed Perdue to use his post office box address in magazine advertisements for mercenary recruits. Perdue claimed that 10 per cent of Nordic Enterprises had been set aside for the money men behind the coup: "They'd finance the coup and they'd get their 10 per cent." Both men denied Perdue's allegations, and their lawyers successfully challenged much of Perdue's testimony. White's defense, for example, was that the money he gave Perdue was for antiques, towing equipment and other items, and their lawyers said that Perdue was an admitted liar. Both men were acquitted.

Perhaps Perdue's biggest blunder was not the invasion, but the target he chose. The U.S. government and American law enforcement agencies have shown little eagerness to hinder mercenaries and private armies from using U.S. territory to prepare and launch actions against "unfriendly" nations like Cuba, Grenada and Nicaragua; for example, the existence of military training camps in Florida and California operated by Cuban and Nicaraguan exile groups is well documented.[3] The Dominican government of Eugenia Charles, on the other hand, was staunchly pro-American. According to the *Covert Action and Information Bulletin*, a review which monitors the Central Intelligence Agency and similar organizations, Charles's election victory was aided in part by Canada, the U.S. and Britain. Immediately after elections, the *Bulletin* reports, "diplomats" from the three countries met with "their favorite policemen to

congratulate them" and make special arrangements for contracts;
"the Canadian was overhead specifically promising better
walkie-talkies and police broadcast equipment."[4] Arguably
Perdue's plot was stopped by U.S. authorities not because it was a
racist, violent attack on a third world country, but because it
threatened the stability of American and Western interests in a
region where the U.S. needs all the friends it can get.

Though the initial arrests, trials and convictions of the
Dominica invaders took place in the U.S., the planned coup was
very much a Canadian caper. When the ten mercenaries were
arrested in New Orleans, Alexander McQuirter first denied that
the Canadian Klan had anything to do with the affair. "My
original story was that I didn't know anything about it," he was to
say later. Eventually, however, the full extent of the Canadian
KKK's involvement became known. The trail led not only to
Droege and Jacklin, the two Klansmen arrested, but to McQuirter
and other leaders in Canada's white power movement.

Back in 1979 when Perdue was searching for financial backing
and forces for what was originally an anti-Grenada operation, he
contacted his friend David Duke who referred him to Donald
Andrews. Perdue and Andrews kept in touch until a few months
before the attempted Dominica coup. Andrews took advantage of
a visit by Perdue to Toronto in the fall of 1979 — one of several
which the coup ringleader would make to the city — to introduce
him to Wolfgang Droege, his fellow Western Guard organizer
turned Klan leader. Droege immediately signed up for the
invasion party. "I knew of the possible consequences in the
Dominica affair and was willing to face them because I prefer to
live a full life, with as much excitement and adventure,
experiences as possible," he later wrote from prison.[5] Aside from
the call of adventure, however, the coup offered more material
attractions. According to the plan, the former prime minister,
Patrick John, "was to be a mere puppet, along with his followers,
and would allow their nation to be run by a behind-the-scenes
corporation/government which would have the intention of using
the nation for commerce and base of operations." Droege was sent

to Dominica in December, 1979, to contact John and finalize details of the plan. (Droege failed in his mission, though, and it fell to Perdue to work out the detailed arrangements the following month with some of John's men.) Droege spent some time with Perdue in Las Vegas and other U.S. cities, drumming up investors for the various corporations and tax havens which the conspirators were dreaming of creating on "their" Dominica. And, according to trial testimony by a U.S. treasury department agent, Droege himself also planned to cash in by setting up a cocaine processing laboratory that would export to the U.S. This was all going on at a time when Droege, as an official spokesperson for the Canadian Klan, was telling newspaper interviewers that "we're against violence" and "it's one of our oaths not to commit illegal acts."

The other Canadian Klan organizer in Perdue's band was Larry Jacklin, a man in his early twenties from Listowel, Ont. Jacklin was a former member of the Western Guard who became the Klan's organizer in the Kitchener-Waterloo region under the alias Doug O'Hare. Jacklin's main concern at meetings to plan the coup seemed to be how much he was going to be paid and whether he would have to live with blacks during the operation.

Droege and Jacklin were the only Canadians in the group of ten mercenaries arrested in New Orleans, but the Canadian connection did not stop there. Shortly after the arrests, the authorities in Dominica jailed a young woman from Toronto, Marion McGuire, for her role in the coup attempt. McGuire, a friend of Droege and Andrews, had joined the Western Guard when she was eighteen and, like many others, went on to join the Klan. In a 1981 Klan newsletter, she was listed as a "Great Titan, attached to headquarters." McGuire came into the coup picture late, after it was decided to send someone to the island to determine the feasibility of getting Patrick John out of jail. According to the conspirators, "Wolfgang had already been there before so we decided perhaps instead of sending him down even less suspicious would be to send a woman down, Marion McGuire, posing as a nurse."[6] McGuire flew down to Dominica from Toronto to act as an intelligence officer, relaying information back to the waiting invaders.

The Canadian conspirators were able to use the facilities of Toronto radio station CFTR for some of their activities. Tipped off about the plot early, the station decided to keep quiet about the affair and planned to be on Dominica's shores for a "scoop" when the invaders arrived. A reporter, with the approval of his news director, spent many months interviewing the Klansmen and others involved in the coup bid. The station co-operated with the plotters to the point of telephoning Dominica on behalf of Perdue to find out the situation on the island after John's arrest. McGuire also sent a telegram to her fellow conspirators via CFTR. When the details of CFTR's role became public, the reporter and the news director left the station, but no further action by the government or any other authorities was taken.

The arrests of Droege, Jacklin and McGuire raised the question of when, if ever, McQuirter was going to be charged. After all, McQuirter had admitted his role in the planning of the coup in a front-page article in the Toronto *Globe and Mail* less than three weeks after the arrests of his fellow Klansmen; but he claimed he had not violated any Canadian laws by participating in a plot against a foreign government. For almost a year, authorities in Canada did not move against co-conspirators here. The apparent reluctance to prosecute other Klansmen aroused consternation among some observers. Protested one angry editorial in *Contrast*, the newspaper of Toronto's black community:

> Eight months have elapsed since McQuirter's role in the aborted coup was revealed. Eight months later and guess what? McQuirter is still on the loose! Still on the loose to crisscross the country burning crosses and spreading hate messages! Still on the loose to raise funds from secret, monied admirers of his philosophy of racial superiority...Maybe we should point out to you that this man was planning to systematically murder as many people as necessary to achieve his goal in Dominica.[7]

Finally, eleven months after the initial arrests in New Orleans, McQuirter was charged for his part in the conspiracy. What had done McQuirter in were taped interviews he gave to an Ottawa friend and aspiring writer, Lee Brandy, in which he boasted about his role in the plot. Excerpts of the tapes were printed in the *Globe and Mail* and eventually made their way into police hands.* McQuirter had been quite wrong in assuming that he had not broken any Canadian laws; section 423, subsection 3 of the Criminal Code makes it illegal to conspire in Canada to commit a crime outside the country. "I never heard of this stupid law," McQuirter later remarked ruefully.

McQuirter had been brought into the Dominica operation early on by Droege. At first he was doubtful ("I just didn't want anything to do with" Perdue, he said) but soon warmed to the invasion plot. "I actually saw the plan and I began to believe it. This was the biggest thing to hit us or White Nationalists in years." McQuirter was intimately involved in the scheme up until the final days of the conspiracy. Seven days before the mercenaries were to set out from New Orleans, McQuirter attended the final planning session in Toronto, one of several strategy meetings held there. It was the evening of April 20 — the anniversary of Adolf Hitler's birthday, a date celebrated by the Klan — and a small group was gathered in a room at the Ramada Inn. Others in attendance included Michael Perdue, Droege, Jacklin and Charles Yanover.

Yanover, a Jew who favored gold jewelry and fancy clothes, must have looked out of place in the room with Klansmen and Nazi sympathizers. But his presence was vital. He had struck a deal with Perdue: "to provide operational support in return for financial gain," and received an "unknown sum of money" for his promise of aid.[8] Yanover flew down to Dominica and "took a

---

*McQuirter later said his only regret over the Dominica affair was his indiscretion with Brandy. "Our biggest mistake was accepting Lee Brandy. She and I had a contract for a book and the money was supposed to go to a defence fund. Nothing could ever go out of her hands if I didn't say okay. Nothing would have happened if she had lived up to it." McQuirter's talkativeness to Brandy and to the media about the coup bid also upset co-conspirator Droege, who commented wryly: "He sought publicity on the issue of our case, which had the ultimate effect of compromising us to a degree...he did go overboard, showed lack of discretion."

large number of photographs, including photographs of the jail of the police station, the air strip, the harbor and other installations on the island," according to testimony. Yanover, said the other conspirators, wanted a position in the Dominican army. "I want to be a major and once we take over, I'm going to fly to Paris to have Pierre Cardin design a fancy uniform for me," McQuirter quoted him as saying. But according to authorities, Yanover's "sole role in this coup attempt was...to provide photographs of surveillance." At any rate, the plotters apparently had little intention of letting Yanover do much else: they talked of eventually killing "the Jew", as they called him. "We felt personally that once he had outlived his usefulness, he would be eliminated," McQuirter said.

During the Ramada Inn meeting, the conspirators pored over the photographs taken by Yanover. As McQuirter recalled, "Mike (Perdue)...had three large maps of the island, topographical maps stretched out across the room. We went over the plan...We took a look at a lot of photographs of the island, of the installations, etc...[We] went over our plans and everybody's position." McQuirter's job was "to fly down there direct, wait around, bring vehicles to the landing point and put on my uniform." From shore, McQuirter was "to go out to signal with three flashes with a flashlight" to the rented boat carrying Perdue and the other mercenaries. Once the invading group had made its way into the capital city, McQuirter's task was to disable a police communications centre, using violence if necessary. "My code name was Red Dog Three and I and one other man [Jacklin] were supposed to ensure the radio panic button in the communication centre wasn't pressed by the two Negroes who guarded them... [it] would light up to the police station...we didn't want them to know. I was supposed to stop them from pressing that radio to anybody and what it meant, whether blasting them or knocking the door [down]..." McQuirter was supposed to fly to Dominica a week after this Ramada Inn meeting (on the same flight as Yanover) to be in Dominica on May 9, the date the mercenaries were to attack after completing the trip by boat from New

Orleans.* (His stated reason for not joining the other mercenaries for the boat trip was that his known Klan affiliations would make his entry into the U.S. difficult.) McQuirter did drive Droege and Jacklin to London, Ont., to catch a bus to the U.S. to join with Perdue and the others. As he said goodbye to his two fellow Klansmen, they gave him the white power salute, McQuirter later recalled. "That was the last time I saw them."

The Klan leader's motivation for embarking on the Dominica venture was linked to the pursuit of his racialist goals. McQuirter wanted a stable base to finance his operations. "If you have a country and you control that country you can make an awful lot of money," he told Brandy. "Our purpose was to make a lot of money for white nationalist circles . . ." Along with such plans as selling false passports and establishing a gun-running centre, McQuirter said the coup plotters hoped to set up a lucrative lumber operation. "We were going to cut down the majority of the lumber which would have caused immense soil erosion and probably destroyed the island for years to come." Fisheries, banking, casinos and tax havens were other schemes mentioned.†

McQuirter saw a chance to make a fortune and establish a power base for his cause. "I had expected that, had the attempt been successful, I would have spent five years on the island, in some sort of ministry of propaganda (encouraging the Negroes to work and accept the new regime). At the end of five years, I would have returned to Canada and used my thus attained personal fortune (approximately $1 million U.S.) to affect a more professional attempt to articulate the philosophy of White Nationalism."

McQuirter's dreams of power in Dominica remained just that and, two years after joining the conspiracy, he pleaded guilty to his role in the plot. McQuirter's lawyer asked for a light sentence

*McQuirter's $699 plane ticket was purchased with American businessman James C. White's credit card. Perdue testified that White gave him his credit card number to use, and that he had passed it on to Marion McGuire. White said that his credit card had been stolen.

†According to Perdue's trial testimony, Droege and McQuirter were to get 5 per cent of Nordic Enterprises each. McGuire and Jacklin, along with most of the other mercenaries, were to receive 1 per cent each.

for his client, whom he described as "a rather bemused observer" of the coup plot who "never set foot on the island." But judge Patrick LeSage sentenced him to the maximum penalty of two years in a federal penitentiary. LeSage commented upon the fact that McQuirter had provided the main evidence against himself — the taped interviews with Brandy — under the impression that he was immune from prosecution under Canadian law. "It appears you were not quite as good a scholar of the law as you thought you were," LeSage told McQuirter.

McQuirter didn't smile, but doubtless he was happy to have received only a two-year sentence; if Dominica's laws had explicitly stated that overthrowing the government was an indictable offence McQuirter would have been charged under a part of Section 423 of the Criminal Code that carried a maximum of fourteen years in jail. In giving McQuirter two years, LeSage said it was "unfortunate that is the maximum penalty." Nevertheless, justice and the law, it seemed, had finally caught up with McQuirter — though perhaps too slowly and too mildly for most Klan opponents.*

Two colleagues of McQuirter were also in touch with the plotters in the early stages of the conspiracy, while Grenada was still the target. Neither was charged. One of the men was Don Andrews, the first Canadian contacted by Michael Perdue when Perdue was hatching his Caribbean conspiracies. Police and prosecutors maintain that Andrews was only involved with Perdue when Grenada was the coup target and had nothing to do with the Dominica conspiracy. In the middle of 1979, Perdue told Andrews he was looking for a base of operations to launch an attack on Grenada. Perdue later testified in court that Andrews "was quite interested in doing what he could." Andrews himself, in an interview during McQuirter's trial, said it was he who suggested Dominica as "an ideal place" for Perdue's base. As

---

*On June 10, 1983, Charles Yanover pleaded guilty to his role in the Dominica affair. Sentencing was postponed, however, pending the resolution of other cases involving Yanover. In April, 1983, Yanover had been sentenced to nine years for orchestrating — from his prison cell — a 1980 insurance bombing of a Toronto disco. Yanover had also been arrested but cleared of charges in connection to a plot to murder South Korean president Chun Doo-Kwan.

Andrews explained, "What could Dominica do with 30 or 40 well-armed people? They couldn't arrest you."[9] Andrews did more than offer suggestions; he set up a coffee roasting business in Dominica to serve as a front for the group's operations, and introduced Perdue to Wolfgang Droege, who in turn would bring in McQuirter. Andrews also sent a friend, Arnie Polli, to Dominica to "run reconnaissance", as Perdue put it. It was Polli, a stringer for CFTR, who tipped off the Toronto radio station about the coup plot.

By the fall of 1979, Perdue was growing disenchanted with the Grenada caper and began considering Dominica instead. He testified that he phoned Andrews and told him of his change of plans, suggesting "we need to get somebody on the island to have a constant source of information." Again, Andrews helped out, suggesting a French associate of his named Roger Dermee. "The purpose was to...entrench him in Dominica as a source of information," said Perdue. "He was to feed back reports to Don Andrews." Droege confirmed this, describing Dermee as "an aging mercenary living in Toronto who was sent to Dominica to provide reconnaissance." Droege said that Dermee claimed to have "made arrangements with various influential people on the island of Dominica to the effort of a possible business venture which could serve as a front for the takeover of Dominica or serve as a base of operations against Grenada."

At this point tensions began to develop between Andrews and the other plotters, who believed Andrews was leaking their plans to too many people. They were also dissatisfied with the aid and personnel he was providing. Perdue, for example, clashed with Polli over the use of funds, and Droege felt Dermee was "freeloading" and had accomplished nothing. Differences over strategy also began to emerge. Andrews favored an economic takeover by investing in Dominica, while Perdue and Droege had a military solution. Andrews later recalled: "Droege and Perdue went down to Dominica and said, 'This is a pushover.' They started talking to Patrick John. I wanted them to raise funds to give to Charles's election campaign. But they were greedy and myopic." Andrews said from then on he was effectively shut out of any plans because "they felt I couldn't be trusted." He

admitted, though, that he was informed in the winter of 1981 of
the idea to invade Dominica — before Patrick John was arrested
— but was not told of the plotters' plan to go ahead with the coup
after John's imprisonment. Andrews, then, was decidedly not a
Dominica conspirator but it can be argued that he planted the seed
for the selection of Dominica as the final target. He also provided
assistance to Perdue and Droege when their invasion plans were in
the formative stages.

Another figure on the Canadian extreme right with connections
to Dominica was Martin Weiche, the Klan supporter and Nazi
from London, Ont. At the end of 1979, Michael Perdue came to
Toronto for a meeting with Don Andrews. According to Perdue,
"Don Andrews gave me $10,000 to continue the plot. Earlier, he
had introduced me by phone to a man by the name of Martin
Weiche,* who said he was interested in financing. . . I assume the
$10,000 came from him." None of the people named by Perdue
deny such meetings and conversations took place. In fact, Weiche
later admitted in an interview that he had "many telephone
conversations with Perdue [and] met him personally." Said
Weiche: "We have talked about financing a lot. We have talked
about financing from Toronto, from Houston, from Dominica,
from Miami. . . all concerning the coup in Grenada. He [Perdue]
was making it to me how rich I could get if I would put in $10,000
or $20,000. I was seriously thinking."[10] But Andrews and Weiche
deny that any money ever actually changed hands. Weiche
insisted Perdue's allegations were "an outright lie. He didn't get
$10,000 from Don Andrews and he didn't get anything from me
either, direct or indirect." Wolfgang Droege, for his part, said, "I
was at all times fully aware of who was contributing and I know
for a fact that Martin Weiche, who had only showed mild interest,
did not contribute $10,000. Or any amount."

Still, Weiche's denial that he gave money to Perdue seems based
not so much on a moral objection to Perdue's schemes as on a fear
of going to prison: "I personally never thought there was anything

---

*The transcript of Perdue's testimony in a U.S. District Court in Louisiana in
1981 uses the spelling "Martin Winch" but the reference is clearly to Weiche.
This ambiguity was cleared up in an Associated Press dispatch from New
Orleans on June 23, 1981.

wrong with giving anybody any money, and if they [the authorities] could have proven that anybody had given the guy any money it would be 'away in the hole.'" Weiche said he suspected Perdue "was an FBI spy" and "if I go down there, there'll be cops and they'll arrest me for conspiracy." Not that Weiche himself did not have his own plans for Dominica. He admitted he was looking for a haven for right-wing extremists, a colony for "all pure whites — Aryan stock, physically and mentally."[11] For Weiche, Dominica would be "an ideal place" for this "home away from home" for his fellow Nazis. He said the island could support 300,000 people, instead of the mere 70,000 "poor niggers" now there. Weiche added that he had business interests in Dominica, which he had visited at least twice. "I have contacts down there; I own investments on the island." Dominica's problems with foreigners who try to determine its future may not be over yet.

A little over four months after he had been sentenced for his part in the Dominica plot, McQuirter again found himself in court, pleading guilty to another bungled conspiracy. On February 8, before judge John O'Driscoll of the Ontario Supreme Court, McQuirter and fellow Klan member Jean MacGarry pleaded guilty to several counts of fraud. The two of them, along with Klansman Armand Siksna, also admitted to plotting to kill their former colleague Gary MacFarlane, MacGarry's common-law husband.

Like the Dominica affair, in which an indiscreet word to a boat captain tipped the authorities off to the planned invasion, the new case had its ironies and chance mishaps. For five months starting in early 1982, the Ontario Provincial Police had been trying to break up a ring responsible for forging passports and birth certificates. One of the people they were investigating was McQuirter. Undercover OPP constable Gary MacDonald contacted McQuirter under the guise of being a fugitive from the law in need of false papers. According to court testimony, McQuirter explained to MacDonald how he and MacGarry — working out of the Klan headquarters on Springhurst Avenue — were making "use of forged items of identification in order to perpetrate a fraud and forgery involving many, many thousands of dollars on banks

and other financial institutions."[12] McQuirter sold a false passport
and birth certificate to the undercover policeman. (Other forged
documents found by police when they arrested McQuirter
included certified cheques totalling $134,000, credit cards and
bank cards.)*

As their business relationship solidified, McQuirter took
MacDonald into his confidence, telling him about his drug deals
and political plans and even giving MacDonald an honorary life
membership in the Klan. Suddenly, though, the OPP's fraud
investigation turned more serious. On July 28, 1982, McQuirter
was having breakfast with MacDonald in his hotel room at the
downtown Toronto Holiday Inn. "McQuirter started to speak,
stopped, then asked me if I knew people who would do a hit,"
MacDonald testified. "I asked McQuirter if he wanted the person
beat up or killed. McQuirter replied killed." Over his meal of
steak and scrambled eggs, toast and orange juice, McQuirter told
MacDonald how he and Jean MacGarry were planning to kill
Gary MacFarlane with an overdose of pills. A motorcycle gang
offered to dismember the body for $1,000, McQuirter said.

How much would MacDonald's friends charge? he asked.

Probably $2,000, maybe $1,500, MacDonald replied. It would
be no problem to arrange.

Go ahead, said McQuirter, it's well worth $2,000.

McQuirter had several reasons for wanting MacFarlane killed.
MacFarlane was jealous of the relationship that had developed

*McQuirter had been involved in other scams over the years. In various press
interviews, the Klan leader described himself as a businessman, a book
salesman, and the owner of a landscape firm and management consultant
company. The only books McQuirter ever sold were neo-Nazi publications
through a 1978 operation called Victory Books, which folded quickly. If his
management and landscaping firms ever existed, there is no evidence that
McQuirter spent time on them. McQuirter did work briefly as a security
guard at a company warehouse, before he was convicted of theft on the job
and sentenced to 90 days in jail. Late in 1981, Toronto police stopped
McQuirter's car and found what they said was cocaine. He was charged with
possession for the purpose of trafficking, but the charge was dropped when
the product turned out to be a high-caffeine drug which was legal in Canada.
Curiously, though, McQuirter told undercover man MacDonald that he
"buys large quantities of caffeine pills in the United States and makes
approximately $1,000 a month clear." He also told MacDonald that "he was a
money man in the trafficking of cocaine and hashish."[13]

between MacGarry and McQuirter since the latter had moved into their Springhurst Avenue home. MacFarlane had resigned as security chief of the Klan early in the year. Still, McQuirter considered him "crazy and very dangerous" and a liability to the organization, not to mention a risk to his fraud schemes. The Klan boss, MacDonald testified, described Jean MacGarry as his "good friend" and business partner in his forgery ring, and said they both had "a common interest in killing MacFarlane." Remarked MacGarry about her common-law husband's death: "Nobody will really miss him." Added McQuirter: "He's a pain in the ass until the day he dies."

During July and August, the details of the murder plot were finalized. MacDonald introduced McQuirter and MacGarry to a supposed professional contract killer, actually another undercover police officer, William Campbell. The plan was for Campbell to be introduced to MacFarlane as a friend of McQuirter. MacFarlane would be asked to go with Campbell to pick up some drugs; at that point he would be killed. On August 14 the meeting took place. MacFarlane left the house with Campbell as planned, but once outside was told by the policeman of the murder plot. McQuirter and MacGarry were told the killing had been carried out. At eight o'clock that night, McQuirter phoned MacDonald. "How are things?" he asked.

"Good — he's dead," was the reply.

"Excellent," said McQuirter.

Later, McQuirter and MacGarry came to MacDonald's hotel room to inspect some of MacFarlane's personal belongings — a belt buckle, a knife sheath and a lighter — as proof he was dead. They drank beer to toast the killing. "So did he — this is just out of curiousity — did he struggle?" McQuirter asked.

The evidence against McQuirter and MacGarry was overwhelming. Much of their plotting had been taped or videotaped by police. Oddly enough, the authorities did not even know about Armand Siksna's role in the affair until, after McQuirter's arrest, Siksna went to the police and confessed that he took $900 out of his bank account to help pay for the hit man. He also told police that "although he felt it would be an unpleasant job, he would and could have done the job himself" to save the Klan some expense.*

McQuirter was sentenced to eight years for his role in the murder plot, to be served after he completed his two-year sentence for conspiring to overthrow the government of Dominica. Judge O'Driscoll also gave him five years concurrently for conspiring to forge several documents. Siksna was sentenced to a six-year term for bankrolling and encouraging the attempted killing. Jean MacGarry was given a suspended sentence and put on three years probation; she was ordered to stay at the Clarke Institute of Psychiatry for three years or until she is deemed fit to leave. Medical and psychiatric evidence indicated that MacGarry suffered cardiac arrest, malfunctioning kidneys, lupus disease, and bone and brain degeneration.†

McQuirter's jailing put an abrupt halt to his three-year reign as the star on the political stage of Canada's extreme right. In a somewhat bitter post-mortem, Don Andrews, McQuirter's political mentor and sometime rival, said the Klan leader's downfall was the result of his inexperience and his penchant for get-rich-quick schemes. "He was a little too ambitious. He cut corners," said Andrews. McQuirter insisted that his imprisonment did not spell the end of the Canadian Klan. "I don't think the Klan is dead," he said in an interview in the Toronto jail. "It'll take time to reorganize it, but just because I've dropped the ball, there are people out there to carry it."

But the jailing of McQuirter — along with MacGarry, Siksna and Wolfgang Droege, who was still in an American penitentiary — did create an obvious lack of trained leaders and organizers. Admitted Droege in a letter from prison, "Even though we have

*This was not the first time Siksna's loyalty to his Klan chieftain went to extreme lengths. After police found drugs in McQuirter's car in late 1981, his home — the Klan headquarters on Springhurst — was raided. Police found a gun in his safe, and McQuirter was charged with possession of an unregistered weapon. But in court Siksna claimed the gun was his and took the rap for McQuirter. He was fined $200 and forbidden for five years to possess a firearm.

†The planned victim of the murder plot, Gary MacFarlane, also soon ran afoul of the law. In April, 1983, he was charged, along with another woman, with first degree murder in the death of a Richmond Hill man. The man was found in a school yard and had apparently died of massive head injuries.

membership across Canada, our current problem is effective leadership, which means that people will have to fill the vacuum." That vacuum was supposed to be filled by Ann Farmer, the B.C. Klan leader who had succeeded McQuirter as the Klan's national director. Klan headquarters — or, more accurately, its national mailing address — was moved to a New Westminster post office box. But with strongman McQuirter removed from the scene, it did not take long for dissension to appear in the ranks of the Klan. Farmer's appointment came under fire from several quarters. John Gilroy, a Toronto Klan leader during McQuirter's reign, led a split of disgruntled Ontario Klansmen. Called the National Knights of the Ku Klux Klan, Gilroy's new group was headquartered in Oak Ridges, Ontario. "We didn't stay with the Canadian Knights because there were too many of us against having Farmer as Grand Wizard," explained Gilroy, a 39-year-old commercial diver and truck driver, who claimed his Klan had "most of the old Klan here in Ontario with us and quite a few from the other provinces as well." One Klansman he did not impress was Wolfgang Droege, who said, "The Klan in Toronto is falling apart [and] has become virtually ineffective." Another, smaller splinter group was created in B.C., when a provincial organizer named Dan Wray set up a survivalist-oriented Imperial Knights of the Ku Klux Klan, based in rural Aldergrove. From his jail cell, McQuirter tried to make the most out of the three-way split by claiming that the KKK "has now increased threefold, in terms of leadership, enthusiasm and regional diversity." In fact, the Klan stood divided and demoralized.

Ann Farmer insisted her group was "very much larger" than her "miniscule" rivals. Certainly Farmer's group was in the best position to assert itself as the dominant force on the extreme right in Canada. For one thing, the Canadian Knights had the most experienced leaders, including Al Hooper. Farmer herself, though only 26, had a few years of organizing behind her. Her first assignment for the Klan in the late 1970s, even before a distinct Canadian branch of the organization had been set up, was to handle the correspondence which American Klan leader David Duke received from Canadian applicants. She was a founding member of the Canadian KKK and its original membership secretary, eventually becoming one of the chief spokespersons for the B.C. Klan. Rounding out the leadership team would be Wolfgang Droege, Farmer's boyfriend, who moved to Vancouver upon his release from prison in May, 1983.

Farmer's Klan also benefitted from having been given the offical franchise for Canada by a revitalized and united American Klan. Six independent Klan organizations in the U.S. had banded together to form a Confederation of the Klans in Stone Mountain, Georgia, in September, 1982. Don Black, the leader of the Knights of the Ku Klux Klan, with which the Canadian Klan had been affiliated, was elected to a four-year term as Grand Wizard of the confederation. Black was still out on appeal of his three-year sentence for his role in the Dominica plot. James Venable, a 76-year-old leader of another Klan group who traced his family heritage back to founding members of the post-Civil War Klan, was given the honorary title of Imperial Emperor. David Duke, who had handed his Klan organization over to Don Black in order to set up his National Association for the Advancement of White People, addressed the Stone Mountain rally, and it was expected that the NAAWP might affiliate with the confederation. Black called the confederation "the biggest step toward Klan unity in 50 years." The American media estimated that 6,000 people belonged to the new body.* Ann Farmer represented the Canadian Klan at the Georgia rally. Getting the stamp of approval from a large American Klan organization gave Farmer the same organizational, political and financial backing that McQuirter had received from Duke's Klan when the former was trying to establish his Canadian Klan four years earlier. In addition to her Stone Mountain visit, Farmer had spent several weeks in the U.S. as part of a "Leadership Training Program" with Don Black. She toured various Klan regional headquarters and took part in local Klan events across the U.S., visiting New Orleans, Seattle,

---

*The U.S. Klan was still not entirely united. Missing from the rally were Robert Shelton of the United Klans of America and Bill Wilkinson of the militaristic Invisible Empire, Knights of the Ku Klux Klan. These two Klans at their peak accounted for about a third of the entire KKK membership in the States. Wilkinson had been ostracized by other Klans since it was revealed that he had been an FBI informer. In early 1983, his group filed for reorganization under U.S. federal bankruptcy laws.

Denver, Dallas, Birmingham, Milwaukee, Chicago, New York, Washington, Arlington and Philadelphia. She also visited the headquarters of Duke's NAAWP. "During my stay in the United States, I learnt how to organize the Klan on a larger scale than presently exists in Canada," said Farmer. "I gained from the knowledge of Klan leaders who have many years of experience in Klan administration."

Farmer wasted little time in applying her training. Plans were made to resume publication of *The Spokesman.* Its operations were moved to New Westminster, and a promotional letter which carefully described the newspaper as "not primarily a Klan publication," urged KKK supporters "to subscribe to the fastest growing White Nationalist newspaper in the country." Farmer's Klan also began to put out a newsletter, *Canadian KKK Action*, similar to the bulletin McQuirter had produced in 1981. Aside from ads for Klan paraphernalia, a glowing tribute to the imprisoned McQuirter and news of Klan activities, the newsletter presented a new, twenty-point program of the Canadian Knights. This was the first time the Klan had officially formulated a program. Many of the points were the standard calls of the KKK: "a return to the traditional white values on which Canadian society was built;" "a selective immigration policy, which includes the end of non-white immigration;" and the "repatriation" of non-whites "to their country of ethnic origin." The Klan also appealed to a larger conservative constituency by espousing such goals as the restriction of abortion and the expansion of the armed forces. The KKK even threw in some left-sounding positions, pledging "to end the exploitation of Canadian resources by multinational corporations" and to provide "political and economic autonomy to the native Indian and Inuit nations." Farmer claimed the Klan was growing steadily while maintaining a low profile. "Our activities include meetings, the education of members, the dissemination of our ideology to non-members, weapons training and a youth corps," she said. "I am very optimistic about the Klan's future in Canada. I have observed a positive correlation between growth in Klan popularity with an increase in non-white population. Today in B.C., people are becoming more overtly racist because there is a local influx of non-white immigration." Farmer was not completely off the mark. While she was busy reorganizing her troops there had been an increase in local racial incidents. A Richmond house occupied by East Indians was gutted by an arsonist's fire; another East Indian home was burned in Surrey; and a two-metre wooden cross was set on fire in front of a Sikh Temple in Vancouver. Charan Gill, leader of the B.C. Organization to Fight Racism, described the Vancouver area's racial climate as "deteriorating".

The Stone Mountain unity rally also inspired the Canadian Klan to seek its own alliances with other white supremacist forces. Five days after the Georgia meeting, Farmer and Hooper met with Don Andrews, leader of the Nationalist Party of Canada, to discuss ways of working together. Andrews still scorned the Klan's composition and tactics: "The future belongs to white nationalists of a more intellectual order. We're not interested in flash-in-the-pan media publicity stuff," he said. Still, he was prepared to work with Farmer and Hooper, suggesting "joint statements, tactical alliances, but no union." Farmer talked about "co-operation and dialogue amongst white nationalists. . . not an amalgamation of the various groups into a single unit." From his Toronto jail cell, former Klan leader McQuirter also promoted common action. "I've been writing a lot of letters, proposing and pushing unity," said McQuirter. He still clung to his plans to enter the mainstream political arena: "I'm looking for a political party as a vehicle." He said a federal political party of the extreme right could find protection under the law. "We can be exempt from the hate law if we're proposing certain political positions. No one could stop a formal political party." Wolfgang Droege shared McQuirter's desire for unity and political action. Before he returned to British Columbia, Droege wrote from prison that there was "a cohesive bond and a potential unity" on the extreme right in Canada and pledged "to co-operate with both the Klan and the Nationalist Party." Droege also talked of building "an effective political force through the normal, legal political process."

By mid-1983, Farmer's Klan had markedly improved its organization, propaganda and public activities. A second, eight-page Klan newsletter, *KKK Action*, — the largest one ever produced — featured a detailed article on "racial differences in the brain" of blacks and whites and a long shopping list of Klan books, tapes and even video cassettes. "The Klan is continuing to grow in size and to expand its level of activities throughout Canada," the bulletin boasted. It noted that William Lau Richardson, McQuirter's intelligence chief, had been named a "Great Titan" in Farmer's Klan and had "organized a membership drive" in Toronto. A certain R. Bradford was congratulated for his appointment as Great Titan, or organizer, for the Prince George area in B.C. The Klan also began to renew its public activities. In Vancouver, it paraded in front of bookstores, handing out anti-immigrant pamphlets and the latest issue of *The Spokesman*. In Alberta, the so-called Keegstra affair gave the Klan and its ideology a much-needed boost. James Keegstra was the elected mayor of the small town of Eckville and a teacher at the local school. For fourteen years, he taught his Grade 9 and 12 students that the Holocaust was a myth and that there was a world-wide Jewish conspiracy. Many students believed him and even wrote essays on the subject. Keegstra used literature he had obtained from an Ontario direct mail distributor of right-wing material named Ron Gostick, who had connections with the Western Guard crowd of the 1970s. Keegstra was fired as a teacher at the end of 1982, but his case raised a national scandal when he made a highly-publicized judicial appeal to regain his job. Judge Elizabeth McFayden dismissed his appeal in April, 1983, but it was clear that Keegstra's anti-semitic views were widely held, or at least tolerated. No less than 96 of the 116 students in the Eckville school where he taught signed a petition calling for Keegstra's reinstatement. Keegstra also retained his post as mayor; a bid to oust him in a non-confidence motion was defeated by a 4-2 city council vote. Keegstra was suspended temporarily from the Alberta branch of the federal Social Credit Party, of which he was vice-president, by a narrow executive vote of four to three. But shortly after that he and two other executive members of the party who supported him were reinstated at a general meeting of Alberta party members. Martin Hattersley, leader of the federal party, resigned after Keegstra's reinstatement, warning that "we cannot be a successor to the Nazi party of Germany." Kenneth Sweigard, the man elected as interim national leader of the Social Credit Party, described Keegstra as "a fine Christian gentleman."* Meanwhile, in Edmonton, the Ku Klux Klan was quick to jump on the Keegstra case in order to fan its own flames. Posters appeared, advertising an "Aryan World Congress" in Idaho and featured a pair of white knights and a call for a "new crusade".

By August, with Droege replacing Farmer as leader, the Klan was again making itself heard in British Columbia. The RCMP asked police forces throughout the province to update information on Klan operations, and the attorney general's office said the upsurge in Klan activity warranted a new probe. One police estimate put the KKK's B.C. membership at 150.[14] The BCOFR revealed that six Klansmen had recently returned from the U.S. where they had received training in recruitment techniques. At the same time, two houses occupied by members of racial minorities were firebombed.

This renewal of Klan activity in Vancouver, Edmonton and Toronto, coupled with plans by Droege and others for political action and future right-wing unity, was disturbing. However much government and police authorities claimed that they had broken up the Klan by sending some of its leaders to jail, the Klan remained basically intact — smaller, perhaps, but not dead. The fact was that most of the arrests and jailings of Canadian Klansmen had been carried out not on the basis of their racial activities or violations of civil rights legislation as part of the Klan organization, but on criminal activities arising from their individual greed. Law enforcement agencies had little to be proud of when it came to curbing the Klan. McQuirter's arrest in the Dominica affair came as a spinoff of investigations and arrests made in the United States, not Canada. His arrest and jailing over the attempted murder of MacFarlane came about as an

---

*This was not the first example of the Social Credit party flirting with right-wing racial extremism. In February, 1972, Jack Morrison, head of the Ontario Social Credit party, was one of the Canadian participants — along with Canadian Klansmen Jacob Prins and other Toronto fascists — at a Klan banquet in Michigan (see page 86). A few months later, at a Western Guard rally in Toronto where the Klan's presence in Canada was announced (see page 87), Guard speaker Paul Fromm told the crowd of 130 that the Ontario Social Credit party was the tool to use to capture power in the province.

unexpected twist in an OPP investigation of a fraud scheme, not an investigation of the Klan's political activities.

What this meant was that Farmer, Hooper, Andrews and Droege were more or less free to pursue their peculiar and dangerous brand of politics without fear of prosecution under the law.

"The promise of the federal and provincial governments remains largely unfulfilled."
— The McAlpine Report

13. Legal loopholes

WITHSTANDING PUBLIC OUTCRY AND demonstrations, leadership changes and internal splits, botched coup plots and murders, the Canadian Klan was still functioning. Its survival raised the obvious question: why had the authorities done so little to curb the KKK? Of course, if the war against racism and the Klan could be won through fine speeches alone, provincial and federal politicians would be decorated with medals. In February, 1981, federal and provincial ministers responsible for human rights met in Ottawa. They issued this statement:

> Ministers unanimously endorsed a resolution calling upon all Canadians to reject unequivocally the racist principles articulated by persons associated with organizations such as the Ku Klux Klan. Further, Ministers underscored the fact that theories of white supremacy and racial superiority are scientifically false, morally condemnable, socially unjust and dangerous, and have no place in Canadian society.

The ministers also pledged to take the necessary legal action against the Klan:

> Ministers undertook to be vigilant with regard to all manifestations of racism, and will effectively enforce the provisions of the criminal law and anti-discrimination

legislation to counter those manifestations whether they emanate from the Ku Klux Klan or any such group.

It would take more than ringing declarations to beat back the Klan. As the McAlpine report put it, "the promise of the federal and provincial governments remains largely unfulfilled. The [federal] Minister of Justice has not seen fit to introduce amendments to the Criminal Code of Canada to declare it an offence punishable by law to disseminate ideas based on racial superiority, nor to declare illegal and prohibit organizations which promote and incite racial discrimination."[1]

The federal House of Commons resolution against the Klan had called for the use of the "full force of the law," and the ministers' conference on human rights pledged their governments to "effectively enforce the provisions of the criminal law and anti-discrimination legislation." Unfortunately, the "full force" of both the Criminal Code and provincial anti-discrimination laws has little punch.* They contain legal loopholes large enough to drive a burning cross through; and the interpretation of these laws by politicians and the courts has been so loose as to be ineffectual against the Klan.

The only part of the Criminal Code of Canada as it presently is written which can be used directly against the Klan is Section 281, concerning hate literature. Subsections (1) and (2) of 281.2 make it an indictable offense, punishable by up to two years' imprisonment, for "everyone who by communicating statements in any public place, incites hatred against any identifiable group where such incitement is likely to lead to a breach of the peace" or for "everyone who by communicating statements, other than in private conversation, wilfully promotes hatred against any identifiable group." This section of the law was added in 1970, a watered-down version of a proposal by a Special Committee on Hate Propaganda which had studied the issue since 1965. Lawyer McAlpine noted in his study on the Klan and the law that "Parliament did not enact the full recommendations of the Committee. The communication of statements that wilfully promote contempt, as distinct from hatred, were excluded...In

---

*See Appendix for the full text of the relevant laws and codes.

practical terms, the offensive statements of the Klan to date appear immune from the criminal law."

There are several reasons why Section 281.2 is a cumbersome weapon against racism. The law talks about a prospective guilty party as "everyone", thereby apparently excluding prosecutions of groups or organizations. When the furor over Klan distribution of hate literature in public schools erupted in the fall of 1980, Ontario attorney general Roy McMurtry stated that only if the individuals giving out the literature are identified could charges be laid. He said the organization as such cannot be charged unless it can be shown to be a legal entity with officers or directors. McMurtry let the Klan off the hook this way:

> "But the very fact that somebody puts the name Ku Klux Klan on the letterhead [means] there's nobody to charge unless you have an individual who you can prove is responsible for printing or distributing the material. So you need a live body, in other words."[2]

The law also states that the hatred must be "wilfully promoted"; section 3 of the law in fact allows the accused to use the defence that his or her statements "were relevant to any subject of public interest." This "wilfully" caveat of the law has been ably exploited by the Klan. *The Spokesman* publishes a disclaimer in every issue stating that it "does not wilfully promote hatred against any identifiable group... *The Statesman* believes all statements made on its pages to be true with respect to any that would be prosecutable under Section 281.2 of the Criminal Code." McQuirter himself has been a beneficiary of this loophole. Back in 1978, police seized eleven boxes of office supplies, pamphlets and white supremacist material from the apartment of Armand Siksna, which they had entered to search for a stolen typewriter. McQuirter and Siksna at the time were both members of the Western Guard. Siksna and McQuirter, whose membership card in the KKK was also found in the raid, were charged with two counts of conspiring to distribute hate literature. The racist literature which the two men admitted to owning included pamphlets comparing blacks to apes, and stickers reading "Jews are parasites". The case finally came to trial in March, 1980. Said McQuirter in his defense: "I don't hate any groups, I don't feel any hatred toward Jews or blacks." The judge ruled that there was no evidence of a conspiracy between the two men to distribute the literature, saying that the material was given only to people "of similar political persuasion" and therefore not likely to incite hatred against an identifiable group. He made explicit reference to the importance of the word "wilfully" in the hate propaganda law.[3] McQuirter and Siksna were acquitted.

There are other weaknesses in the law as well. It requires an "identifiable group" to be a victim, rather than making the promotion of race hatred in general illegal; the dissemination of hate propaganda must be in a "public place" and there must also be the likelihood that there will be a "breach of the peace." Finally, subsection 6 specifies that the consent of the attorney general is required before any proceedings may begin. Few other sections of the Criminal Code have this requirement. Presumably, its purpose is to prevent frivolous prosecution and thus protect freedom of speech; in effect, given the reluctance of attorneys general to move against racist groups, this clause has given organizations like the Klan a freer hand.

At an April, 1982 federal government-sponsored symposium on race relations and the law held in Vancouver, lawyer Israel Ludwig of Winnipeg underlined the failings of Section 281. Canada, he noted, "has gained a reputation as being one of the world's capitals for distribution of hate literature. Not only has hate literature been circulated in Canada, but this country is one of the largest mailing centres of hate literature to the rest of the world."[*] In the twelve years since this section was introduced in the Criminal Code, "convictions are few and the number of prosecutions have been minimal," Ludwig said. Indeed, the two

---

*When West German police raided homes and seized literature in March, 1981, during the biggest post-war crackdown on that country's neo-Nazis since the war, they identified Ernst Zundel of Toronto as one of the main sources of the anti-semitic pamphlets and leaflets. Zundel, owner of Great Ideas Advertising and Samisdat Publishing, said he mailed literature from his Toronto office to 45,000 people worldwide. Klan chieftain McQuirter would refer reporters to Zundel as a good source for information to back up the KKK's race theories. Ontario attorney general McMurtry, responding in June, 1983, to a question in the Ontario legislature, declared that authorities are monitoring Zundel's activities and had "a reasonable chance of successful prosecution of Mr. Zundel." But he cautioned that aspects of the Criminal Code were inadequate and that prosecution was not possible in all cases.

best known cases of the application of Section 281 were not aimed
at eliminating the race hatred of groups like the Klan. In one case,
a group of young people were charged after distributing literature
at a Shriners' parade in Toronto which said "Yankee go home."
The charge was eventually dropped. In 1977, two men were
charged with promoting race hatred against French Canadians in
Ontario's Essex County through the distribution of handbills.
Oddly enough, the two charged were Franco-Ontarians
themselves who had written an anonymous anti-French leaflet
with the hope of rekindling interest among their fellow
francophones in a fight for a French-language school in the area.
They were convicted, but a higher court overturned the verdict.
What was significant was that the appeal judge based his
argument on the fact that while the two Franco-Ontarians were
reckless they did not "intentionally promote hatred." This decision
set an important judicial precedent in interpretation of Section
281, strengthening the "wilfully" caveat and obliging the
prosecution to prove beyond a reasonable doubt that the accused
specifically intended to promote hatred. The judge who in 1980
acquitted McQuirter and Siksna of charges under the hate
literature section of the Criminal Code made direct reference to
the precedent set by the Franco-Ontarian ruling when he handed
down his decision.

The inability or unwillingness of the political and judiciary
system to use the hate literature law against the Klan is all the
more disturbing considering the Klansmen's open admission of
guilt at times. Klan leader McQuirter obviously knew he was
spreading hate propaganda, but was equally sure he could get
away with it. In one interview, he went out of his way to state
that he was contravening the hate literature laws with impunity:
"I never said we'd never break *any* laws, just those concerning
violence. The reason I say that is because we have hate laws. So I
couldn't say that I will knowingly not break the law."[4]

Human rights legislation in the country, as distinct from the
criminal law, is equally ineffective against the Klan. For example,
the B.C. Human Rights Code, like most provincial codes,
prohibits discrimination in public facilities, housing, and
employment on the basis of race, religion or color. But the Klan

cannot be accused of these offences because the KKK itself does not deny lodging or jobs to non-whites. The only section of the B.C. Code which affords a possible action against the Klan is Section 2 which prohibits the "display before the public" of a "notice, sign, symbol, emblem or other representation indicating discrimination." McAlpine pointed out that this section does not encompass racist statements made in the written or electronic media. Any broad interpretation of the code is also undermined by a "notwithstanding" caveat which immediately follows the section quoted above and guarantees that "a person may . . . freely express his opinions on a subject." Wrote McAlpine: "My conclusion is that there is no case in law against the Klan under the Human Rights Code of British Columbia as currently drafted."

The failure of existing criminal and civil law and the interpretations of that law by authorities were driven home forcefully to B.C. opponents of the Klan. Following the Klan's appearance in the province in the fall of 1980 and some particularly offensive statements against blacks made by McQuirter on television, separate complaints were filed against the Klan by leaders of two black community groups — one under the hate section of the Criminal Code and another under the B.C. Human Rights Code. Both actions failed. As McAlpine concluded: "It soon became evident to these groups that the door to the court room was closed, and that access to a Human Rights Commission board of inquiry was precluded."[5]

Faced with public skepticism of existing legislation and criticism of their unwillingness to prosecute, governments were obliged at least to give the appearance of doing something. In June, 1981, B.C. attorney general Allan Williams introduced a Civil Rights Protection Act. In Ontario, a beleaguered McMurtry was quick to hail the B.C. example and suggested that maybe such a law should be in the Criminal Code. He promised to raise the matter with other provincial ministers and with federal cabinet ministers.

Just how good was this law, presumably the best that the governments have been able to come up with to deal with the Ku Klux Klan? The act prohibits the promotion of contempt or doctrines of superiority based on race, color, ethnic origin or religion. It allows civil action against an individual or organization that interferes with a person's civil rights by promoting racial hatred. It also permits prosecution under summary conviction and provides maximum fines of $2,000 for individuals or $10,000 for a group or a corporation. "It gives people a chance to fight their case in the courts rather than in the streets," said NDP MLA Emery Barnes, who is black and who lobbied hard for the law. "The bill is directed at what the Klan is doing — being violent, abusing justice and so on, and is out to punish the acts they commit."

But other people involved in fighting the Klan were dubious about the new law. "It is an ineffectual and legally cumbersome piece of legislation that will not provide any remedies for people who have suffered attacks of racism," said Vancouver lawyer Stuart Rush of the B.C. Organization to Fight Racism. "It is highly unlikely that anybody will be convicted of any offense under it. To prove a civil wrong under the act is going to be about as hard as proving the earth is flat."

The skepticism of Rush and the BCOFR was based on several weaknesses in the law. To bring a suit against an organization like the Klan, it is necessary to prove that the Klan has committed what the law defines as a prohibited act:

> Any conduct or communication by a person that has as its purpose interference with the civil rights of a person or class of persons by promoting:
> (a) hatred or contempt of a person or class of persons; or
> (b) superiority or inferiority of a person or class of persons in comparison with another or others,
> on the basis of colour, race, religion, ethnic origin or place of origin.

The passage "has as its purpose interference with the civil rights of a person" is what lawyer Rush called "the Achilles' heel of the act." It means that it has to be shown in court not that the Klan said or did something racist against a group or individual, but that its *purpose* was to interfere with the rights of those people (similar to Section 281's caveat of "wilfully"). It is very difficult in law to show purpose. Direct evidence is out, because no racist will say that his or her words or deeds are aimed at anything but the betterment of mankind ("We're not anti-anybody, we're just pro-white," was McQuirter's standard refrain). "It will be well-nigh impossible to prove that any racist's comments are for the purpose of interfering with another's civil rights," complained Rush. He cited the example of a cross burning ceremony in B.C. where new Klan members took an oath thanking God for the "superior intelligence" of whites.* Rush pointed out that the words clearly express contempt and inferiority of a class of persons, but it can't be proven that their purpose was to interfere with somebody's civil rights.

The law had other weaknesses. The "civil rights" of the victim are not defined, making it more difficult to prove their rights are being infringed upon. The word "promoting" in the law also suggests something more than simply stating or expressing a racist comment; it implies an element of repetition or salesmanship. A Klan leader who appears on television to denigrate blacks can claim he is only stating his opinion, not actively promoting hate. Critics of the law also point out that the cost and complexity of bringing forth a legal suit would deter many. The attorney general of the province could, of course, intervene himself and lay a charge of racism against the KKK, but the government's past reluctance to move against the Klan gives little hope the authorities would move to prosecute under the new act.

The Civil Rights Protection Act does not prevent the Klan or any other racist organization from having access to the public media, organizing and holding meetings, publishing and circulating their literature, advertising or otherwise promoting their ideas, recruiting and organizing their members and possessing or owning weapons. "The situation is still fairly explosive in B.C.," says BCOFR leader Charan Gill. "The KKK is still distributing its leaflets. They are coming more and more out into the open. So obviously the Civil Rights Protection Act didn't do a good job of stopping the Klan from pushing their hate literature in our schools, our communities and in the streets." Within three months after its implementation, the CRPA had proven itself inadequate. In one case, police arrived at the scene of

*See page 141.

a Klan cross burning while Klansmen were chanting white supremacist slogans. Two rifles and a shotgun were seized, but no charges under the new law were laid. Nor were charges laid when Klan material was inserted into literature given to the public at a multicultural booth at the Pacific National Exhibition. The Klan itself was openly contemptuous of the law. When B.C. KKK spokesperson Ann Farmer suggested in February, 1982, that the organization was going to beef up its presence in Vancouver, she pointedly remarked that the new civil rights act could not prevent the KKK from setting up its office in B.C.

The way the new law was being (or rather not being) applied, its content, and the manner in which it was drafted suggest it may have been much more a public relations exercise than a serious attempt to deal with the threat of the Klan. McAlpine, who had been commissioned to study the Klan and the effectiveness of existing legislation on racism, proposed much tougher laws. He suggested legislation to ensure that no person or group be allowed to use any statement, notice, sign, symbol or other representation that is likely to expose people to hatred, contempt or discrimination or that is based on the idea of racial superiority, and that these regulations by accompanied by injunctive and criminal sanctions for failure to comply. "The government could have produced substantially better and stronger protection for victims of racism in the legislation had they allowed public discussion of the McAlpine document during the process of drafting the legislation," commented Stuart Rush. Instead, the act was produced hurriedly in an atmosphere where the authorities were coming under increasing fire for doing nothing about the Klan. "The act is an attempt by the provincial government to appease those who are raising the demand for government action to ban the Klan's activities," concluded Rush. "It will not work. It's completely wrong to say that the issue of the Klan has been dealt with."

Rush, the BCOFR and other anti-racism activists argue that, in the face of the current legal loopholes which the Klan exploits, one of the most effective weapons would be to ban the Klan itself. Debate over this issue has been stormy ever since the hooded empire arrived in Canada. Few people, even among those opposed to banning the Klan, would argue that the KKK is not a distasteful and revolting organization. But opponents of a ban on the Klan insist that the Klan has not yet broken any laws and that outlawing it would set a dangerous precedent for freedom of speech in Canada. The Toronto *Star* summed up these arguments in a series of editorials. "The Klan has a long and bloody history of terrorism, brutality and murder in the U.S.," the newspaper admitted. "It is, however, a presence that must be tolerated — though by absolutely no means encouraged — as long as it remains within the law."[6] In another editorial, the *Star* elaborated:

> To use the force of law to stifle free speech which does not actually run afoul of the prohibition against disseminating hate, no matter how repulsive that speech may be, would merely accomplish what the Klan itself has set out to do: To weaken the fabric of Canadian democracy.[7]*

The British Columbia Civil Liberties Association echoed these arguments when it opposed attempts to prohibit the licensing of the Klan in Vancouver. "Our group is opposed to disallowing any group, although we are, of course, appalled at their [the KKK's] ideas," said an association spokesperson. Much the same reasoning was invoked by B.C. attorney general Williams and his Ontario counterpart McMurtry to explain their reluctance to move against the Klan. "They will be watched, but until they break the law there is nothing we can do," McMurtry said.

Similar positions are held by some within the anti-Klan movement itself, who add that the demand to ban the Klan could be used as a pretext by government to crack down on progressive and left-wing groups. This point of view was most clearly elaborated in British Columbia, where the provincial New Democratic Party and the B.C. Federation of Labour declined to support the BCOFR's ban-the-Klan campaign. "No matter how distasteful and hateful the Klan may be," Tom Fawkes wrote in a

---

*There is a curious double standard at work here. For instance, when Jean-Claude Parrot, leader of the Canadian Union of Postal Workers, was sent to jail in 1979 for advising his striking members to defy a back-to-work order, no cries were ushered by the *Star* defending his freedom of speech. But when the Klan urges its members to arm and prepare for race war, editorials insist it must be tolerated in the name of freedom of speech.

special B.C. Federation of Labour pamphlet on the Klan, "they are not such a threat that they should be responsible for altering the cornerstone of our basic freedoms."[8] Calling a ban on the Klan an "easy solution" and a "tempting one", Fawkes argues that outlawing the KKK would make it all too easy for a government to ban other groups it didn't like:

> The Klan has every right to exist and function in our community as labor does; that is the way our system works and — if it is to continue to work — it must work equally for all.

Fawke's arguments were repeated in a four-page criticism of the BCOFR campaign which appeared in the *Democrat*, the newspaper of the B.C. NDP. *Democrat* editor Stephen Brewer pointed out that legislation passed in the United States in the late 1960s made it a federal crime to cross state lines to enter into a conspiracy to commit illegal acts. The law was supposedly intended to "get" the KKK and other racist groups, but has been used by law enforcement agencies mainly to stop anti-Vietnam war activists. Brewer concluded that "education and elections are the only answer acceptable to New Democrats," and urged "vigorous criminal prosecution" of any Klan member who broke the law.

> But, distasteful as it is, defend the right of the inciters to incite, because it is impossible to defend *our* right to preach social democracy without defending *their* right to preach their message of hate.
> Their right to swing their arms ends when their fist reaches our noses . . . but not before.[9]

On the other hand, proponents of a ban on the Klan argued that to hold off from prosecuting the Klan "until they break the law" (as McMurtry put it) or until "their fist reaches our noses" (as the NDP said) was to ignore reality in favor of technicality. If a group of ex-bank robbers, upon their release from jail, set up an organization to encourage and aid bank robberies, would the authorities hesitate to crack down on them? The Klan is very similar — an organization led by and composed of many people who have already been convicted of racially-motivated, at times violent, crimes; an organization devoted to encouraging and aiding the growth of racism. McMurtry himself noted that the Canadian KKK is "a highly dangerous, despicable criminal group of individuals with a treacherous, destructive history." He admitted that Canadian Klansmen were not exactly virgins when it came to law-breaking; he noted the Klan is made up of people who "are basically an outgrowth of the Western Guard, many of whom engaged in criminal activity." Every single top leader of the Klan in Ontario — McQuirter, Droege, Prins, MacFarlane, Richardson, Siksna — had previous criminal charges or convictions. Several Klan members were arrested in 1981 for breaking a public mischief law; several other Klan members were arrested in Canada, the U.S. and Dominica for the attempted coup. The fact that no Klan member has been formally charged with violating the hate propaganda sections of the Criminal Code — despite the inflammatory contents of Klan pamphlets, newspapers and media comments — reflects more on the inadequacies of the law than on the virtues of the Ku Klux Klan. The authorities' reluctance to prosecute the Klan should not be interpreted to mean that the KKK has honored and respected Canadian law, much less public morality and human rights. Why, say observers of the Klan's long history of law-breaking and violence, should we offer them our noses to be bloodied without taking sensible precautions? If you know someone is going to swing their fist at you — because they have already beaten up many of your friends — doesn't it make sense to stop them before they hurt you too?

What about the argument that banning the Klan would infringe upon freedom of speech? This is a more complicated matter, over which civil rights activists are themselves divided. "There is a split," acknowledged Lawrence Greenspon, former president of the Civil Liberties Association in Ottawa. He notes that the American Civil Liberties Union and other groups defend the rights of Nazis and the Klan. "But our association took the position that there is no such thing as absolute freedom of speech. With every freedom, there is a limit. The limit is dictated when one group preaches the destruction or hate of other groups or persons in society." Greenspon does not see "any difficulty in putting limits on freedom of speech, or freedom of association, where a group is preaching the elimination of other groups, if they go against the law," though he prefers the use of existing laws against the Klan rather than a specific legislation against the organization.

Carol Tator, president of the Toronto-based Urban Alliance on Race Relations, has no qualms about the need for a ban on the Klan. "I feel that it is very important the government acts to eliminate the existence of a group which has as its first and foremost principle the incitement of violence against racial and ethnic groups," she says. "However the Klan dresses itself up, it still stands for what they have done for a hundred years; they have a long history of incitement to violence. By allowing the group to exist, we are giving tacit approval to what they stand for."

Tator sympathizes with those who hesitate to ban the Klan. "I'm a civil libertarian and I understand the civil liberties argument. Freedom of speech is important and there is a serious and delicate balance between the rights of an individual and society. But I don't think this is a question of freedom of speech. There are certain standards that a society has to have.* The act of racial hatred presents a threat to society and certain groups. You have to weigh freedom of speech and the right of people to be free from racial harassment."

The problem with the NDP's defence of "the right of the inciters to incite," say its critics, is that this means protecting the right of the Klan to deny the rights of a large number of Canadians. The Klan is not merely a vocal political group but, as the BCOFR puts it, an organization "whose sole platform is to deny the basic democratic rights to all ethnic, cultural and national minorities." There is a basic contradiction between the rights of blacks, Jews, Catholics, immigrants and others targetted by the Klan, and the "right" of a tiny minority to carry out violent acts against these people. The BCOFR, in a rejoinder to the NDP's criticism of its "Ban the Klan" campaign, stated:

---

*There are, for example, at least fifteen sections of the Criminal Code which infringe on "freedom of speech" when it comes to inciting mutiny, publishing obscene materials, causing a disturbance, or engaging in libel.

Censorship and restraint exist, and must exist, in many forms without thereby eroding the basis of democratic society. To defend the democratic rights of people it is sometimes necessary to deny these rights to those who are engaged in abusing and destroying them.[10]

The same point had been made a decade earlier by the federal government-created committee on hate propaganda. The committee's report noted that "in our public discussion and settled practice, there is very little support for individual freedom as an absolute right...there is a strong presumption in favour of freedom of expression...But this presumption can be rebutted by showing that certain kinds of expression in words or writing will, in certain circumstances, imperil seriously vital community interests." The report also suggested that restricting the literature distributed by racists would hardly hamper free speech since the material distributed is so "abusive, insulting, scurrilous [it] could not in any sense be classed as sincere, honest discussion contributing to legitimate debate..."[11]

The BCOFR and others advocating banning the Klan acknowledge that such a law could be used to attack progressive organizations. But they argue that history shows governments do not need an excuse to crack down on progressive or left-wing movements; in 1918, the federal government banned thirteen radical trade unions and foreign workers' associations; in 1931, the state outlawed the Communist Party. The question is not whether governments will again try to suppress progressive groups, but how these organizations can protect themselves from repression. The BCOFR argues that the strongest protection lies in opposing, not defending, the rights of the Klan:

> The state and the government always have the power to use repressive measures and to do so whenever it suits their purpose. The only adequate defence of democratic rights is resolute opposition of fascistic forces, not a defense of their rights. The best defence...is surely the trust of the Canadian people and not [the] championing of the rights of the Ku Klux Klan.[12]

It has been proposed that any new anti-racist law make illegal the promotion of race hatred and violence and the existence of groups based on racial superiority. Lawyer Ludwig calls for legislation that strikes out at racist activity rather than a specifically named group. "With such a definition, the moment any group commenced practising any racist activity a prosecution could be levelled at all members of that group," he said. Without such a definition, the Klan could simply change its name and operate with impunity.

Since the second world war, the protection of minority rights from genocidal and hate policies has become an accepted principle of international justice. Several countries that were occupied by the Nazi forces during the war have laws which make fascist groups illegal. Canada is also a signatory to many international treaties which gives it the legal basis to act against the Klan, including:

• **The United Nations Convention Against Genocide** (1948), the most widely ratified convention in the world. Genocide, the convention says, "is a crime under international law" which can include acts besides physical massacre. Genocide is also defined as the "intent to destroy, in whole or in part, a national, ethnical or religious group" by "causing bodily or mental harm to members of the group." Genocide can also mean "deliberately inflicting on the group conditions of life calculated to bring about its physical destruction" (such as the Klan's call for the massive deportation of all non-whites). Article III of the U.N. convention stipulates there should be punishment for the actual act of genocide but also for "direct and public incitement" of the hatred and destruction of a particular group.

• **The International Convention on the Elimination of All Forms of Racial Discrimination** (1965). Article 4 states that signatories "shall declare illegal and prohibit organizations, and also organized and all other propaganda activities, which promote and incite racial discrimination, and shall recognize participation in such organizations or activities as an offence punishable by law."

• **The International Covenant on Civil and Political Rights** (1966). The covenant enshrines freedom of speech, but notes that "it may be subject to certain restrictions" necessary "for respect of the rights and reputations of others . . ." The covenant adds that "the law shall prohibit any discrimination and guarantee to all

persons equal and effective protection against discrimination."
• **The Declaration of Race and Racial Prejudice (1978).**
Subsection 2 of the declaration states that governments should take all appropriate steps "to prevent, prohibit and eradicate racism, racist propaganda...."[13]

Ottawa could move against the Klan by adding to the Criminal Code a ban on groups and individuals carrying out the kind of activities the Klan has promoted; and by cleaning up the wording of Section 281, concerning hate literature, so it is enforcable. CRTC regulations which forbid radio and television from broadcasting "abusive comment" on races could be more vigorously enforced to deny Klan leaders access to the media. Similarly, access to the mail system and the pubic telephone network by the Klan and similar groups could be restricted. Provincial and municipal governments, for their part, could toughen existing human rights codes or bring in other legislation which would make it difficult for groups like the Klan to function.

Measures to deal with racism are not likely to be instituted without tremendous public pressure. Even when some reforms have been implemented, that pressure has to be sustained, for the authorities have displayed an amazing leniency when it comes to applying those anti-hate laws already on the books. Popular vigilance is all the more important since racism, as historical experience has shown, cannot be fought only or even principally with laws. Racism, after all, is not a legal problem, but a much deeper political, social and economic one. It has to be tackled in a much wider way. As the BCOFR put it, " 'Ban the Klan' should not only mean a *legal* ban. It also means creating the necessary popular conditions which would make it impossible for the Klan to acquire any effectiveness in its activities. We should impose a *people's ban* on the KKK." Widespread education, mass actions and public outcry should be used to silence groups like the Klan, says the BCOFR. "Every time the Klan raises one head, there should be a thousand to match it. Every time the Klan raises its voice, a thousand people's protests and indignation should be able to drown it."

*"Ignoring or laughing at the Klan is the best
way of furthering their aims."*
— Toronto Board of Education

Conclusion: A deeper sore

THREE YEARS AFTER IT burst onto the public scene in 1980, the
modern Canadian Ku Klux Klan may have been somewhat
divided and partly demoralized — but it was far from dead.
Skeptics, of course, could point a righteous finger south of the
border and console themselves with the fact that the Canadian
Klan had never been an imposing menace on the same scale as its
American namesake. True, Canada's Klan is much too small
numerically and too marginal politically to wield the kind of clout
enjoyed by the American KKK. Still, the modern Canadian Klan
was and is vocal and active enough to put society — its
institutions and its values — to the test. Some players in our
society are failing the test miserably.

Governments at all levels, with the exception of a few city
councils, have refused and continue to refuse to confront the
Klan's racism in any serious or systematic fashion. The parallel
between their negligence in the 1920s and in the 1980s is striking:
in both periods we see governments hiding behind narrow
interpretations of the law. In the 1920s, premier Brownlee of
Alberta declared: "If the KKK or any other organization observes
the laws of the land...it will not be molested." In 1980, Ontario
attorney general Roy McMurtry reiterated: "They will be
watched, but until they break the law, there is nothing we can

do." For Canada's political leaders, countering racism has never been a high priority. This is predictable, if only because government policies themselves — whether dealing with immigration, civil service hiring or the settlement of native land claims — are often tainted with racism. When governments do move on the racism issue, it often seems they are more concerned with the appearance of doing something rather than actually solving a problem. The highly-touted British Columbia Civil Rights Protection Act, for example, was essentially an effort to placate a burgeoning anti-Klan movement in the province; as a judicial impediment to the KKK and racism in general it has been a lamentable failure. Similarly, on the federal scene, the establishment of a special parliamentary committee on racism appears to be more smoke than substance. Amidst much fanfare in May, 1983, James Fleming, then multiculturalism minister, told a national press conference that there was an "urgent need" for such an all-party inquiry to tour the country. Fleming stated that 8 to 11 per cent of Canadians were "hardcore bigots" and that racial intolerance was increasing in part because of "hard economic times." He based his statements on government-commissioned studies in eleven Canadian cities. While some minority leaders were enthusiastic about an inquiry that could sensitize Canadians to the problems of racism, others felt the priorities in fighting racism lay elsewhere. Waheed Malik, author of Ottawa's survey on racism in Montreal, said the money for an inquiry might be better spent on local community groups directly involved in countering racism or protecting minority rights. Added Donald Dutton, the University of British Columbia psychology professor who co-ordinated the eleven regional studies which included Malik's: "I'm not sure if there is anything more we can learn about racism. We know it is there. It has always been there. It may be better to inject that money at the grass roots." Civil rights lawyer Charles Roach called on Ottawa instead to enforce and improve anti-racism laws and affirmative action programs. Unfortunately, Fleming hinted that the inquiry would not necessarily lead to major legislative reforms but instead — like an earlier committee on the handicapped — the racism probe "would be an exercise in public exchange and education." Ironically, Fleming said the proposal for such a committee stemmed mainly from the government-sponsored seminar on racism in the law held in Vancouver in 1982. But several keynote speakers at that seminar had also called for major legal reform and tougher laws — not simply declarations and words from ministers — to deal with the Ku Klux Klan, hate literature and racial discrimination.* Whether these badly needed changes will come out from the special parliamentary inquiry into racism remains an open question.

Perhaps the most glaring example of government insensitivity to the problems of racism came in July, 1983, when British Columbia's newly re-elected Social Credit government abolished the provincial Human Rights Commission. Bill 27 — part of a sweeping budget reform of the Bill Bennett administration — also eliminated the Human Rights Board of the provincial labor department. The Bill loosened the human rights act and replaced the Human Rights Commission with a five-member council appointed by cabinet. The Bennett government promptly fired all three members of the Human Rights Commission and Hanne Jensen, the director of the human rights branch of the labor ministry. The measures were widely condemned by provincial, national and even international organizations concerned with civil and human rights. "I'm scared for the state of affairs in this province," said Jensen. "There's no system in place for people to exercise their rights." Concluded Charan Gill of the BCOFR: "The government has trivialized human rights and sent a message to minorities saying their rights are not a priority."

While governments fail to take action against the Klan and racism, law enforcement agencies are equally unwilling or unable to act. Various police forces play a dubious role in countering the Klan and its fellow racial extremist groups, paying informers who commit acts of racial violence while never really bringing the full force of the law down on the Klan. Fighting the KKK, for some policemen at least, appears to be a big joke. In October, 1982, several black Ontario Provincial Police officers found KKK application forms in their lockers; OPP officials dismissed the incident as a prank. Police forces in general have shown little readiness to

*See pages 154, 193.

clean up their own house when it comes to institutionalized racism.

The media, for their part, displayed some improvement and discretion in handling the Klan only after much of the damage of free publicity and sensationalist exposure had already been done.

It falls then to ordinary Canadians from various backgrounds, grouped in a loose, diverse anti-racism movement, to arrest the modern Klan's growth. Undeniably, the Klan of the 1980s has been weakened by its own internal problems — the arrests of leaders for fraud and other crimes, the jealous battles for power and the personality clashes — which also plagued the Klan of the 1920s. But the anti-racism forces in Canada, immeasurably stronger today than they were in the 1920s, have dealt the heaviest blows to the Ku Klux Klan. While it is undoubtedly true that racism remains widespread in Canada, recent decades have also seen an upsurge in efforts by nationalities and ethnic groups to have their rights recognized. The various nationalities and immigrant groups are much more organized and better equipped to respond to the Klan's assault than they were 50 years ago. Among the general population, too, things have changed — at least in some quarters. The trade unions today speak out much more forcefully against racism, as do churches, school boards and other community groups. Public attitudes have also evolved, at least toward overt racism. Since the second world war especially, blatant theories of racial superiority and race hatred have become closely identified with the spectre of Nazism; Hitler has given racism a bad name. Political leaders today cannot get away with the kind of statements made by prime minister Wilfrid Laurier, who said at the turn of the century that "little good" could come of Asian immigration, or by British Columbia premier John Oliver, who sought the "final elimination" of the "Oriental menace" through massive deportation.*

---

*This is not to suggest that many politicians or prominent citizens do not hold these views privately. Occasionally their prejudices do slip out. In 1982, Conservative MP Dan McKenzie, upon return from a trip to South Africa, condoned apartheid on the grounds that blacks "cannot keep up with whites intellectually." In April, 1983, during the height of the so-called Keegstra affair, Stephen Stiles, a Conservative backbencher in the Alberta legislature was quoted as saying he also doubted the Holocaust occurred: "I haven't seen anything in terms of documentary evidence to prove to me that they

By tapping this revulsion against extreme racism, the anti-Klan movement has had some effect. Its educational seminars and meetings have drawn hundreds of people; its protest marches have attracted thousands; and its petitions against the Klan have been signed by over 30,000 people. School boards, city councils and the media were obliged to take a tougher stand against the Klan because of this kind of pressure.

The anti-Klan, anti-racism movement may have won a battle, but not the war. Lurking in the shadows, the Klan and its like-minded allies are still active. The KKK or a similar group could easily become — through a rejuvenated, B.C.-based Klan, or Don Andrews's Nationalist Party and Taylor's Western Guard in Toronto — a formidable national force. After all, in 1921 the Klan had begun as a small, isolated group which many ignored. When exposures of Klan violence and lawlessness in the United States reached Canada at the time, one newspaper remarked with premature righteousness that "it is fortunate that Canada has nothing of the kind within its borders."[1] Within a few short years, the Ku Klux Klan in Canada had become a movement of at least 30,000 members. Can something like that happen again in Canada? Certainly the conditions exist. In 1965, the special parliamentary committee set up to prepare Canada's hate propaganda laws warned that while the amount of hate literature at the time was small and its effect minimal, "given a certain set of circumstances, such as a deepening of the emotional tensions or the setting in of a severe business recession, public susceptibility might well increase significantly."[2] That set of circumstances is more present than ever; as the Toronto board of education pointed out, "the KKK thrives when times are tough, when it can blame problems shared by all on a particular group of people. During times of recession or crisis, when people are insecure, the Klan is to be found. They try to provide scapegoats for society's ills."[3]

It is far too easy to dismiss McQuirter, Droege, Farmer and their followers as a crazy group of isolated fanatics. But as the

(European Jews) were necessarily persecuted." A public uproar later forced Stiles to apologize for his remarks, but premier Peter Lougheed rebuffed calls for Stiles's resignation.

school board noted, "they are more than an isolated band of extremists. A simple fringe group could never last over a century with the impact on society they have had. Ignoring or laughing at the Klan is the best way of furthering their aims." Far from being an aberration in a supposedly just and equal society, the Klan arguably is more of a reflection — however exaggerated — of the racism endemic in that society. The Klan combined the standard anti-black racism of its American parent with a blend of prejudice that was uniquely Canadian. In the 1920s, its special targets were Asians, southern and central European immigrants and the French Canadians — much the same targets of abuse in society as a whole; in the 1980s, adapting to the changing times, the Klan's favorite scapegoats were the third world immigrants and the Jews. The Klan of the 1920s was strongest in the prairies where feelings against immigrants and Catholics ran the highest; the modern Klan has its strongest bases in the cosmopolitan urban centres of Toronto and Vancouver where racism and other social tensions had been festering for years. The Klan fed on the racism deeply rooted in Canada. "We were just championing a lot of opinions people had expressed on their own and we went a little further," said Klan leader McQuirter. Indeed, a controversial Gallup Poll released by the federal government in mid-1982 showed that 31 per cent of Canadians "would support laws that worked towards preserving Canada for whites only."* Such surprising endorsement for Klan goals could be explained in part by the fact the Klan was, after all, only putting officially-sanctioned racist notions in more vulgar terms. If the "Green Paper" which preceded federal changes to the immigration law warned of "the consequences for national identity" resulting from high immigration, the Klan simply "went a little further" and painted a bleaker picture of immigrants seizing control of "white" society: "As soon as they

---

*The poll was criticized by many groups including the Canadian Labour Congress, which called it "insidious" because it "gives life to latent racism." Critics of the survey pointed out that its questions were posed in a loaded manner. "The structuring and the language of the questionnaire is destructive and calculated to provoke people to be negative," said the CLC. The initial question, which set the tone for the survey, asked people if they agreed or disagreed with the statement that riots and violence increase when non-whites are let into a country.[4]

become the majority, they will become the ruling power,"
said McQuirter in one interview. "We'll be threatened and forced
out of our country. We'll lose control of our laws and lose control
of our destiny." If Ottawa was making it harder for non-white
immigrants to come into Canada, the Klan had a better idea:
massive deportation of all non-whites. If, through a variety of
government, media and police statements or policies, immigrants
and the so-called visible minorities are seen to be stealing
Canadians' jobs, crowding schools and causing crime, the drastic
solutions proposed by the Ku Klux Klan can be appealing.

The appeal of racism — be it the Klan's more vulgar brand or
the more subtle forms permeating society — is simple. A real
problem that is of great concern to Canadians in a crisis-ridden
economy is identified: unemployment, poor education, social
decay, the gap between rich and poor. But instead of a profound
criticism of government and the social system responsible for
these ills, the blame is shifted to an easily identifiable scapegoat.
On unemployment, a federal immigration minister warns
immigrants are a "burden" on the job market and the KKK says
that unemployment among white workers is caused by hiring
practices which favor minorities. What the Klan ignores, of
course, is that nine out of ten blacks in Toronto's Regent Park
area are unemployed; that in 1976, Indians and Pakistanis in
Toronto had an unemployment rate double the average rate.
According to projections made by the Economic Council of
Canada in 1975, Canada would have the same unemployment
rate *whether there was net immigration of 200,000 or no
immigrants at all.*[5] Moreover, the "flood" of immigrants to
Canada is hardly a tidal wave: according to the 1981 census 84 per
cent of Canadians were born here. On education, a CTV public
affairs program warns of classrooms being overrun by Chinese,
and the Klan says the deterioration of schools is caused by
minorities taking the place of whites. Yet 97 per cent of
Saskatchewan's native people do not finish high school; one 1973
study of Nova Scotia blacks showed that 94 per cent never got
beyond grade eleven. The Klan prefers not to see that minorities
are the victims, not the cause, of injustice in the education system.
On social decay, police authorities are willing to suggest that

immigrants cause more crime, and the Klan blames "blacks, East Indians and other minorities" for "an increasing rate of brutal crime." Yet a study prepared for the federal solicitor general in 1974 showed that the crime rate for new residents in Canada was half that among native-born Canadians.[6] On the gap between rich and poor, the Klan likes to play on the widespread myth that Jews control the country's purse strings. "When people have a certain amount of despair they will blame the Jews and other minorities," said Alan Shefman of B'nai Brith when that organization released a study showing anti-semitism in Canada is the worst it has been in years. Despite the myth of a "Jewish conspiracy" and the presence of such high-profile millionaires as the Bronfmans, Canada's ruling business and financial elite remains as WASPish as it has always been: one study indicated Jews made up only eight per cent of the elite.[7]

Because of its extreme virulence and violence, the Ku Klux Klan must be singled out; its defeat or at least containment can be a rallying cry for an outraged public, a symbol and a warning to others that prejudice and discrimination will not be tolerated. But for all its ugliness, the racism of the Ku Klux Klan is not the most dangerous threat to Canada. After all, it is not the Klan, but businesses which profit from paying immigrants and minorities lower wages. It is not the Klan, but landlords who deny people decent housing because of the color of their skin. It is not the Klan, but the real rulers of society who benefit when people blame minorities rather than the system for their problems. Racism is no stranger to Canada; it was not born with the Klan and it will not die with it. From the theft of native lands to the little-known system of slavery which existed in Canada for two centuries, from the anti-Asianism of the 1900s to the internment of Japanese Canadians and the exclusion of Jewish refugees in the second world war, from the discrimination against minorities today to the Keegstra affair, racism has been part of the country's history. It is an integral part of a system in which the powers that be can hold onto their privileges only so long as the people they rule are divided.

Canada's Ku Klux Klan is only a visible scar, a trace of a much deeper sore that runs deep in a society with many ills. In that sense, any fight against the Klan has to be part of a wider effort to change a system where prejudices, inequalities and injustices persist.

Appendix: Canada's hate laws

1. The Criminal Code

The Criminal Code provisions with regard to hate propaganda are contained in Sections 281.1, 281.2, and 281.3 of the Criminal Code of Canada. They are as follows:

281.1
(1) Everyone who advocates or promotes genocide is guilty of an indictable offence and is liable to imprisonment for five years.
(2) In this section, "genocide" means any of the following acts committed with intention to destroy in whole or in part any identifiable group, namely:
   (a) killing members of the group, or
   (b) deliberately inflicting on the group conditions of life calculated to bring about its physical destruction.
(3) no proceedings for an offence under this section shall be instituted without consent of the Attorney General.
(4) In this section, "identifiable group" means any section of the public distinguished by colour, race, religion or ethnic origin.

281.2
(1) Everyone who by communicating statements in any public place, incites hatred against any identifiable group where such indictment is likely to lead to a breach of peace, is guilty of
   (a) an indictable offence and is liable to imprisonment for two years; or
   (b) an offence punishable on summary conviction.
(2) Everyone who by communicating statements, other than in private conversation, wilfully promotes hatred against any identifiable group is guilty of
   (a) an indictable offence and is liable to imprisonment for two years; or
   (b) an offence punishable on summary conviction.
(3) No person shall be convicted of any offence under subsection (2)
   (a) if he establishes that the statements communicated were true;
   (b) if, in good faith, he expressed or attempted to establish by argument an opinion upon a religious subject;
   (c) if the statements were relevant to any subject of public interest, the discussion of which was for the public benefit, and if on reasonable grounds he believed them to be true; or
   (d) if, in good faith, he intended to point out, for the purpose of removal, matters producing or tending to produce feelings of hatred toward an identifiable group in Canada.

(4) Where a person is convicted of an offence under section 281.1 or subsection (1) or (2) of this section, anything by means of or in relation to which the offence was committed, upon such conviction, may, in addition to any other punishment imposed, be ordered by the presiding magistrate or judge to be forfeited to Her Majesty in right of the province in which that person is convicted, for disposal as the Attorney General may direct...
(6) No proceeding for an offence under subsection (2) shall be instituted without the consent of the Attorney General.
(7) In this section
"communicating" includes communicating by telephone, broadcasting or other audible or visible means;
"identifiable group" has the same meaning as it has in section 281.1;
"public place" includes any place in which the public have access as a right or by invitation, express or implied;
"statements" includes words spoken or written or recorded electronically or electromagnetically or otherwise and gestures, signs, or other visual representations.

2. The B.C. Civil Rights Protection Act

In July, 1981, the Legislative Assembly of British Columbia passed the following act:

Prohibited act is actionable
1. (1) In this Act, "prohibited act" means any conduct or communications by a person that has as its purpose interference with the civil rights of a person or class of persons by promoting
(a) hatred or contempt of a person or class of persons, or
(b) the superiority or inferiority of a person or class of persons in comparison with another or others,
on the basis of colour, race, religion, ethnic origin or place of origin.
(2) A prohibited act is a tort actionable without proof of damage,
(a) by any person against whom the prohibited act was directed, or
(b) where the prohibited act was directed against a class of persons, by any member of that class.
(3) Where a corporation or society engages in a prohibited act, every director or officer of the corporation or society who authorized, permitted or acquiesced in the commission of the prohibited act may be sued by the person referred to in subsection (2) and is liable in the same manner as the corporation or society.
(4) In an action brought under this section, the commission of a prohibited act by any director or officer of a corporation or society shall be presumed, unless the contrary is shown, to be done, authorized or concurred in by the corporation or society.
(5) An action under this section shall be commenced in the Supreme Court.

Attorney General may intervene in action
2. (1) The Attorney General may intervene in an action commenced under section 1, and where the Attorney General intervenes, he becomes a party to the proceedings.
(2) Where a person commences an action under section 1, he shall serve the Attorney General with a copy of the writ of summons within 30 days after

commencing the action.

Remedies
3. (1) A party to an action brought under section 1 may be awarded damages or exemplary damages.

(2) Where the court awards damages or exemplary damages in an action brought by a member of a class of persons under section 1, the court may order payment of the damages to any person, organization or society that, in the court's opinion, represents the interests of the class of persons.

(3) In an action brought under section 1, the court may, in addition to any other relief, grant an injunction.

Offence
4. (1) A person who engages in a prohibited act commits an offence and is liable to a fine of not more than $2,000 or to imprisonment for not more than 6 months, or to both.

(2) A corporation or society that commits an offence under subsection (1) is liable to a fine of not more than $10,000.

(3) Where a corporation or society commits an offence under subsection (1), every director or officer of the corporation or society who authorized, permitted or acquiesced in the commission of the prohibited act commits an offence and is liable to the penalties under subsection (1).

3. Human Rights Codes

a) The Canadian Human Rights Act

Sec. 13. Hate messages.—(1) It is a discriminatory practice for a person or a group of persons acting in concert to communicate telephonically or to cause to be so communicated, repeatedly, in whole or in part by means of the facilities of a telecommunication undertaking within the legislative authority of Parliament, any matter that is likely to expose a person or persons to hatred or contempt by reason of the fact that that person or those persons are identifiable on the basis of a prohibited ground of discrimination.

(2) *Exception.*—Subsection (1) does not apply in respect of any matter that is communicated in whole or in part by means of the facilities of a broadcasting undertaking.

(3) *Interpretation.*—For the purposes of this section, no owner or operator of a telecommunication undertaking communicates or causes to be communicated any matter described in subsection (1) by reason only that the facilities of a telecommunication undertaking owned or operated by that person are used by other persons for the transmission of such matter.

b) The Ontario Human Rights Code

PART I
Services
Sec. 1. Every person has a right to equal treatment with respect to services, goods and facilities, without discrimination because of race, ancestry, place of origin, colour, ethnic origin, citizenship, creed, sex, age, marital status, family status or handicap.
PART II
Announced intention to discriminate
Sec. 12.—(1) A right under Part I is infringed by a person who publishes or

displays before the public or causes the publication or display before the public of any notice, sign, symbol, emblem, or other similar representation that indicates the intention of the person to infringe a right under Part I or that is intended by the person to incite the infringement of a right under Part I.

Exception as to matters of opinion
(2) Subsection (1) shall not interfere with freedom of expression of opinion.

c) The Manitoba Human Rights Act

Discrimination prohibited in notices, signs, etc.
Sec. 2. (1) No person shall
   (a) publish, display, transmit or broadcast, or cause to be published, displayed, transmitted or broadcast; or
   (b) permit to be published, displayed, broadcast or transmitted to the public, on lands or premises, in a newspaper, through television or radio or telephone, or by means of any other medium which he owns or controls;
any notice sign, symbol, emblem or other representation (1976, c. 48, s.2.)
   (c) indicating discrimination or intention to discriminate against a person; or (1976, c. 48, s. 2.)
   (d) exposing or tending to expose a person to hatred; (1976, c. 48, s. 2.)
because of the race, nationality, religion, colour, sex, marital status, physical or mental handicap, age, source of income, family status, ethnic or national origin of that person.

Exception as to matters of opinion
(2) Nothing in subsection (1) shall be deemed to interfere with the free expression of opinion upon any subject.
Exception
(3) Subsection (1) does not apply to the display of a notice, sign, symbol, emblem or other representation displayed to identify facilities customarily used by one sex.

d) The Manitoba Defamation Act

(1) The publication of a libel against a race or religious creed likely to expose persons belonging to that race, or professing the religious creed, to hatred, contempt, or ridicule, and tending to raise unrest or disorder among the people, entitles a person belonging to the race or professing the religious creed, to sue for an injunction to prevent the continuation and circulation of the libel; . . .
(2) The action may be taken against the person responsible for the authorship, publication, or circulation of the libel.
(3) The word "publication" used in this section means any word legibly marked upon any substance or any object signifying the matter otherwise than by words, exhibited in public or caused to be seen or shown or circulated or delivered with a view to be seen by any person.

e) The Saskatchewan Human Rights Code

Prohibitions against publications
Sec. 14. (1) No person shall publish or display, or cause or permit to be published or displayed, on any lands or premises or in a newspaper, through a television or radio broadcasting station or any other broadcasting device or

in any printed matter or publication or by means of any other medium that he owns, controls, distributes or sells, any notice, sign, symbol, emblem or other representation tending or likely to tend to deprive, abridge or otherwise restrict the enjoyment of any person or class of persons of any right to which he is or they are entitled under the law, or which exposes, or tends to expose, to hatred, ridicules, belittles, or otherwise affronts the dignity of, any person, any class of persons or a group of persons because of his or their race, creed, religion, colour, sex, marital status, physical disability, age, nationality, ancestry or place of origin.

(2) Nothing in subsection (1) restricts the right to freedom of speech under the law upon any subject.

4. The Canada Post Act

Prohibitory Orders
41. (1) Where the Minister believes on reasonable grounds that any person
    (a) is, by means of mail,
        (i) committing or attempting to commit an offence, or
        (ii) aiding, abetting, counselling or procuring any other person to commit an offence,
    (b) with intent to commit an offence, is using mail to accomplish his object, or
    (c) is, by means other than mail, aiding, abetting, counselling or procuring any other person to commit an offence by means of mail,
the Minister may make an order (in this section called an "interim prohibitory order") prohibiting the delivery, without the consent of the Minister, of mail addressed to or posted by that person (in this section called the "person affected").

5. The McAlpine Proposal

In his report commissioned by the B.C. government in March, 1981, Vancouver lawyer John D. McAlpine proposed the following formulation for an amendment to the human rights code:

"No person or persons acting in concert shall communicate any statement, or disseminate or display any notice, sign, symbol, emblem, or other representation before the public
    (a) that is likely to expose a person or class of persons to hatred, contempt or discrimination, or that ridicules, belittles or otherwise affronts the dignity of a person or class of persons by reason of their race, religion, colour, ancestry or place of origin; or
    (b) that is based upon the idea of racial superiority, and is likely to expose a person or class of persons to hatred, contempt or discrimination, or that ridicules, belittles or otherwise affronts the dignity of a person or class of persons."

Notes and sources

THIS IS, TO THE BEST of my knowledge, the first book devoted exclusively to the history of the Ku Klux Klan in Canada. Because the Klan was active in Canada for about a decade in the 1920s and has only recently started up again, there is not an enormous amount of literature on the organization in our country.

There is a wealth of books on the American Klan. One of the standard, and most complete, histories is David M. Chalmers's *Hooded Americanism* (Chicago: Quadrangle Books, 1965). His study has many vital facts and statistics, though less analysis of the social conditions surrounding the Klan's birth and growth.

A good examination of the modern American Klan is Patsy Sims's *The Klan* (New York: Stein and Day, 1978). Written as a first-person account of her travels through the Klan world, Sims's book provides a revealing look at the men and leaders concealed beneath the Klan's hoods, and their frightening ideas. The National Education Association has put together a very useful teaching kit called "Violence, the Ku Klux Klan and the struggle for equality." The Klanwatch group in the U.S. produced a graphic and informative magazine entitled "Special Report: The Ku Klux Klan, a history of racism and violence." There is also a short educational pamphlet on the KKK's violent track record in the U.S. produced by the Southern Equal Rights Congress in Mobile, Alabama, entitled "We Won't Go Back: The Rise of the Ku Klux Klan and the Southern Struggle for Equality."

The history of the Klan in Canada is mostly contained in unpublished university theses, although mention of the Klan is often made in books which examine the social and political conditions of Western Canada in the 1920s. The most helpful theses, upon which much of the early chapters of this book are based, are William Calderwood's *The Rise and Fall of the Ku Klux Klan in Saskatchewan* (University of Saskatchewan, 1968); Raymond Huel's *La Survivance in Saskatchewan — Schools, Politics and the Nativist Crusade for Cultural Conformity* (University of Lethbridge, 1975); Howard Palmer's *Nativism and Ethnic Tolerance in Alberta: 1920-1972* (York University, 1973), which appeared in revised form as a book, *Patterns of Prejudice: A History of Nativism in Alberta* (McClelland and Stewart, 1982); and, for a look at the Klan and the Crowsnest Pass strike, Allen Seager's *A History of the Mine Workers' Union, 1925-36* (McGill University, 1977). There are also several articles on the Klan in Canadian historical journals, most notably Calderwood's "Religious Reaction to the Ku Klux Klan" in *Saskatchewan History*, Autumn, 1973, and Tom Henson's "Ku Klux Klan in Western Canada" in *Alberta History*, Autumn, 1977. Information on the Klan and the Saskatchewan elections is available in Patrick Kyba's "Ballots and Burning

Crosses — The Election of 1929" in *Politics in Saskatchewan*, edited by Norman Ward and Duff Spafford (Don Mills: Longmans Canada Ltd., 1968). An examination of the right-wing extremists who succeeded the Klan in the 1930s is contained in Lita-Rose Betcherman's book, *The Swastika and the Maple Leaf: Fascist Movements in Canada in the Thirties* (Toronto: Fitzhenry and Whiteside, 1975).

There is, fortunately, a much richer and more available literature on racism in general in Canada. Recent years have seen an impressive crop of books dealing with traditionally-ignored topics such as black Canadians, Chinese Canadians and immigration laws. An understanding of the deep roots of racism in Canada can be gleaned from Daniel G. Hill's *Freedom Seekers — Blacks in Early Canada* (Agincourt: Book Society of Canada Ltd., 1981). Peter Ward looks at anti-Asiatic racism in B.C. over the past century in his *White Canada Forever* (Montreal: McGill-Queen's University Press, 1978). Canada's biased immigration policies — in the past and present — are excellently dissected by the Law Union of Ontario in the *Immigrant's Handbook* (Montreal: Black Rose Books, 1981). Donald Avery's *Dangerous Foreigners* (Toronto: McClelland and Stewart, 1981) gives a valuable perspective on immigration in the 1920s.

Material on the modern Klan in Canada is much harder to come by. The only original Klan material (aside from its internal *Handbook* and interviews with members) which can be used for research are issues of the *KKK Canada Action Report* and copies of *The Spokesman* newspaper. The only government study on the Canadian Klan to be made public is John D. McAlpine's *Report arising out of the activities of the Ku Klux Klan in British Columbia*, April, 1981. It briefly treats the Klan's history and strength in Canada and then examines in depth the consequences of its race hatred and the policy options open to government. To keep tabs on the latest developments and actions of the KKK in Canada today, the alternate and progressive press is generally a better source of regular information than the commercial media. Finally, information on the Klan and similar groups — and, more importantly, what people are doing to stop them — can be obtained from the various anti-racism organization across the country, such as the BCOFR, the Native Rights Coalition in Regina, the Parkdale Action Committee Against Racism, the Committee for Racial Equality and other groups in Toronto, and the National Black Coalition of Canada.

Part I: The Birth of an Empire

CHAPTER ONE: THE KLAN HEADS NORTH

1. David M. Chalmers, *Hooded Americanism* (Chicago: Quadrangle Books, 1965), p. 40.
2. Richard O. Boyer, *Labor's Untold Story* (New York: UE, 1955), p. 316.
3. Chalmers, pp. 312, 316.
4. Montreal *Standard*, July 19, 1930, p. 1.
5. Montreal *Daily Star*, October 4, 1921.
6. Tom M. Henson, "Ku Klux Klan in Western Canada," *Alberta History* (Autumn 1977), p. 2; *La Presse* (Montreal), November 28, 1922.
7. *Spectator*, March 24, 1923.

8. William Calderwood, *The Rise and Fall of the Ku Klux Klan in Saskatchewan* (Unpublished Ph.D. thesis, University of Saskatchewan, 1968), p. 15.
9. *The Worker*, May 9, 1924.
10. Henson, p. 2.
11. Calderwood, p. 20.
12. *Spectator*, March 24, 1923.
13. Toronto *Star*, September 15, 1923.
14. Toronto *Globe*, November 19, 1924, p. 1.
15. Calderwood, pp. 17-18.
16. Calderwood, p. 18.
17. Toronto *Mail and Empire*, August 18, 1924, p. 1.
18. Toronto *Globe*, March 1, 1930, p. 1.
19. *Canadian Forum*, April 30, 1930, p. 232. Later reports said the man was an Indian, not black.
20. Toronto *Globe*, March 11, 1930, p. 1.
21. *Saturday Night*, August 26, 1930, p. 1.
22. *Canadian Forum*, April 30, 1930, p. 232.
23. Toronto *Globe*, March 4, 1930, p. 4.
24. *The Worker*, February 28, 1925, p. 1.
25. Cited in *Literary Digest*, February 3, 1923.

CHAPTER TWO: KEEPING B.C. WHITE

1. *B.C. Federationist*, November 24, 1922, p. 2.
2. *B.C. Federationist*, October 11, 1924.
3. Calderwood, p. 11.
4. W. Peter Ward, *White Canada Forever* (Montreal: McGill-Queen's University Press, 1978), p. 25.
5. House of Commons speech, 1882, cited in exhibit at Chinese Canadian Heritage Festival, Toronto, October, 1980.
6. Ward, p. 58.
7. Cited in John D. McAlpine, *Report Arising out of the Activities of the Ku Klux Klan in British Columbia* (Victoria: B.C. Ministry of Labour, 1981), p. 15.
8. Ward, p. 126.
9. Law Union of Ontario, *Immigrant's Handbook* (Montreal: Black Rose Books, 1981), p. 9.
10. Ward, p. 138.
11. Vancouver *Province*, February 5, 1927, p. 1.
12. *Canadian Annual Review* (1925-26), p. 516.
13. Vancouver *Province*, February 5, 1927, p. 1.
14. Calderwood, p. 167.
15. *B.C. Federationist*, November 24, 1922, p. 2.
16. *House of Commons Debates* (1926), I, p. 573.
17. Calderwood, p. 12.
18. Vancouver *Province*, February 16, 1927.

CHAPTER THREE: SCAPEGOATS IN ALBERTA

1. Donald Avery, *Dangerous Foreigners* (Toronto: McClelland and Stewart, 1981), p. 94. Much of the discussion here on immigration policy is based on Avery's book.
2. Howard Palmer, *Patterns of Prejudice: A History of Nativism in Alberta* (Toronto: McClelland and Stewart, 1982), p. 101.
3. Palmer, p. 102.
4. Palmer, p. 102.
5. Palmer, p. 103.
6. Palmer, p. 105.
7. Edmonton *Journal*, August 9, 1980, p. B2.
8. Howard Palmer, *Nativism and Ethnic Tolerance, 1920-72* (Ph.D. Thesis, York University, Toronto, 1972), p. 200.
9. Palmer, p. 107.
10. Henson, p. 6.
11. Henson, p. 5.
12. Henson, p. 5
13. Palmer, p. 106.
14. Palmer, p. 106; Palmer, *Nativism and Ethnic Tolerance*, p. 198.
15. Edmonton *Journal*, August 9, 1980, p. B2
16. Henson, p. 6.
17. This account of the Crowsnest Pass strike is drawn largely from Allen Seager, *A History of the Mine Workers Union of Canada, 1925-36* (Unpublished thesis, McGill University, 1977).

CHAPTER FOUR: POLITICAL CLOUT IN SASKATCHEWAN

1. Calderwood, p. 37.
2. Calderwood, p. 38.
3. Calderwood, p. 57.
4. Montreal *Gazette*, July 7, 1928.
5. William Calderwood, "Religious reactions to the Ku Klux Klan in Saskatchewan," *Saskatchewan History* (Autumn 1973), p. 104.
6. Raymond J.A. Huel, *La Survivance in Saskatchewan: Schools, Politics and the Nativist Crusade for Cultural Conformity* (Unpublished Ph.D. thesis, University of Lethbridge, 1975), p. 116.
7. Huel, p. 142.
8. "The Ku Klux Klan in Saskatchewan," *Queen's Quarterly* (1928), p. 597.
9. Huel, p. 153.
10. "The Ku Klux Klan in Saskatchewan," p. 597.
11. Montreal *Gazette*, July 7, 1928. As the Klan put it, "The plain people of Canada realize that merely stopping the Alien Flood does not restore Canadianism nor even us against final utter defeat. Canada must also defend itself against the enemy within or we shall be corrupted and conquered...The first danger is that we shall be overwhelmed by the Alien's mere force of breeding." Quoted by Patrick Kyba, "Ballots and Burning Crosses: The Election of 1929," in Norman Ward and Duff Spafford, eds., *Politics in Saskatchewan* (Don Mills: Longmans Canada, 1968), p. 110. The Klan in the 1980s would echo this warning about the "force of breeding" of immigrants.
12. Calderwood, *The Rise and Fall of the Ku Klux Klan*, p. 129.

13. Calderwood, *The Rise and Fall of the Ku Klux Klan*, p. 190. See also Calderwood, "Religious Reactions to the Ku Klux Klan" and Calderwood, "Pulpit, Press and Political Reaction to the Ku Klux Klan in Saskatchewan" in S.M. Trofimenkoff, *The Twenties in Western Canada* (National Museum of Man, Ottawa, 1972).
14. Montreal *Standard*, July 19, 1930.
15. Huel, pp. 138-9.
16. Calderwood, *The Rise and Fall of the Ku Klux Klan*, p. 216.
17. Huel, p. 184, and Kyba, p. 110.
18. Huel, p. 179.
19. Huel, p. 277.
20. Montreal *Gazette*, March 25, 1981, p. 1; *House of Commons Debates* (1931), I, p. 252; (1934), III, p. 2701; (1930), II, p. 1557.
21. Montreal *Standard*, July 19, 1930, p. 1.
22. Calderwood, "Religious Reactions to the Ku Klux Klan in Saskatchewan," p. 109.
23. Interview with author.
24. Calderwood, "Religious Reactions to the Ku Klux Klan in Saskatchewan," p. 113.
25. Calderwood, "Religious Reactions to the Ku Klux Klan in Saskatchewan," p. 113.
26. Calderwood, *The Rise and Fall of the Ku Klux Klan*, p. 109.

CHAPTER FIVE: WHITE ROBES AND BROWN SHIRTS

1. Ward, p. 139.
2. Lita-Rose Betcherman, *The Swastika and the Maple Leaf: Fascist Movements in Canada in the Thirties* (Toronto: Fitzhenry and Whiteside, 1975), p. 13.
3. Betcherman, pp. 103-5.
4. Betcherman, pp. 10, 11, 42.
5. Betcherman, p. 163.

Part II: The Modern Klan

CHAPTER SIX: THE FASCIST CONNECTION

1. Don Whitehead, *Attack on Terror: The FBI Against the Ku Klux Klan in Mississippi* (New York: Funk and Wagnalls), p. 143.
2. Patsy Sims, *The Klan* (New York: Stein and Day, 1978), p. 107.
3. Chalmers, p. 383.
4. Sims, p. 113.
5. Sims, p. 180.
6. Sims, p. 180.
7. Sims, p. 182.
8. Sims, p. 215.
9. Toronto *Globe and Mail*, July 27, 1981.
10. "The Ku Klux Klan tries for a comeback," *Facts* (Anti-Defamation

League), November, 1979, p. 4.

11. Toronto *Star*, September 30, 1979. See also *Newsweek*, October 6, 1980, p. 52.
12. Toronto *Globe and Mail*, August 12, 1965, p. 4; August 13, p. 4.
13. Edmonton *Journal*, August 9, 1980, p. B2.
14. Calgary *Herald*, December 17, 1975. See also Toronto *Globe and Mail*, December 9 and 10, 1975.
15. John Garrity, "My sixteen months as a Nazi," *Maclean's*, October, 1966, p. 9.
16. "Secretary's Report," in *Nationalist Report* (Nationalist Party of Canada), 37-38, undated, p. 9.
17. Sims, pp. 162-63.
18. Letter to author.
19. Interview with author.
20. Letter to author.
21. Interview with author.

CHAPTER SEVEN: THE REBIRTH OF THE KLAN

1. "Fact sheet on the Ku Klux Klan," (Toronto: Ad Hoc Committee for Racial Equality, 1980).
2. Toronto *Sun*, May 4, 1972.
3. Sims, pp. 195-200.
4. Toronto *Sun*, January 22, 1978, p. 24.
5. Toronto *Sun*, December 9, 1979.
6. McAlpine, p. 22.
7. McAlpine, p. 15.
8. Law Union, *Immigrant's Handbook*, p. 382.
9. Toronto *Globe and Mail*, February 4, 1982, p. 5.

CHAPTER EIGHT: SPREADING THE FLAMES

1. *The Democrat* (New Democratic Party of B.C.), September, 1980.
2. McAlpine, pp. 7-8.
3. Edmonton *Journal*, September 5, 1980.
4. Letter from the Toronto board of education to all school principals, March 15, 1981.
5. Winnipeg *Free Press*, January 24, 1980, p. 2.
6. McAlpine, p. 17.
7. Interview with author; Toronto *Sun*, November 9, 1980.
8. Toronto *Sun*, November 11, 1979.
9. Ottawa *Citizen*, July 8, 1980.
10. Toronto *Star*, November 20, 1980.
11. Montreal *Gazette*, December 6, 1980.
12. Dean Calbreath, "Kovering the Klan," *Columbia Journalism Review*, March-April, 1981, pp. 42-45.
13. "The Ku Klux Klan tries for a comeback," p. 15.
14. McAlpine, p. 5.
15. Toronto *Sun*, June 30, October 17, and November 25, 1980.

CHAPTER NINE: INSIDE THE INVISIBLE EMPIRE

1. Ottawa *Citizen*, July 8, 1980.
2. McAlpine, p. 19. Cook and McQuirter appeared to differ on the exact size of the B.C. Klan, demonstrating the unreliable nature of claims of membership. Cook told McAlpine that there were fourteen dens each with four to ten members; McQuirter claimed more than 50 dens with six to twenty members each (New Westminster *Columbian*, June 26, 1981).
3. "The Ku Klux Klan tries for a comeback," p. 7.
4. Interview with author.
5. Letter to author.
6. Interview with author.
7. Letter to author from Siksna; interview with Macdonald by author.
8. Interview with author; Toronto *Star*, July 10, 1981.
9. Interview with author.
10. Toronto *Globe and Mail*, February 8, 1982.
11. John Turner et al, "Special Report: The Ku Klux Klan — A History of Racism and Violence," (Montgomery, Alabama: Klanwatch, 1981), p. 22; *New York Times*, February 18, 1980, November 17, 1981, November 29, 1982.
12. Sims, pp. 221-3; The *Crusader*, Issue No. 23, undated, p. 1.
13. Transcript, Judicial District of York, Preliminary Inquiry, Donald Andrews, Dawyd Zarytshansky, Wayne Elliott, November 22, 1976, Judge S. Tucker.
14. *Commission of Inquiry Concerning Certain Activities of the RCMP*, (Ottawa: Queen's Printer, 1981), III, p. 325.
15. Toronto *Globe and Mail*, July 8, 1981; Toronto *Star*, July 10, 1981, p. 8.
16. Transcript, *Regina v. McQuirter et al*, Ontario Supreme Court, Justice John O'Driscoll, February, 1983.
17. Toronto *Globe and Mail*, July 8, 1981.
18. *Commission of Inquiry*, III, p. 317; II, p. 295. Other Klan officials aside from Richardson have had intriguing connections with law enforcement agencies of one sort or another. Gary MacFarlane, the Klan's security chief, worked for a private company as a security guard — as did his wife and fellow Klan member Jean MacGarry — and was licensed by the Ontario Provincial Police to carry a gun even though he had been convicted several years earlier of fatally shooting a man. McQuirter himself worked for a while as a security guard, before he was convicted of theft on the job and sentenced to 90 days in jail (Toronto *Star*, July 10, 1981, p. 8). In March, 1981, McQuirter even helped undercover Toronto police officers arrest a man for an attempt to kill a lawyer and "kneecap" a businessman. A man named Joseph Fabian apparently contacted the Ku Klux Klan in Toronto to ask them to help him carry out this operation. McQuirter instead made contact with the police and a trap was set. Sergeant James McGivern, a plainclothes officer who worked in the intelligence bureau of the Metro Toronto Police, was introduced to McQuirter at a tavern by a fellow Toronto policeman, Sergeant Maywood. "Mr. McQuirter and I spoke for a short time outlining the plan of action...Mr. McQuirter was aware I was a police officer," Sgt. McGivern testified about his collaboration with the Klan leader (Transcript, Preliminary Inquiry, Judge F.C. Horowitz, August 25, 1981). The Klan chief later introduced McGivern to Fabian as a hit man

who could do the job for him. Fabian fell for the ruse and was then arrested. There was, to say the least, something incongruous about the public leader of the Canadian Ku Klux Klan working so intimately with the police.

19. Toronto *Star*, July 10, 1981.
20. Montreal *Gazette*, February 4, 1981; February 17, 1981.

CHAPTER TEN: STANDING UP TO THE KLAN

1. Vancouver *Sun*, March 12, 1981.
2. It is regrettable, though typical of how the media has handled the Klan issue, that the legitimacy of the BCOFR was undermined by sensationalist and distorted reporting. On October 4, 1981, a rally of several hundred people organized by the BCOFR was attacked and disrupted by a small group calling itself the People's Front Against Racist and Fascist Violence — a front group for the Communist Party of Canada (Marxist-Leninist). The CPCML is widely suspected in progressive and trade union circles of being heavily infiltrated by provocateurs (its long history of disrupting and at times violently intimidating progressive movements bolsters this view). The CPCML attack sent one BCOFR marshall to hospital with a concussion; two other people suffered broken arms. Two weeks later another BCOFR demonstration, this time with 600 people, was attacked by about 60 CPCML members and supporters armed with two-by-twos. The stick-swinging melee was widely covered in the local and national media, which played it up as a brawl between two "anti-racist groups" and quoted a gleeful Alexander McQuirter commenting on how gratified he was to see the groups fighting each other instead of the Klan.

  This type of coverage served to create an image of anti-racist groups as small, sectarian factions prone to violence. (There were exceptions; some more astute newspaper columnists, and an editorial in the New Westminster *Columbian*, defended the BCOFR.) The media in general ignored the CPCML's questionable background compared to the respect and legitimacy already accorded the BCOFR by many in B.C.; the fact that the CPCML never had more than a few dozen people in its contingent, compared to the hundreds marching with the BCOFR; and the fact that the BCOFR demonstrations were supported by more than ten community groups, including trade unions and the Union of B.C. Indian Chiefs. After the CPCML attacks, the BCOFR received endorsements from the New Democratic Party, the Vancouver and District Labour Council, and several East Indian community associations. But little if any of this was reported in the national media, which had seen fit to report only the "brawl" between "two anti-racist groups."

  There is a revealing postscript to this story. About three months later, B.C. Klan official Al Hooper admitted to *Columbian* reporter Terry Glavin that Klan members "carrying clubs of their own" had joined with stick-swinging members of the CPCML in the October 17 attack on the BCOFR demonstration (*Columbian*, January 18, 1982). Apparently the Ku Klux Klan knows very well who its real friends and enemies are.
3. Toronto *Globe and Mail*, March 11, 1981.
4. Transcript, verdict of coroner's jury, February 26, 1982; File no. R23155/80.

5. Vancouver *Sun*, June 1, 1981.
6. Toronto *Sun*, November 27, 1981, p. 56.
7. Toronto *Globe and Mail*, March 11, 1981.
8. *House of Commons Debates* (1981), p. 124, p. 8117.
9. Toronto *Globe and Mail*, October 27, 1980.
10. Vancouver *Sun*, June 2, 1981.

CHAPTER ELEVEN: PLOTTING NEW STRATEGIES

1. Toronto *Sun*, October 1, 1980.
2. Vancouver *Province*, October 24, 1980.
3. Toronto *Globe and Mail*, April 28, 1981.

CHAPTER TWELVE: THE TRIALS

1. Testimony of Michael Perdue, October 6 and 8, 1981, *U.S. v. L.E. Matthews and James C. White*, U.S. District Court, Eastern District of Louisiana, New Orleans. All Perdue quotes in this chapter are taken from this transcript.
2. Charges read by Paul Culver, crown counsel, County Court, Judge Patrick LeSage, September 24, 1982.
3. Toronto *Globe and Mail*, December 6, 1982.
4. "Elections in Dominica: RCMP, MI-6, CIA Manipulation?" *Covert Action and Information Bulletin*, 10, August-September, 1980, pp. 33-4.
5. Letter to author.
6. Quoted in charges read by Paul Culver, crown counsel, September 24, 1982.
7. *Contrast*, October 23, 1981, p. 6.
8. Transcript, *Regina v. Yanover*, Judicial District of York, Judge H.R. Locke.
9. Interview with author.
10. Interview with author.
11. Interview with author; see also Toronto *Globe and Mail*, June 23, 1981.
12. Charges read by Harry Black, prosecutor, *Regina v. McQuirter et al*, Ontario Supreme Court, Justice John O'Driscoll, February, 1983.
13. Testimony by Gary MacDonald, *Regina v. McQuirter et al.*
14. Toronto *Globe and Mail*, August 6, 1983, p. 8.

CHAPTER THIRTEEN: LEGAL LOOPHOLES

1. McAlpine, p. 54.
2. Toronto *Globe and Mail*, October 17, 1980.
3. Toronto *Star*, March 27, 1980; Toronto *Sun*, March 25, 1980; Transcript, *Regina v. Armand Siksna and James Alexander McQuirter*, County Court Judges' Criminal Court, Judicial District of York, Judge Coo, March 25, 1980.
4. Interview with author.
5. McAlpine, p. 34.
6. Toronto *Star*, June 29, 1980.

7. Toronto *Star*, October 16, 1980.
8. Stephen Brewer, "Getting rid of the Klan," *The Democrat*, March, 1981.
9. Brewer, "Getting rid of the Klan."
10. *BCOFR Newsletter*, 2, April, 1981, p. 4.
11. McAlpine, pp. 48, 50.
12. *BCOFR Newsletter*, 2, April, 1981, p. 4.
13. Excerpts from 1965, 1966 and 1978 declarations are taken from McAlpine, pp. 52-3.

CONCLUSION: A DEEPER SORE

1. Montreal *Star*, February 13, 1922, p. 10.
2. McAlpine, p. 51.
3. "Where we stand on the Ku Klux Klan," Toronto board of education, February, 1981.
4. "CLC says racial poll 'insidious'", *Briarpatch*, June, 1982, p. 17.
5. Law Union of Ontario, *Immigrant's Handbook*, p. 40.
6. Law Union of Ontario, *Immigrant's Handbook*, p. 40.
7. Wallace Clement, *Canadian Corporate Elite* (Toronto: McClelland and Stewart, 1975), p. 237.

Also from New Star

ANTHONY B. CHAN

GOLD MOUNTAIN
The Chinese in the New World

The story of Canada's Chinese has been told
before but almost always from the perspective
of the white "host" society. Anthony B. Chan's
Gold Mountain is the first popular account of
Chinese Canadian history written by a Chinese
Canadian.

Chan, a Victoria native who has a Ph.D. in
history from York University and most recently
taught at the University of Saskatchewan,
describes the horrific conditions in nineteenth
century China which drove thousands of
Chinese to North America—Gold Mountain.

Gold Mountain, however, did not offer up
the riches of the gold rush; instead it turned out
to be a labyrinth of coal mines, railroads,
logging camps and racism. Chan also describes
the political currents swirling within Chinatown's so-called "apolitical" community, a
perspective skimmed over by earlier chroniclers
of Chinese Canadian history. Chan's book is a
loving and angry look at his own community,
and an important contribution to Canada's
ethnic history.

*"Exposes as fiction many of the assumptions
and half truths held as immutable by that
mythical beast, the tolerant white Canadian . . .
Gold Mountain is a book to celebrate."*
—Vancouver *Sun*

$ 7.95 paper ISBN 0-919573-01-0
$14.95 cloth ISBN 0-919573-00-2

RONALD WARDHAUGH

LANGUAGE & NATIONHOOD
The Canadian Experience

In this ambitious study, Ronald Wardhaugh
examines a broad range of issues which persist
in dividing the Canadian people. A linguist by
profession, Wardhaugh brings a rare
perspective to the task of understanding the
politics of language and ethnicity. In the
process he challenges many Canadian myths.

The scope and severity of the problem are
not underplayed. Now constitutionally
bilingual, Canada faces a series of entrenched
antagonisms between the two "charter groups,"
the French and English. The Official Languages
Act of 1969, designed to establish harmony
between them, has fallen far short of a solution.
And legislative measures aimed at promoting a
"multicultural mosaic" fail to address the basic
needs of cultural minorities, in particular the
need for language maintenance.

"It is not an optimistic book," says the
author, "but no one who looks seriously at such
matters in Canada can be heartened by the
view." If Wardhaugh does not provide
optimism, he does present a clear and
thoughtful portrait of the tangle of problems.
With *Language and Nationhood* he has added
an important voice to the dialogue.

$ 9.95 paper ISBN 0-919573-17-7
$17.95 cloth ISBN 0-919573-16-9

Also from New Star

MANUEL ALVAREZ

THE TALL SOLDIER
My 40-Year Search for the Man
Who Saved My Life

The first popularly priced paperback edition of
this modern-day Canadian classic, which
evoked universal acclaim on its first appearance
in 1980.
   In the Spanish Civil War, a ten-year-old boy
is saved from drowning by a Canadian—a
soldier in the volunteer Mac-Pap battalion
fighting Franco's Nazi-backed fascist army. The
boy, Manuel Alvarez, vows to find his "tall
soldier", whose name he does not know, whose
face he only glimpsed, who might not even
have survived the war.

*"Reaffirms the power of the human spirit and
provides proof that in an era dominated by
darkness and despair, there is still evidence of
kindness and compassion."*
                              —William French,
                         Toronto *Globe and Mail*

*"The first literary classic in the full sense of the
term that [Vancouver] has produced."*
                         —Alan Morley, Vancouver *Sun*

*"An exciting, fast-paced account of one man's
experiences in one of the most ideologically
savage of the 20th century's wars."*
                              —London *Free Press*

$ 6.95 paper ISBN 0-919573-19-3
$15.95 cloth ISBN 0-919573-18-5

Also from New Star

MANUEL ALVAREZ

SEVEN YEARS AT SEA

In this companion to *The Tall Soldier*, Manuel
Alvarez tells the story of the seven years he
spent as a sailor trying to enter Canada. At the
end of the war Alvarez, still a youth, bribed a
job broker to get a position on a leaky freighter
and fled Franco's Spain. But without a passport
from the fascist regime, Alvarez had no way of
legally entering Canada to find his Tall Soldier,
the Mac-Pap who had saved his life during the
Battle of Ebro in the Spanish Civil War.

Three freighters, dozens of embassies and
consulates, thousands of miles and scores of
ports-of-call later, Alvarez finally reached his
new home. *Seven Years at Sea* takes the reader
on a global adventure which, together with *The
Tall Soldier*, completes the author's astonishing
mission to find his Canadian soldier.

$ 7.95 paper ISBN 0-919573-21-5
$15.95 cloth ISBN 0-919573-20-7

MARY ASHWORTH

THE FORCES WHICH SHAPED THEM
A History of the Education of
Minority Group Children
in British Columbia

Mary Ashworth, professor of education at the
University of B.C., examines the B.C. school
system and how it has treated—and mistreated
—native Indian, Chinese, Japanese,
Doukhobor and East Indian children.

*"Mary Ashworth's book is a challenge to
Canada to incorporate into its social and
multicultural pattern all the beautiful and
worthwhile aspects of the many heritages we
have found here or have brought along with us
when we settled in this great land."*
—McGill Journal of Education

$ 6.50 paper ISBN 0-919888-91-7
$14.95 cloth ISBN 0-919888-92-5

Also from New Star

STAN PERSKY

AT THE LENIN SHIPYARD
Poland and the Rise of the
Solidarity Trade Union

The uprising of Polish workers against their
government is perhaps the most important
development in Eastern Europe since World
War II. In a narrative based largely on
interviews with Solidarity members and other
Polish workers, Stan Persky renders the
complex and confusing events in Poland into a
readable and moving report on a nation's
continuing battle for freedom.

*"An excellent introduction to recent Polish
affairs for those baffled by the profusion of
shallow information appearing in the daily
media. . . a first-rate piece of reflective
journalism."*
—Toronto *Globe and Mail*

*"Captures the sense of excitement and tension
in the nine-month period it covers, and there
are lively close-ups of the people and ideas that
gave the movement its impetus and definition.
It is an excellent antidote to the fragmentary
coverage of events in the daily press."*
—*Books in Canada*

$ 7.95 paper ISBN 0-919888-45-3
$14.95 cloth ISBN 0-919888-46-1